Over the Earth I Come

Over the

Earth I Come

The Great Sioux Uprising of 1862

Duane Schultz

St. Martin's Press   New York

The assistance of the Division of Library and Archives, and the Audio Visual
Library, of the Minnesota Historical Society is grateful acknowledged.

DESIGN BY DAWN NILES

Library of Congress Cataloging-in-Publication Data

Schultz, Duane P.
    Over the earth I come : the great Sioux uprising of 1862 / Duane Schultz.
        p.   cm.
    "A Thomas Dunne book."
    ISBN 0-312-07051-9
    1. Dakota Indians—Wars, 1862–1865.   I. Title.
E83.86.S36   1992
973.7—dc20   91-36453
                                                                        CIP

10 9 8 7 6 5 4 3 2

CONTENTS

A very nice and pretty bird of all colors came and sang beside our village. A voice said, "Listen not to him; pay no heed to his song; look not on his colors." He went away.

He came again with finer colors and sweeter songs, and he continued to do so until we heard him, and he led us away to die.

The bird is the big knives—the white man; his songs are his fair words and lying promises; his colors are his paints, the beads and goods he gives for our land.

Woe to us, for the day we hear the big knives' words, we go to our graves.

—A TALE OF THE SANTEE SIOUX

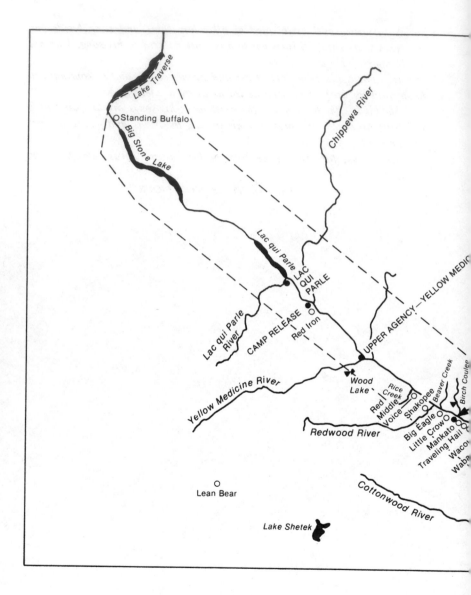

MINNESOTA IN 1862

▼ Battle
○ Indian village
● Town
— — Sioux Reservations

Mississippi River

FOREST CITY ●

ACTON ●

MINNEAPOLIS ●

ST. PAUL ●

FOnT SNELLING ●

MENDOTA ●

● HUTCHINSON

SHAKOPEE ●

Minnesota River

LOWER AGENCY—REDWOOD

FORT RIDGELY

MILFORD TOWNSHIP

HENDERSON ●

○

NEW ULM ▼

ST. PETER ●

TRAVERSE DES SIOUX ●

MANKATO ●

1

EVERYTHING WENT
OFF QUIETLY

The Indians are chained by their ankles to the bare wooden floor. Some crouch quietly, smoking their pipes. A few try to sleep while others chant the words the missionaries had taught them a few days before.

> Jesus Christ, *nitowashti kin,*
> *Woptecashna mayaqu.*
> Jesus Christ, thy loving kindness
> Boundlessly thou gavest me.

As the morning grows lighter, the men sit up and examine their reflections in tiny pocket mirrors. It is important that their painted faces and feathers be perfectly arrayed. Some adjust their eagle plumes and owl tail feathers and run their fingers over the lines and circles daubed on their faces with vermilion and ultramarine blue. To the Sioux Indians, there is a proper way to appear and dress for every occasion, a ceremonial routine to be rigidly observed, and never is it more vital than when it is time to die.

Outside the stone jail, the weather is unusually mild for December, and everyone agrees that it is a fine day for a hanging. The town is jammed. As many as four thousand people line the rooftops and windows of every building and stand patiently on the hard ground of the town square. All of the onlookers are white. It is an orderly crowd—the army has seen to that. Two days earlier, martial law had been declared and the saloons were closed. As the ultimate guarantee that the spectators will not become unruly, 1,419 armed troopers stand shoulder-to-shoulder, facing the crowd. In the white world, too, there is a proper procedure, a correct form and ceremony for officially orchestrated death, and it is being adhered to scrupulously this day.

Behind the ring of soldiers, a large wooden platform rises some six feet off the ground. Stout wooden beams stand atop the platform, forming an elevated square. From the beams, rope nooses dangle and sway in the breeze. There are thirty-eight of them.

It is the day after Christmas in the year 1862. The place is Mankato, Minnesota.

Many in the crowd are disappointed by the small number of nooses. They had hoped to see all 307 Indians sentenced by the military court to death hang by their necks today. President Lincoln had commuted all but thirty-nine of those sentences, however, and one man had won a reprieve only the day before.

At ten o'clock, a squad of soldiers enters the prisoners' room. Father Augustin Ravoux, a Catholic priest, is kneeling on the floor in the center of a circle of Indians, leading them in prayer. He speaks first in their own language, Dakota, then in French, pausing while one of the condemned, a French-speaking mixed-blood, translates his words.

The Indians rise so that the soldiers can knock off the leg irons. Unprotesting, each man waits calmly while the soldiers bind his wrists in front of him, tying them together about six inches apart. One Indian asks that he not be tied—he will keep his hands down, he vows—but his wrists are trussed like the others. He tells the soldiers that Little Crow and other chiefs are responsible for the uprising. It is unfair, he says, that he must die for their actions, while they go free. He knows that his words will make no difference, but by speaking out, his sense of honor is satisfied.

Most of the condemned seem cheerful, and even shake hands with the soldiers. They believe they are about to embark on a journey to a pleasant place, a better place. They begin to chant now, the slow, rhythmic "Hi-yi-yi" of the Sioux death song, the lament of their own religion, not that of the white man.

But when the soldiers start to place white muslin skullcaps on the Indians' heads, they grow restless. They glance at one another, embarrassed and ashamed. Manacles and ropes do not humiliate or dishonor them, but those white caps that look like little flour sacks do, and they stop chanting.

The provost marshal, Captain Redfield, opens the cell door and the Indians form a single line quickly, almost eagerly. No one lags. No one has to be pushed or shoved into place. The group rapidly moves outside and through a cordon of soldiers to the foot of the platform steps. The Indians scramble after the officer, almost as though they want to see who can reach the top first, who can win this last race. They bump into one another in their haste to mount the steps, and each takes his position under one of the dangling nooses.

As the ropes are placed around their necks, they begin to wail their mournful, discordant death song again. The muslin caps are rolled down over their faces, cutting off their final view of this world. Their singing grows louder, and some call out their names and the names of their friends who will die with them.

"Their bodies swayed to and fro," wrote an eyewitness, "and their every limb seemed to be keeping time. . . . The most touching scene was their attempt to grasp each other's hands, fettered as they were. They were very close to each other, and many succeeded. Three or four in a row were hand in hand, and all hands swaying up and down with the rise and fall of their voices. One old man reached out each side, but could not grasp a hand. His struggles were piteous."

The white spectators, along with hundreds of other Indian captives who peer at the scene through cracks in their prison walls, are silent. The only sounds are the shouts and chants of the condemned. The colonel in charge of the execution surveys the site. Everything is in order. He nods to the drummer. The first beat of the drum is barely heard over the voices of the Indians. The next two beats boom louder. A man holding a long knife steps up to the rope stretched taut beneath one side of the platform. His name is William Duley. Three of his children are dead, killed by the Sioux, and his wife and two other children are still missing.

Duley hacks at the rope, but it does not break. He brings the knife down again with a quicker motion, and this time slices the rope through. The trap drops with a clatter. The thirty-eight bodies fall and jerk to a stop. A long yet subdued cheer fills the air as the bodies gyrate, some still clasping the hands of their neighbors. One rope breaks. Soldiers quickly carry the body up to the platform and attach another noose. This one holds. A few torsos twitch; here and there legs draw up spasmodically and some tethered arms continue to move. The crowd falls silent. One Indian is observed to be still breathing after ten minutes. The noose is adjusted. He breathes no more.

A half hour later, several physicians mount the steps and, one by one, confirm the death of each of the thirty-eight men. The onlookers disperse noiselessly, a few people casting backward glances at the gallows as the bodies are cut down and dumped into four mule-drawn army wagons. A burial party of soldiers escorts the wagons to a sandbank along the Minnesota River not far from town.

A common grave has already been dug thirty feet long, twelve feet wide, and four feet deep. The bodies are placed in two rows and covered with blankets and a layer of dirt and sand. That night, doctors from Mankato and neighboring towns dig up the corpses and take them home—cadavers for dissection are hard to come by. One of the doctors, forty-three-year-old William Worrall Mayo, keeps the bones of his subject, an Indian named Cut Nose, in a huge iron kettle in his office, and one day will use them to teach anatomy to his two sons, William James and Charles Horace.

The following day, a telegram is sent to President Lincoln.

I have the honor to inform you that the 38 Indians and half-breeds, ordered by you for execution, were hung yesterday at Mankato, at 10 A.M. Everything went off quietly, and the other prisoners are well secured.

Respectfully,

H. H. Sibley
Brigadier General

It was the largest mass execution ever to take place in the United States, and it was carried out in retribution for the most savage Indian uprising in the nation's history. In less than one week in August, the Sioux went on a rampage throughout Minnesota that left hundreds of white people dead. The exact number will never be known. Life on the frontier was unregulated and unregistered, and many settlers were slaughtered in their isolated cabins and their remains never recovered. Estimates of the death toll range from four hundred to two thousand.

Whole families were burned alive in their farmhouses. Children were nailed to barn doors, girls raped by a dozen braves and hacked to pieces, babies dismembered in front of their horrified mothers. More than 260 women and children, whites and mixed-bloods, were dragged off to a brutal captivity that lasted for forty days. Nearly forty thousand settlers became refugees, abandoning their possessions and their farms and towns over a ten-thousand-square-mile area. In ten Minnesota counties, not a house or a store or a living white person remained untouched.

The uprising had ramifications that went far beyond the killing ground. It marked the outbreak of a series of wars between whites and Indians over the Great Plains that did not end until 1890, almost thirty years later, at a place called Wounded Knee in South Dakota. These conflicts, taken together, coalesced into the longest war United States troops would ever fight.

Few people foresaw the horror. Few predicted that the Sioux would one day rise up and exact such a terrible vengeance for the way they had been treated over so many years. The seven thousand Santee Sioux in Minnesota were peaceable Indians, tame Indians, who had lived on a reservation for more than a decade. Some were successful farmers who wore shirts and trousers, like white men, and who had been baptized by the Christian missionaries. Little Crow, the fifty-two-year-old Sioux chief who believed that his people needed to adopt white ways if they were to survive, regularly attended Episcopal church services. The very morning the massacre began, he had been seen shaking hands with the minister.

The Sioux were neighbors, in some cases friends. And even after the uprising started and smoke from burning farmhouses stained the sky, many white families refused to believe the wild tales borne by their neighbors, who arrived on panting horses. Many settlers waited until it was too late to flee, trusting to the good relations they thought existed with the Indians.

The Sioux of Minnesota had long harbored resentment, however. They brooded over the lands appropriated by the whites, over the disappearance of the buffalo and other game, the broken treaties, the lies and deception of the government and its representatives. Frequently cheated out of their annuity payments by crafty traders and dishonest Indian agents, their hatred smoldered for years and finally surfaced in that awful summer of 1862.

The previous winter had been severe, with widespread failures of the precious corn crop. The Indians were hungry, some were starving, and the traders' warehouses were stuffed with food. As soon as the annual stipend promised by the government arrived from Washington, the Indians would be able to buy enough food to survive. But that year, the annuity did not come at the end of June, when it was due. July passed, and the calendars were turned to August, and still there was no money. The Sioux were increasingly desperate, increasingly angry. Without the money for food, they might all starve.

What had happened to the annuity payment for the year 1862? First, the U.S. Congress was a month late in appropriating the money. When the legislators finally did act, bureaucrats at the Treasury Department dithered over whether to pay in gold, as usual, or to substitute paper money. Gold coins were in short supply because of the demands of the Union army, at war with the Confederates. By the time government officials made up their minds that the payment would be made in gold, it was too late. The Sioux had gone to war—one day before the money was delivered.

2
LET THEM EAT GRASS

Hunger and rumors stalked the reservation during the spring and early summer of 1862, and they fueled the Sioux's growing hatred not only of the whites but of some of their own people, as well. By June, the situation was critical. Malnutrition was widespread, and many Indians looked hollow-eyed and gaunt. One tribe had been reduced to eating its horses and dogs. Others had subsisted for weeks on only roots and shriveled ears of corn, which, in their desperation, they ate raw. A few had already died of starvation. Little Crow, the chief who preached harmony with the whites, was forced to trade weapons for food and occasionally relied on his white friends for a meal.

This was not the first year the Indians had known hunger when spring turned to summer, but in the past they had always been saved from starvation by the timely arrival of the federal annuity payment. They had believed that they had only to hold out until the end of June, until the annuity and the provisions specified in the latest treaty would be distributed. As the end of June 1862 approached, however, rumors spread among the Sioux camps that the payment would be late, or would be smaller than expected, or would not be made at all.

"The paymaster did not come," Big Eagle recalled, "and week after week went by and still he did not come. The payment was to be in gold. Somebody told the Indians that the payment would never be made. The government was in a great war, and gold was scarce, and paper money had taken its place, and it was said that the gold could not be had to pay us."

The Sioux knew that the government troops were fighting the rebellious Southerners and that, so far, the Northerners were being beaten.

The merchants and traders, and the mixed-bloods who worked for the traders, were also worried about survival. Their livelihoods depended on the annuity, too, and in their fear they exaggerated the magnitude of the disaster facing the government in Washington, thus fostering panic and increasing the Indians' concerns. The "niggers," said the traders, were special friends of President Lincoln, the Great Father, and would get all the Indians' money that year—and maybe forever. There would be nothing left for the Sioux.

The Indians easily found evidence to support the tales that the U.S. government was exhausting its resources in the war. In every white settlement they passed on their hunting trips, they saw primarily women, children, and old men—almost all of the young men of military age were gone. And on the reservation, many of the young mixed-bloods and the white government employees—the blacksmiths and carpenters, the clerks, teamsters, and warehousemen—had left to enlist in the army.

As the weeks passed, the traders grew more anxious about the money. Although the Sioux depended on them for food and supplies, the traders suddenly cut off the Indians' credit. By then, the traders believed the rumors, too, and they knew that if Washington failed to pay the annuity, their highly profitable businesses would fold. It was their custom to sell goods to the Indians almost entirely on credit, keeping elaborate books of accounts. Although some Indians could pay for their purchases with pelts and furs, most ran up debts that would be deducted from their portion of each annuity payment. By selling inferior goods at inflated prices, the traders could count on huge profits, and they habitually claimed virtually the entire annuity amount every year, a sum approaching eighty thousand dollars. While the traders prospered, the Indians fell further into debt. An individual brave's share of the government's largess seldom amounted to more than twenty dollars in the best of years.

The Sioux rarely had the chance even to see their money. Each year, as they lined up to be paid by the Indian agent, the traders would step forward with their account books, filled with pages of symbols that were meaningless to the Indians, and tell the government representative how much each man owed. No one checked the accuracy of the traders' records, and the agent simply handed over the requested funds.

The Sioux had become economic prisoners, constantly being told that they owed more and more money to the storekeepers. As the buffalo, deer, and game birds on which they had once lived so well became scarce, because of the encroaching white settlements, the Indians were ever more dependent on the goodwill of the traders and the promises of the federal government. All too often, the merchants cheated them shamelessly, and the government willfully ignored its solemn treaty commitments.

The yearly payments of the Indians for their debts were only a small portion of the profits the traders and others were making from the Sioux tribes. Every time the government ratified a treaty with the Indians, middlemen seized the opportunity to act as agents, negotiating agreements or expediting paperwork and effectively scheming to steal most of the money the tribes were to receive as compensation for selling their land. In 1851, the Indians had been tricked into signing what became known as the "traders' paper." After each chief had signed the government agreement, he was given another paper to sign and told it was simply an extra copy of the treaty. Actually, it was an agreement acknowledging certain debts to the traders and pledging to repay them.

There was no indication in the traders' paper of the amount of money involved, no written record or accounting of any obligation. The amounts allegedly owed by the Indians were substantial, and in due course they were deducted from the annuities. By the terms of the 1851 treaty, most of the $495,000 promised the Indians as compensation for their removal from the 24 million acres of their former land, which they had sold for a ridiculously low amount, was claimed by the traders. The governor of the Minnesota Territory, Alexander Ramsey, had negotiated that treaty in his capacity as ex officio Superintendent of Indian Affairs. He and his secretary, Hugh Tyler, took a 15 percent fee for handling the transaction. Tyler received an additional $55,000 for arranging Senate approval of the treaty.

The infamous traders' paper became a standard practice. In 1857, the Sioux agreed to sell a tract of approximately 1 million acres to the government, but they received little cash once the traders' phony claims were settled. Among those with prior claims on the Indians' money was Henry Hastings Sibley, a fur trader soon to be governor, congressman, and the man chosen to quell the Sioux uprising. His demand was for $145,000.

"My Great Father was to give me money and goods," Standing Buffalo recalled. "I know that my Great Father is good and that he wishes only my good, but some of his children are not all as good as him. They are traitors. I was to receive a great quantity of money every year. The money left the hands of my Great Father but in passing from hand to hand, each one taking his part, nothing reached my hand more than a dollar. My heart was sad in seeing that."

The Sioux had long ago learned to distrust the traders and the mixed-bloods who worked for them, and by June of 1862, they had also become wary of the reservation's new Indian agent. There were two agencies on the Sioux reservation: the Upper Agency, known as Yellow Medicine, and the Lower Agency, called Redwood. Whereas the Upper Agency Sioux were generally pleased with their portion of the reservation, because it included more woods and better hunting grounds, the Lower Agency Sioux were dissatisfied with theirs, a condition that contributed to their dislike and suspicion of the whites. The Indians at both agencies, however, were suffering similarly from hunger and from the trickery of the traders and the insensitivity of the latest administrator, Maj. Thomas J. Galbraith. He was not really a major of anything; that was an honorary title given to all Indian agents to enhance their authority among Indians and their prestige among whites. Galbraith, who arrived in 1861, lived at the Upper Agency.

Like all agents, Galbraith was a political appointee, and, like far too many of them, he knew nothing about Indians. In addition, he lacked the commitment or dedication to fair treatment for the Indians that some of his predecessors had demonstrated. Those who knew Galbraith described him as a man "supremely confident of his own rectitude, scornful of advice, inclined to oversimplify situations, and doggedly determined to cling to his interpretation of a situation and to justify his course of action afterward, regardless of the consequences." He was considered to be "arrogant, stubborn, emotionally unstable, and a hard drinker." Little Crow would later charge that Galbraith was entirely to blame for the Sioux uprising. He was the wrong man in the wrong place at the wrong time.

Nevertheless, Galbraith was the only white man to whom the Sioux could appeal for relief of their desperate situation. The chiefs of the Upper Sioux did just that in person on June 20 at Yellow Medicine, asking when the annuity money and provisions would be distributed. They reported the rumor they had heard that there would be no payment that year because of the war. Galbraith told the chiefs that their fears were unfounded, that they would definitely receive their money. However, he did not know for certain when it would come, or whether it would be the full amount promised. In truth, Galbraith knew no more about the payment than the Indians did.

The chiefs requested that the food and provisions then stored in the agency's large brick warehouse be made available to the Indians. That merchandise was due to be distributed with the annuity payment, but their people were hungry now. The chiefs could not understand why they should starve when flour, pork, lard, and sugar—all things they sorely needed— were kept behind the storehouse's locked doors.

Galbraith refused to issue the goods until the annuity money arrived. Not a blanket, a pot, a hatchet, or a bolt of cloth would be released. To do so would be to flout established procedure, which called for a single distribution of money, food, and provisions. Besides, it was easier to distribute everything at once. The process was cumbersome enough; the Indians lined up and individually received their goods and made their marks on the agency roll books. Just because they were hungry was no reason to take any extra trouble.

Galbraith instructed the chiefs to return to their villages and to send their young men out on hunting parties—let them feed themselves. The chiefs should come back to the agency in a month, on July 20, he told them. By then, Galbraith said, the annuity would surely have arrived. However, he was expressing only a hope, not a conviction, although he promised to distribute money and provisions then.

After the Indian delegation left, Galbraith traveled to the Lower Agency, covering the thirty miles on horseback. He had government business to attend to and did not return to Yellow Medicine until July 14, three weeks later. When he arrived, he found some five thousand destitute Sioux waiting to greet him, encamped around the agency buildings and demanding to be fed. The chiefs repeated the rumors they had heard that the annuity would not come that year, and said if they did not get food from the warehouse soon, they would die.

Galbraith remained adamant about adhering to established procedure, but this time the Indians were prepared. They had someone else to plead their case, twenty-five-year-old Lt. Timothy J. Sheehan of the Fifth Minnesota Regiment at Fort Ridgely, forty miles to the southeast. Anticipating trouble after the chiefs' June 20 visit, Galbraith had asked for soldiers to protect the agency and safeguard the food in the warehouse. Sheehan had arrived with two companies, numbering one hundred men, a few days before Galbraith returned from his trip to the Lower Agency.

Feeling more secure with the troopers on hand, Galbraith again told the Indians to go home and wait. He would let them know when the annuity arrived. The Sioux refused to leave. If they were going to starve to death, they would do so on his doorstep. Lieutenant Sheehan, either out of compassion for the Indians' plight or fear for the safety of his outnumbered men, eventually persuaded Galbraith to open the warehouse. The agent reluctantly consented, and for three weeks he doled out just enough food to keep the Sioux from dying.

*   *   *

Not all of the Indians were in danger of starving. Those who had adopted the white ways of living were doing quite well, and that angered the rest of the Sioux. The ones who observed the old customs, the ways of their ancestors—roaming free, hunting game, and living off their own land—had always been hostile toward the whites who tried to "civilize" them. However, they truly despised those of their own kind who heeded the white man's call, regarding them as nothing less than traitors. And when so many of the Indians were desperate for food, the traditionalists, the so-called blanket Indians, hated the well-fed farmer Indians even more.

The blanket Indians who abided by the old ways believed that the white settlers were trying to destroy the cohesiveness that characterized Indian tribal life. They were right; that was precisely the intent of the federal program designed to entice the Sioux to become farmer Indians. The government hoped to substitute private ownership and competition for the Indians' standard of communal ownership and cooperation, and they offered powerful incentives to adopt this new way of life.

The program, begun by an Indian agent in 1856 and encouraged by the missionaries, involved giving Indian families up to five acres of land and building them brick houses in which to live. Initially, white farmers plowed the land and planted the crops until the Indians learned the rudiments of farming. The farmer Indians were offered more food and clothing than the blanket Indians, paid for from the common fund intended to benefit the entire reservation. The farmer Indians were also given two men's suits, a cow, a yoke of oxen, cook stoves, and other household items such as tubs, buckets, and churns. They were well supplied with coffee, tea, salt, sugar, soap, molasses, rice, and lard, enough to provide for a more luxurious life than that of the blanket Indians. In all, each farmer Indian received supplies valued at ten times that of the other Sioux.

In return, the farmer Indians were required to keep their hair short, dress in trousers and shirts, attend church, and send their children to the mission schools. They pledged never to drink liquor, to cultivate the soil, and to elect a president and a body of representatives to govern them. As more Sioux joined this movement—and by the summer of 1862 some 10 percent of the families had done so—their natural sense of community began to deteriorate. The farmer Indians sold their crops to the government agent rather than distributing them among their relatives. They kept the profits for themselves, too, rather than sharing them. Living as separate families rather than as part of a group, they no longer had time for or interest in tribal ceremonies and feasts. After several prominent chiefs joined the farmer movement, the old Indian villages dwindled significantly. Two-story houses were fast replacing the deerskin lodges. Little Crow and a few other chiefs viewed these changes with despair. If the trend continued, they believed, the culture that had nurtured and protected the Sioux nation for centuries was marked for extinction.

When Tom Galbraith became the Indian agent to the Sioux in 1861, he worked hard to foster the farmer program. He issued provisions to the blanket Indians only once a year, adhering to regulations, but freely gave food and other goods to the farmer Indians whenever they demanded them, as often as once a month. He believed that Indians should not be paid and fed for maintaining what to him was a slothful way of living. They should be rewarded only when they farmed and behaved the way they were supposed to, like decent Christian white men.

During the summer of 1862, when the majority of the people on the Sioux reservation were going hungry, the farmer Indians ate well and continued to receive food from the agency warehouse, sometimes within sight of their starving brothers.

The blanket Indians resented the special privileges enjoyed by the farmers and were jealous of them. Still, they remained opposed to the abandonment of the tribal customs and sacred rituals. At first, they were content to ridicule those who lived in brick houses, but when that proved ineffective, they turned to more violent forms of intimidation. They harassed the farmer Indians by setting fire to stables and haystacks. They killed their cows and oxen. And when that did not work, they threatened to kill the farmer Indians themselves. In the winter of 1860, a spokesman for the blanket Indians warned the farmers that anyone caught wearing white man's trousers

by the following summer would not live to see the leaves fall.
After several farmers were murdered, there were some defec-
tions. Others survived by wearing white man's clothing only
when they needed to see the agent.

Galbraith called in troops to protect the farmer Indians,
and he continued the practice of distributing generous amounts
of food to them but barely subsistence rations to the others.
He wanted the blanket Indians to understand clearly what they
were missing by refusing to give up their ways; that is, their
freedom, dignity, and identity, everything that defined them
as Sioux. They saw it clearly enough, however. They saw the
well-fed Indians among the starving, and they understood that
the whites wanted to destroy their culture and turn them into
something alien.

As the end of July approached and the annuity payment did
not arrive, the Indians grew weaker and more resentful, nursing
their grievances against the whites. And in their fear, confusion,
and uncertainty about the future, they had many grievances on
which to feed. The whites had already taken their land and were
now trying to take away their identity as a people.

How good life had been to the Sioux before the whites
came, how fruitful and abundant, how free! The lands inhabited
by the Indians included nearly all of what became Minnesota,
plus western Wisconsin and parts of North and South Dakota.
Judge Charles Flandrau, an early white settler in the area, described it as "an Indian paradise. It abounded in buffalo, elk,
moose, deer, beaver, wolves, and, in fact, nearly all wild animals
found in North America. It held upon its surface eight thousand
beautiful lakes, alive with the finest of edible fish. It was dotted
over with beautiful groves of the sugar maple, yielding quantities
of delicious sugar, and wild rice swamps were abundant. An in-
habitant of this region, with absolute liberty . . . certainly had
very little more to ask of his Creator."

The first white men who came to the Sioux territory did
not plan to stay, to settle the land, cut down the forests, dig
up the earth, fence in their farms, build houses and towns, or
run off the buffalo and other game. They did not desire to
push the Sioux off their land or destroy their culture. They
came only to trade, to offer valuable goods in return for valu-

able goods—guns, steel tools and knives, shiny brass kettles, and arrays of trinkets in return for furs.

These initial encounters between whites and Indians had occurred some two hundred years before, in the spring of 1660. The earliest visitors were French explorers and traders, and the Indians welcomed them with elaborate ceremonies. When a chief threw a handful of tobacco into the ritual fire, the French reciprocated by tossing in a handful of gunpowder. The result was impressive. Obviously, these whites had powerful medicine.

The French built trading posts and missions and learned the Indian language. Some married Sioux women and were accepted by the community. They bestowed on the Indian nation the name by which it became known. Among themselves, these Indians were known as Dakotas, a term meaning "union" or "ally," thought to refer to the union of several bands—the Wahpeton, Sisseton, Mdewakanton, Wahpekute, Yankton, Yanktonai, and Teton. The first four constituted the Eastern or Santee Sioux; the others, the Western Sioux. Among the eastern tribes, the Wahpeton and Sisseton bands would later settle near the Upper Agency of the reservation and be called the Upper Sioux. The Mdewakanton and Wahpekute would settle around the Lower Agency and be called the Lower Sioux. The enemies of these tribes, the Chippewas, referred to them as Nadouessioux, a Chippewa word meaning "enemy." The French traders shortened the word to Sioux.

In 1760, British traders entered the world of the Sioux. Like the French, they came only to trade. They were few in number, and adapted to the Dakota culture, learning their ways and their language.

Then the Americans arrived, and the world of the Sioux changed forever. The army came first, in 1805, with an expedition led by Lt. Zebulon M. Pike. His mission was to establish a U.S. presence in the area by building a series of forts and laying the groundwork for the development of government-operated trading posts. These posts, which would sell goods to the Indians at lower prices than private traders could, were supposed to make the Indians dependent on American handouts and reduce the influence of the French and British traders. To accomplish these goals, Pike held a council with the chiefs of the various Dakota bands to purchase tracts of land for the forts and trading posts.

The chiefs agreed, but they took offense at being asked to sign a paper to sell the land. They believed that their word of honor, which had always been sufficient in their dealings with other Indian nations, should be enough to bind any agreement with the army. In the end, they agreed to sell approximately one hundred thousand acres, which Pike estimated to be worth two hundred thousand dollars. The treaty paper, however, did not mention any specific amount of money to be paid for title to the land. That clause was left blank, to be filled in later in Washington. When the U.S. Senate ratified the treaty, the amount of two thousand dollars was inserted. Only two of the seven chiefs meeting with Pike had been willing to sign the treaty, but the government considered it binding on the entire Sioux nation. One of the two who signed was Little Crow, whose namesake would be chief during the hunger summer of 1862.

During the War of 1812, the Sioux, like other Indian nations in the northwestern territories, sided with the British against the Americans. They had had little contact with Americans, but for fifty years they had been trading with the British, who had always treated them fairly. In return for the Indians' pledge of support, the British rashly made promises of future benefits to accrue to the Indians, promises they were unable to fulfill when they lost the war. Feeling betrayed, the Sioux held a council with the British and refused to accept their offer of gifts in consolation.

"After we have fought for you," the elder Little Crow told the British, "endured many hardships, lost some of our people, and awakened the vengeance of our powerful neighbors, you make a peace for yourselves and leave us. . . . You no longer need our services, and offer us these goods as a compensation for having deserted us. But no! We will not take them; we hold them and yourselves in equal contempt!" This marked the beginning of the Indians' disillusionment with white men. Their words could not be trusted. Their words held no honor.

The Americans did not return to the Sioux to pay even the paltry two thousand dollars in goods for the land the Indians had ceded until fourteen years after the agreement had been signed. Then the army came to construct their first fort on Dakota land. Named Fort St. Anthony, later renamed Fort Snelling, it occupied a commanding position on bluffs over-looking the juncture of the Minnesota and Mississippi rivers. The garrison was small—the Americans felt no need for a large military presence—but the fort also housed the first U.S. Indian agent to the Sioux, Maj. Lawrence Taliaferro. For nineteen years, an unusually long tenure for an Indian agent, he was the sole representative of the President, the Great Father in Washington, to the Sioux.

Enlightened, fair, forceful, and incorruptible, Taliaferro proved to be a rarity among Indian agents. Unfortunately, during his time, the Sioux suffered serious economic reverses. By the late 1820s, the lucrative trade in furs and pelts was declining. The demand had been so great that too many beavers and deer had been killed, and the traditional hunting grounds were rapidly being depleted. The Sioux were running out of food, and the traders were refusing them credit. There was only one source of help—the U.S. government.

After much discussion with the Sioux chiefs, Taliaferro persuaded them that the only sensible course was to sell more of their land. With the annuities from the sale, they would be guaranteed sufficient food and provisions to live comfortably for many years. In the meantime, he hoped to teach them about farming so that they might be able to support themselves. Taliaferro had little trouble persuading the government to deal with the Indians, because there was growing pressure from eastern business interests to exploit the huge timber stands in Wisconsin and Minnesota, the eastern portion of Dakota lands.

In August 1837, Taliaferro left for Washington, D.C., with a delegation of twenty-six Indian chiefs. They traveled by steamboat to Pittsburgh and by canal barge, stagecoach, and train to the capital, taking four weeks to cover the distance. They stayed at the Globe Hotel and were shown all the sights of the city to impress on them the power and splendor of the white man's way of life. Six chiefs had their portraits painted, and all were given medals.

At meetings held in a Presbyterian church, government representatives proposed buying 5 million acres for $1 million, to be paid in installments over twenty years. Part of the money would be spent on medicine, livestock, and farm equipment. It would also pay for the services of a physician, farmers to teach the Indians how to grow crops, and blacksmiths to repair guns and kettles and fabricate tools and animal traps. The traders were not forgotten—ninety thousand dollars was set aside for payment of the debts they said the Sioux owed.

The Indians signed the treaty and went home, expecting to receive their money and goods soon. They waited an entire year. It took nine months for the U.S. Senate to ratify the treaty and three more months to assemble the goods and ship them west. When the provisions finally arrived, the Indians found them to be inferior. Many of the items were worthless to a hungry people. They had no need of beads, ribbons, castanets, handkerchiefs, and bolts of silk, no matter how colorful they might be. As an additional insult, the cash payment was not made. The Indians were told that they would have to wait another twelve months. They did not understand the explanation that the annuity was to be paid out of interest on investments that had not yet matured.

Although the government was slow in honoring its treaty commitments, it acted swiftly to take the Indians' land. Within days of the signing, white merchants flooded the newly acquired territory. Among the first to arrive were purveyors of whiskey, who set up shop on the perimeter of the Indian territory. The Sioux had already been exposed to hard liquor by earlier traders, but now it became more easily obtainable, and the results were disastrous.

"At some of the villages they were drunk months together," wrote a Minnesota pioneer. "There was no end to it. They would have whiskey. They would give guns, blankets, pork, lard, flour, corn, coffee, sugar, horses, furs, traps, anything for whiskey." The high incidence of drunkenness quickly led to violence. "They killed one another with guns, knives, hatchets, clubs, firebrands; they fell into the fire and water and were burned to death, and drowned; they froze to death, and committed suicide."

The situation became so intolerable that Major Taliaferro persuaded some of the younger men in each village to take turns abstaining from drink so as to prevent their drunken brothers from harming themselves or others. The sober ones would collect the weapons and hide them. Whenever the drunkards became too threatening, they would be tied up until they recovered.

Whiskey was only one destructive legacy of the treaty of 1837. The white settlers also brought their diseases. Cholera and malaria swept the Sioux villages. Whooping cough killed uncounted numbers of children. The Indians had no resistance to these plagues, and the government provided little in the way of care or medicine.

Before too long, the dynamic, self-supporting Sioux nation turned into a welfare state. The Indians became increasingly dependent on the government for their survival, abetted by traders who were liberal in granting credit—now that they knew the U.S. government would reimburse them—while charging outrageous prices for their goods.

Each year, the Sioux obtained more and more of their food directly from the government or the traders and less from their own hunting and gathering. As the pressure to find game eased, many hunters, freed of the obligation to supply food for their families and their camps, left the region in search of adventure farther west. The young men of the villages knew that if a hunt proved unsuccessful, or was not even undertaken, the agency would still feed their families.

In one sense, this situation offered a kind of freedom, but it was also dispiriting because it took away from the Indians their work, their sense of purpose. A primary task in the lives of Indian braves was hunting. They were trained from an early age to hunt not only for food but to gain a sense of pride. It was a pillar of their culture and identity. Now the braves could loaf about the camps, drink whiskey, or wander out west. A downward spiral had begun, spinning into a cycle of dependence, dismay, and despair, continually fueled by anger over the power and presence of the whites.

In 1849, Minnesota became a U.S. territory. The newly appointed governor, Alexander Ramsey, arrived in the capital city of St. Paul with one overriding ambition: to open up the territory for settlement by whites. To accomplish that, he would have to induce the Sioux to sell most of their remaining land and move to a small reservation. Another treaty would have to be negotiated. The local traders were also clamoring for a new treaty because they knew it would include more funds to be set aside to pay the Indians' debts. Henry Sibley, the fur trader who was now a congressman in Washington, urged that the Indians be paid a higher price for their lands than the offer being considered. His reason was not an altruistic one; he was simply being practical. The more money the Indians received from the government, the more the traders would get.

There was no trip to Washington this time. In the summer of 1851, the Indians gathered at Traverse des Sioux, a few miles north of the town of St. Peter on the Blue Earth River. "It was a grand affair," recalled Nancy Faribault, a fifteen-year-old mixed-blood. "All bands of Indians were there in great numbers. The commissioners came up, and with them a number of other white men traders, attorneys, speculators, soldiers, etc. They had great times, to be sure, and I have always wondered how so much champagne got so far out on the frontier!"

It was not such a grand affair for the chiefs when Governor Ramsey and Luke Lea, the one-legged Commissioner of Indian Affairs, presented their terms. The Sioux were hungry, the government representatives noted, and their game had all but disappeared. For those reasons, the Great Father in Washington was willing to help them by exchanging money and goods worth $1,665,000 for 21 million acres, land that was surely of no use to the Indians.

"Everything we promise will be faithfully performed," Lea assured the chiefs when he sensed that they seemed reluctant to dispose of the majority of their homeland. They had been deceived before, and they expressed their concern that the treaty terms would be altered in Washington.

Referring to their last trip to the capital in 1837, one chief said, "When we were at Washington, the chiefs were told many things, which when we came back here and attempted to carry out we found could not be done. At the end of three or four years, the Indians found out very different from what they had been told, and all were ashamed."

Governor Ramsey said that he was hurt by the chiefs' lack

of trust. How could they suggest that he had come there to cheat them! He said again that the Great Father wanted to help them. If the government was only after their land, it would send in the soldiers to drive the Sioux away. When Little Crow, Wabasha, and other chiefs refused to sign, however, Ramsey decided to switch tactics. Commissioner Lea, tired of trying to persuade the chiefs by arguing how beneficial the new treaty would be, reminded them instead how bad it would be for them if they did not sign. He hinted that perhaps the present annuities might stop if they refused to cooperate.

"No man puts any food in his mouth by long talk but may often get hungry at it," Lea said. "Let Little Crow and the chiefs step forward and sign."

They affixed their marks and, as usual, Sibley and the other traders summoned them over to sign another traders' paper, assuring them it was merely an additional copy of the government treaty.

Within days, white speculators and settlers invaded Sioux territory, staking claims and building houses on land that legally still belonged to the Indians, because it would take another year for the U.S. Senate to ratify the treaty. When they did so, they struck out the provision calling for a reservation for the Sioux, leaving thousands of Indians with no legitimate home. The amended treaty required the consent of the chiefs, who quickly understood that they had been cheated and betrayed yet again. When they met with Governor Ramsey, Wabasha expressed their outrage.

"There is one thing more which our Great Father can do," he said. "Gather us all together on the prairie and surround us with soldiers and shoot us down."

Ramsey was in a difficult position. If the chiefs did not sign the amended treaty, the whites now occupying the land might have to be evicted and development of the territory would cease. A careful reading of the Senate's version of the treaty, however, solved his problem. He found a loophole. The Senate had authorized the President to permit the Indians to remain on a portion of the land until such time as the government wanted to use it. Based on that most tenuous of assurances, Ramsey told the chiefs that they could stay on the acreage designated as their reservation. He did not mention that their occupancy could be terminated at any time and that it was not protected by the treaty.

Based on his remarks—the full import of which the chiefs may not have understood, either because Ramsey was circumspect or because of inaccurate translation—the chiefs signed the amended treaty of 1851 and began moving their people to the small part of their homeland that remained open to them.

Five years later, even that tract of land was considered too generous. Whites wanted half of it, nearly a million acres. Immigrants were pouring into Minnesota in record numbers, thirty thousand in 1855 alone. In 1850, there were only six thousand whites in the entire territory; by 1856, there were two hundred thousand, and they all wanted land.

Told that the Great Father wanted to see them to make adjustments in the last treaty, twenty-nine chiefs of the Upper and Lower Sioux, led by Little Crow and Wabasha, made the long journey east in 1858. They stayed in Washington for three months, meeting with Charles Mix, the Acting Commissioner of Indian Affairs.

Uncertain about whether to agree to sell more of their land, Little Crow, Wabasha, and Shakopee called on the only white friend the Sioux had known, Maj. Lawrence Taliaferro, who had been their agent for nearly twenty years.

"My old father," Little Crow addressed him, "we have called upon you; we love you; we respect you. Our old chiefs are all gone. We don't know what to do. They want us to divide our lands and live like white people. Since you left us, a dark cloud has hung over our nation. We have lost confidence in the promises of our Great Father and his people. Bad men have nearly destroyed us."

The chief reminded Taliaferro that he had brought Little Crow's grandfather to Washington in 1824 and his father in 1837. Both men had told Little Crow that he must always heed the agent's words. "I loved you from my youth," Little Crow continued, "and my nation will never forget you. If ever we act foolish and do wrong, it is because you are not with us. . . .

"Since you left we have had five agents. We failed to get

a friend in any one like you; they all joined the traders. We know your heart. It feels for your old children."

Taliaferro, aging and out of touch with Indian affairs, no longer had any influence in Washington. He advised the chiefs to make the best treaty they could and to live in peace with the whites. If ever the Sioux should go to war against the whites, he warned, they would be destroyed forever.

"Bear all things," he told the chiefs. "Hope all things, and the Great Spirit will never leave you in the hands of bad men long."

In the middle of June, the chiefs, dressed in full regalia, held their final meeting with Commissioner Mix. It lasted all night and unleashed much bitterness. Little Crow made a long, impassioned speech about the wrongs the Sioux had suffered from broken treaties and unkept promises. Mix reminded him that the chiefs had no legal right to the land they now occupied and that they lived there only through the goodwill of the Great Father. Now the Great Father desired to help the Indians by granting them permanent title to a new reservation. Tribal villages would be abolished, but each Indian family would be assigned an eighty-acre farm and would be paid for the land they would have to give up. There would be no money, however, unless the chiefs signed a new treaty.

Little Crow continued to resist, citing a catalogue of grievances, until Mix accused him of acting like a child, the worst insult that could be inflicted on a Sioux chief. In the end, Little Crow consented, reluctantly, to the terms of the treaty—he had no choice—even though they did not mention any specific amount of money to be paid for the land. At seven o'clock in the morning, the papers were signed, and Little Crow expressed the hope that Mix would never again call him a child. Mix said only that he hoped he would not have occasion to do so.

To attempt to mollify the chiefs, each was given a new suit of clothing, and they were taken on a visit to New York City, where they were presented with a variety of gifts, including flags and ceremonial swords. Little Crow was given two thousand dollars in cash and the other chiefs were promised the equivalent in presents to distribute to their people on their return to Minnesota.

Little Crow was also invited to a gala dinner party attended by the cream of Washington society. He was a welcome curiosity to those whose only knowledge of Indians had been gleaned from colorful and not always accurate books and magazines. One can only wonder what Little Crow thought of the glittering assemblage, and what he thought of himself, having just signed away half of his people's land, and perhaps all of their way of life.

The following March, the U.S. Congress appropriated $266,880 for the Sioux land, much of which was claimed instantly by the traders. The Sioux's agent, Maj. Joseph R. Brown, had estimated the value of the land at five dollars per acre. The government paid thirty cents.

By the end of July 1862, when the latest annuity payment still had not arrived, some of the younger Sioux warriors decided that it was time to act. About 150 of them formed a Soldiers' Lodge, a secret organization that the warriors could convene whenever the tribe faced some danger that they believed the chiefs were not dealing with properly. The prospect of continued starvation without the annuity was seen as sufficient threat to justify taking this action.

The braves of the Soldiers' Lodge were determined that when the payment arrived, they would claim it all for their people and not allow it to be dispersed among the traders. When the chiefs were presented with the warriors' plan, none of them voiced any opposition. The chiefs had no absolute dictatorial power over their people at any time, and certainly not in the face of a popular ruling by a Soldiers' Lodge. Wabasha, a chief considered to be a moderating influence, said that he would not speak against the plan because the traders and the agents had been cheating the Dakotas long enough. It was time to take a stand.

Shortly after the lodge was formed, it sent a delegation to Fort Ridgely to ask Capt. John Marsh, the post commander, what he would do if the Indians refused to allow the traders to be paid first when the annuity money arrived. Would he order his troops into action? No, Marsh assured them. "My boys are soldiers," he said. "They are not collection agents for the traders."

Some of the more radical men in the Soldiers' Lodge were not satisfied, however. It was not enough to prevent the traders from taking their money. The time was ripe for war against the whites. With fewer troops than usual at Fort Ridgely because of the demands of the Union army, the Great Father was too busy fighting the Confederates, they argued, to bother about the Sioux in Minnesota. They could clear the white settlers out of all former Indian lands before the army could muster enough soldiers to try to stop them. Most of the Sioux were not ready to accept the idea of war, however. Their need for food was more urgent and overwhelming than any desire for revenge or to reclaim their lost lands.

August came, and their desperation increased. Agent Galbraith remained adamant about preserving the stockpiles of food in his warehouse. By August 4, the Indians decided that they had waited long enough.

In the early-morning hours, two Sioux braves rode to the Upper Agency to speak to Lieutenant Sheehan, who was based there with his two companies of one hundred men. They told him that a group of Indians would be coming soon to fire a salute and to hold a demonstration, something they had done before as a harmless way of venting their aggression. The braves wanted to reassure the soldiers of the Indians' peaceful intentions.

Shortly thereafter, eight hundred warriors descended on the agency, shouting and firing their guns in the air. One band rushed to the warehouse and split open the door with an ax. The rest of the Indians surrounded the soldiers, outnumbering them eight to one. Sheehan kept the troopers calm when he realized that the Sioux were only after the food. If the Indians had been intent on killing the soldiers, they would have opened fire immediately, while they had the advantage of surprise.

Sheehan ordered the tarpaulin removed from one of his two howitzers and wheeled the gun around to face the warehouse door. The Indians, who were hauling out sacks of flour, gave way at once, forming an open corridor between the howitzer and the door. The lieutenant led a squad of sixteen men in a quick-march step between the lines of Indians and into the warehouse. Once inside, he detailed his men to escort the remaining Indians out of the building, and he went off to find agent Galbraith.

Sheehan tried to persuade Galbraith to issue more food to the Indians. He felt it was the only way to prevent bloodshed. Galbraith refused, arguing that if he caved in, he would henceforth lose all control over the Sioux.

Outside, the troops and the warriors faced each other uneasily, weapons at the ready. Finally, Sheehan prevailed on Galbraith to distribute some pork and flour to the Indians if they agreed to leave the agency and send their chiefs back the following day for a council.

Lieutenant Sheehan sent a message to Fort Ridgely asking Captain Marsh to come as quickly as possible. Sheehan's firmness may have saved them this time, but who knew what the Indians would do next.

The following morning, Sheehan posted his men in the best defensive positions he could find. The chiefs had come prepared to talk, however, not to fight, despite the urgings of some of their braves for an armed attack on the agency. Little Crow had come from the Lower Agency to take charge of the council. So far, the Indians at the Lower Agency had not made any threats, but Little Crow knew that if fighting broke out at the Upper Agency, he would not be able to prevent his warriors from joining in.

Present at the meeting between the Sioux chiefs and agent Galbraith were some clerks from the traders' stores; John Williamson, a missionary who had grown up among the Sioux and knew their language; Andrew Myrick, a trader who owned stores at both agencies; and Peter Quinn, the agency interpreter.

Little Crow stated the Indians' concerns. "We have waited a long time," he told Galbraith. "The money is ours, but we cannot get it. We have no food, but here are these stores filled with food. We ask that you, the agent, make some arrangement by which we can get food from the stores, or else we may take our own way to keep ourselves from starving. When men are hungry they help themselves."

Quinn, thirty years on the job as an interpreter, appeared upset by Little Crow's threat, and he refused to translate the chief's words, fearing their impact on Galbraith and on the influential trader Andrew Myrick. Galbraith asked the missionary to translate instead.

"Williamson, you tell us what Little Crow says."

Williamson delivered a full and accurate account of Little Crow's words. Galbraith turned to the clerks, who were there to act on the traders' behalf.

"Well," he said, "it's up to you now. What will you do?"

The clerks drew aside to confer quietly and then announced that they would go along with whatever Myrick decided. Myrick said nothing and started to walk out of the room. Galbraith stopped him, insisting that he tell them his decision. Would he give the Indians food from his stock or not?

"So far as I am concerned," Myrick said, "if they are hungry, let them eat grass or their own dung."

Once again, the interpreter declined to translate the inflammatory words, this time fearing the reaction of the chiefs. Williamson relayed the message instead. When the missionary had finished, the Indians remained motionless and silent for a moment, then leaped to their feet, shouting, and stalked out of the room. Andrew Myrick would pay for that remark.

Soldiers remained on alert for the rest of the day. When Captain Marsh arrived at the Upper Agency, he invited the chiefs to meet with him the next day. Marsh knew he had to defuse their anger. If the Sioux decided to attack the agency, his one hundred soldiers would not stop them for long. He ordered Galbraith to give the Indians all the food he was hoarding and threatened the traders with immediate arrest if they said or did anything to cause unrest.

Marsh's actions, and the issuance of 130 barrels of flour and 30 barrels of pork, seemed to placate Little Crow and the other chiefs. Believing the crisis to be over, Marsh led his troops back to Fort Ridgely. By the following week, Galbraith thought the situation was calm enough to leave the agency for a while. The Union army, facing heavy losses that summer, had issued a call for more soldiers. Thirty mixed-bloods and whites at the Upper Agency had volunteered, and on August 13, Galbraith led the new recruits to the Lower Agency to join twenty additional volunteers. Two days later, he escorted them all to Fort Ridgely.

The view that all was now well on the reservation was shared by many, both white and Indian. On August 13, the

Reverend Stephen R. Riggs, who had lived among the Sioux for almost 30 years, wrote from his home at the Upper Agency: "All is quiet and orderly at the place of the forthcoming payment." A few days later, Galbraith told his wife and children, whom he had sent to the fort for protection, that they could go home to the agency. Clearly, the danger was past.

Galbraith held a long discussion with Little Crow at the Lower Agency. The chief expressed his pleasure at the distribution of food and the prospect of the large corn crop that was ready to be harvested on the government farm. The threat of imminent starvation seemed behind them. The Indians had enough food to sustain them until the annuity payment arrived. Little Crow was also impressed with the construction work on the fine brick house that Galbraith was having built for him in the hope of ensuring Little Crow's continued cooperation. The agent was reassured by Little Crow's apparent friendship and goodwill. The chief even told Galbraith that he desired to live like the white man.

On Sunday, August 17, Little Crow awoke early, went hunting, and attended church services at the Episcopal mission of the Reverend Samuel Hinman at the Lower Agency. Hinman remarked on how attentive the chief was and how interested he seemed in the message of the sermon. After the service, Little Crow politely shook hands with the clergyman and several other white men and walked home.

At approximately the same hour, a government wagon left St. Paul. Among the supplies it carried were two heavy wooden kegs that contained $71,000 in gold coins. The long overdue annuity payment was finally on its way to Fort Ridgely, a one-day trip.

3

HE IS NOT A COWARD

There were four of them.

Their names were Brown Wing, Breaking Up, Killing Ghost, and Runs Against Something When Crawling.

Two were dressed like Indians and two like white men.

They were from the village at Rice Creek of the Lower Sioux.

All were in their twenties.

They went hunting that Sunday morning but with no success. They were hungry.

At eleven o'clock, without intention, design, or desire, they started a war.

The men were forty miles northeast of their village, on their way home. Near the tiny settlement of Acton Township, they came to the property of Mr. and Mrs. Robinson Jones, who ran a combined store and post office. Mr. Jones was at the store with his two adopted children, fifteen-year-old Clara Wilson and her eighteen-month-old half brother. Mrs. Jones was visiting her son by her first marriage, Howard Baker, and his wife and two children. The Bakers lived a half mile away. Staying with the Bakers were a young couple from Wisconsin, the Websters. They were living in a covered wagon located near the Bakers' house while they looked for land to buy.

Near the split-rail fence that marked the boundary of Jones's land, the four Indians found some eggs in a hen's nest. One of the braves picked up the eggs.

"Don't take them," another said, "for they belong to a white man and we may get into trouble."

The first Indian, angered by the remark, threw the eggs down.

"You are a coward," he shouted. "You are afraid of the white man. You are afraid to take even an egg from him, though you are half-starved. Yes, you are a coward, and I will tell everybody so."

"I am not a coward. I am not afraid of the white man, and to show you that I am not I will go to the house and shoot him. Are you brave enough to go with me?"

"Yes, I will go with you, and we will see who is the braver of us two."

"We will go with you," the other two said, "and we will be brave, too."

None of them, it turned out, was sufficiently brave when they got to the store. They were noisy and acted tough, but Jones decided they were no threat. He also believed that they were not going to buy anything, so he left, telling young Clara that he would be at the Bakers' house. He took his rifle with him, but there was nothing unusual about that. Few Americans on the frontier went out unarmed.

The four Sioux followed Jones, the one who took the eggs taunting the others for failing to kill the storekeeper. When they all reached the Bakers' house, the Indians suggested to Jones, Baker, and his friend Webster that they engage in some target shooting, a common pastime in those parts. They took turns firing at a block of wood set atop a tree stump. The Indians reloaded after each shot, but the whites did not. Suddenly, all four Indians turned on Jones and shot him. One took aim at the women watching from the doorway of the house. Baker jumped in front of them and took the bullet instead. The Indians quickly brought down Webster and Mrs. Jones. Mrs. Baker, who was holding her baby in her arms, fainted and fell backward through a trapdoor into the cellar. Neither she nor the baby was injured. Mrs. Webster, who was resting in the covered wagon, was out of the Indians' sight.

The Indians fled immediately, realizing the punishment their action was likely to bring. The settlers would hang them from the nearest tree when they caught them. They ran back toward Acton Township, back past Jones's store. Clara Wilson saw them from the doorway. One Indian stopped, took aim, and fired, killing her instantly. The baby remained asleep inside.

Mrs. Baker and Mrs. Webster tried to comfort the dying men. Jones, a strong, muscular man, died hard, kicking holes in the earth with his heels. He crammed fistfuls of dirt in his mouth to keep from screaming. The women could only wail and sob, fearing that the Sioux would return.

A white man on a horse approached the house. They called to him to stop, but he just laughed and waved. He supposed that the dead men were drunk, and had fallen down and bloodied their noses. He laughed again and rode away, leaving the women alone. He was known in the neighborhood as a demented Irishman who spent his days wandering the trails, and his appearance brought no comfort to the hysterical survivors.

The women made for the nearest house, that of Lars Olson, a few miles distant. Olson responded at once. He sent his twelve-year-old son on horseback to Ripley, a town twelve miles away, to raise the alarm, but few people believed the boy's story. Those who did allow that it might have actually happened said that the Indians must have been drunk. Anyway, they would quickly be caught and dealt with. Justice on the frontier was swift.

The four Indian braves headed south, running until they reached another farmhouse, where a man and his daughter and son-in-law were eating their Sunday dinner. Moving stealthily, while the meal continued uninterrupted, the Sioux took two horses that were already harnessed, hitched them to a wagon, and made for their village on the reservation.

It was almost dark by the time they got home to Rice Creek. They approached their chief, Red Middle Voice, and told him and the other warriors, with great excitement, what they had done. The chief was fascinated by the account of how easily the whites had been killed, and he kept asking for details about how each person had been shot. As much as he seemed to relish the story, however, he knew that his whole band could be in trouble. His braves had killed whites, and among them was at least one woman. Soldiers would come after the killers, and the Indian agent might withhold the annuity payment and provisions from all the Sioux until the perpetrators surrendered. If that happened, other tribes would try to capture the guilty braves and turn them over to the soldiers. If they faced punishment anyway, the chief reasoned, why not go to war now and drive the whites away forever? Red Middle Voice's warriors were among the most militant of the Sioux bands. It was no coincidence that Rice Creek was where the Soldiers' Lodge held its meetings.

The idea was intriguing, but Red Middle Voice knew that it was futile to attack the white settlements with only his small number of braves. Unless he could enlist the help of other Sioux bands, he and his people would be considered outlaws and would be banished. If they were to go to war, they must have support.

Red Middle Voice led his braves eight miles downstream to the village where Shakopee was chief. Many of his men had also joined the Soldiers' Lodge. The news had preceded them. When the Rice Creek warriors reached the camp, Shakopee's braves were waiting to greet them with cheers, war chants, and loaded weapons. The people were eager for war.

But Shakopee, like Red Middle Voice, realized that their combined forces would not be large enough to wage a successful war against the whites. They needed a more powerful chief as an ally, one whose authority and influence were sufficient to commit all the Sioux bands to the war.

"Let us go down and see Little Crow," said Shakopee.

Little Crow did not want to go to war with the whites. Like his father and grandfather before him, he favored conciliation and compromise over confrontation, a policy he had practiced with success during the years he had been a chief. He had adopted many of the customs and habits of the white settlers and had urged his people to accommodate to the changing times by negotiating and signing treaties with the government.

His attitude was based on both practical and personal considerations. He recognized the power of the federal government; twice he had traveled to the capital city and seen for himself the vastness and splendor of the white world. He realized that the Indians could not prevent the westward expansion of the settlers. They were coming, and eventually they would overrun the Sioux lands and there was nothing the Indians could do about it. In Little Crow's view, there was no alternative to working with the whites, to trying to get the best treaty terms possible for his people. In the process, he hoped to become the acknowledged leader of all the Sioux, not just of the Mdewakantons, his own tribe.

Over the years, Little Crow had become, if not yet the leader of the Sioux nation in fact, certainly the most influential of the chiefs in terms of negotiating treaties, developing the reservation, and acquiring and distributing the annuities. He was a dedicated spokesman for his people, and for himself, as well. His biographer wrote that Little Crow had an "insatiable personal hunger for power." And a missionary on the reservation observed about Little Crow that "popularity is his God." He honed his natural abilities as a politician to that end, to achieving popularity, power, and prestige among his people, but always with the goal of improving their situation.

The Sioux called him, in the Dakota language, Taoyate-duta. He was highly intelligent, charismatic, and dignified, a skilled orator possessing a strong sense of his personal destiny. He had the bearing of a gentleman and was an expert in dealing with the media of the day. Both on the reservation and in Washington, he frequently gave interviews to newspaper reporters and editors, charming them with his openness and wit and his subtle use of sarcasm.

He had long been interested in learning about the white culture. In the 1830s, as an adult, he attended a mission school to learn to read and write in the Dakota language and to master the basics of English and arithmetic. He was a skilled card-player, particularly adept at poker. He took great care in his manner of dress. Published descriptions of treaty ceremonies often remarked on his appearance.

For Indian feasts and festivals, Little Crow wore an elaborate headdress of weasel tails, buffalo horns, ribbons, and colored buckskin tied in knots. For important treaty meetings, he favored a solemn black frock coat adorned with a velvet collar. At one gathering in Washington, he appeared with a blue circle painted around one eye, perhaps to indicate to both whites and Indians that he had not fully abandoned his Sioux heritage.

Nor did he intend to abandon it, not until he felt that his own people had abandoned him. Although he lived in a two-story house rather than a deerskin lodge and often wore shirts and trousers, he resisted for a long time the white man's religion. He kept his hair long in the Indian way, and resided with four wives, who were sisters. His family life has been described as happy and harmonious.

A paradox and an enigma in many ways, Little Crow tried to integrate the two cultures, to balance his life and that of his people between them, and to make use of the best from each. In the end, he belonged to neither and felt betrayed by both.

Little Crow, Taoyateduta, had also felt betrayed by his father. As a firstborn son of a chief, he expected to become chief on his father's death. His father believed that Little Crow had "very little good sense," a view shared by some other members of his tribe. They considered Little Crow to be a "lothario in morals, a debauchee in habits, and of a haughty and overbearing disposition."

As a youth, Little Crow had showed a dissolute streak, drinking heavily, selling whiskey to other Indian bands, womanizing, and gambling. Once he married his four wives, his wildness abated and he became a respectable and sober citizen of the community, eventually admired for his good manners and persuasive speech. It was clear, however, that he was also lazy, seldom hunted, and rarely joined the war parties organized to fight the Chippewas, the traditional enemy of the Sioux. Heredity may have given him the right to replace his father as chief, but his behavior and character were deemed by many to be deficient for that leadership role.

In October 1845, Little Crow's father accidentally shot himself, causing a mortal wound that even the white man's powerful medicine could not heal. As he lay dying, he sent for one of his younger sons—fourth in line for succession and a half brother to Little Crow—and gave him his medals and the title of chief. He urged the new chief to adopt the best aspects of the white culture and to help the Sioux accommodate to the whites' demands.

When Little Crow learned of this, he was determined to claim his birthright. He had been living at Lac qui Parle, some distance west of his father's village, and he had to wait for the ice to melt in the rivers before he could set out. Several relatives and friends accompanied him on the journey down the Minnesota River, and men from other camps who supported him joined the party along the way.

As the flotilla of canoes approached the Mdewakanton camp where Little Crow's father had been chief, several hundred people waited for them on the riverbank. They knew that Little Crow intended to claim his inheritance. The new chief, along with another of Little Crow's half brothers, warned him not to come ashore, and the chief's warriors shouted threats on Little Crow's life.

"You are not wanted here," one brother said. "Go and live at Lac qui Parle."

Little Crow boldly stepped ashore and pushed through the crowd of hostile villagers. A few of his braves followed him. Little Crow stopped and folded his arms across his chest.

"Shoot, then," he taunted his brothers, "where all can see."

Someone fired. Little Crow fell back into the arms of his men. His brothers fled. The bullet passed through both forearms, shattering the bones of the wrists. The warriors carried Little Crow back to his canoe and headed out for Fort Snelling. The army surgeon examined him and announced that both hands would have to be amputated if Little Crow was to survive. He refused instantly. He knew that the Sioux people would never follow a chief who had no hands. It would be better to die.

He ordered his followers to take him back to his village. He would trust his life to the tribal medicine men. If they could not save him, then his death was surely ordained. Over many painful weeks, however, the wounds healed, although Little Crow bore the scars for the rest of his life and never regained full use of his fingers. His wrists were permanently deformed, and his hands hung awkwardly at his sides. But he had won—he would now be chief.

Because he had shown such courage in the face of his enemies, the Mdewakanton elders decided to support Little Crow's claim to be their leader. Many of the Sioux also came to believe that his survival from the gunshot wound indicated that the Great Spirit clearly wanted him to be chief. Once this decision was made, it was not long before Little Crow's supporters acted, and the designated chief, along with Little Crow's other half brother, was killed.

The responsibilities of leadership changed Little Crow, and he tried to change his people, as well. He urged them to stop drinking whiskey and encouraged them to work harder. He arranged for the missionaries, who had been banished some years before, to return to his village. When people reminded him of his own wild ways—that he had once done all the things he was now counseling against—he replied that then he had been only a brave. Now he was a chief.

Little Crow worked to bring about an accommodation between the Mdewakanton Sioux and the white settlers, taking a commanding role in treaty negotiations that brought him considerable popularity and influence. By the late 1850s, however, some of the people thought that he had become too devoted to the whites, and a few even accused him of accepting bribes in return for executing agreements that were more favorable to the government than to the Indians. One faction of warriors talked of killing those chiefs responsible for the treaty of 1858, an agreement Little Crow had enthusiastically supported. When he returned to the reservation from his trip to Washington that year, however, he sensed the brewing hostility and quickly changed from his broadcloth coat and kid gloves to traditional Indian dress.

The greatest challenge to Little Crow occurred in the spring of 1862, when the Mdewakantons met to elect a new speaker, following the death of the old one. The speaker held an honored position, one of the highest importance, because he opened all council meetings, decided agendas, and led discussions seeking consensus on the vital issues facing the tribes.

Little Crow was certain that he would be elected speaker, but Traveling Hail, a farmer Indian, was chosen instead. Although Little Crow remained a chief of immense influence, the loss was an assault on his pride.

He felt betrayed by his own people. After years of carefully preserving the ways of his ancestors while adopting the best practices of the whites, years of straddling the fence that separated those two disparate worlds, Little Crow had been rejected. A convert to the white world, a despised farmer Indian, had bested him. It seemed as though the political power of the blanket Indians was at grave risk. Those who cut their hair and tilled the soil held sway, at least among the elders. Indeed, many of Little Crow's relatives had become farmer Indians.

The message of the election for speaker was clear to Little Crow; he would have to join the farmer Indians. That was the only way, he believed, he could retain his authority. He already lived in a house, the two-story wooden structure agent Galbraith had built for him, but he ate and slept like an Indian. Now he requested, and promptly received, a stove and proper furniture.

In late June, Little Crow began to attend church services at the Episcopal mission, abandoning his own religion. He put away his Indian clothing and had his hair cut to shoulder length. Major Galbraith was pleased. Although he had lobbied for Traveling Hail to become speaker, he recognized that Little Crow retained a certain stature. If Little Crow was so openly adopting white ways, other Indians would surely follow his example. As a reward to the chief and an inducement to others, Galbraith decided that a brick house would be built for Little Crow. The chief even worked the earth himself, an act disdained by Sioux warriors, and personally dug out the basement. His conversion seemed complete. He was sure that it would be only a matter of time before his people called on him again.

The call came sooner than he expected, and it came not from his fellow farmer Indians or the elders in the camp but from a Soldiers' Lodge and the blanket Indian warriors. They sought him out not to lead a council or resolve a debate but to lead them in a war against the whites. His was the only voice that might prevent it.

*   *   *

By the time the Indians reached Little Crow's house in the early morning hours of Monday, August 18, they were bent on war. Red Middle Voice, Shakopee, some one hundred warriors from their camps, and several other chiefs were so overcome by their anger and hatred, the resentments that had festered for more years than most could remember, that they believed nothing could stop them. The villagers crowded around Little Crow's house, swelling the throng to several hundred.

Little Crow, asleep in the main room on the first floor, awoke when Shakopee appeared in the doorway, followed by the chiefs, the leaders of the Soldiers' Lodge, and the four Indians who had killed the white farmers. Little Crow sat up in bed, pulled a blanket over his shoulders, and listened to them tell the story of the argument over the eggs and the subsequent events at Acton Township. He grew tense as the tale unfolded and sweat broke out on his forehead. He looked around the room, noting that many of those present had failed to vote for him as speaker.

"Why do you come to me for advice?" he asked. "Go to the man you elected speaker and let him tell you what to do."

"Little Crow is the greatest among the chiefs," Red Middle Voice said. "Where he leads all others will follow."

Outside the house the crowd whooped and shouted, then a ghostly howl erupted, like the cry of some great wounded spirit animal.

"What do you want?" Little Crow asked.

"They want to kill all whites," Red Middle Voice said. "They would drive the Americans from the valley and get back our country."

Little Crow told Red Middle Voice that he was a fool. Wabasha and Big Eagle nodded their agreement, but Shakopee and others showed, by the frowns on their faces, that they thought Little Crow was wrong.

Red Middle Voice fell silent, and Shakopee took his place as spokesman.

"Our people must pay the traders more for pork and sugar than the white man pays in New Ulm. Then the traders put up signs saying they will sell nothing to Dakotas on credit.

They say if the Dakotas are hungry they can eat grass. The money for the land goes to Hugh Tyler, and no Dakota knows who Hugh Tyler is. The annuity does not come. Some say it will never come again. If it does, the white man will say it is his and take it away."

Red Middle Voice found his voice again.

"All the white soldiers are in the South fighting other white soldiers," he said. "The Americans are so hard pressed, the agent must take half-breeds and traders' clerks from the reservation to help them. Before a better time comes for the Dakotas to take the country back, the land will be full of Dutchmen."

Medicine Bottle added that the Sioux would not have to fight alone. Other tribes would join them—the Yanktons, the Yanktonais, the Winnebagos, and even their enemies, the Chippewas. Shakopee added that they could also expect help from the British.

"Little Crow has said the rulers of British America [Canada], after the war of 1812, told his father's father they would help if the Dakotas ever needed help."

"That was long ago," Little Crow said. "Now the English are ruled by a woman. She will know two white women were killed."

Then Red Middle Voice offered what he and the war chiefs thought was the most persuasive argument.

"We have no choice. Our hands are already bloody."

They all knew that the white authorities would demand that the four killers be turned over to them for punishment. If they were not, all Sioux would be held accountable.

Wabasha, whose influence among the Dakotas was almost as great as Little Crow's, stepped forward.

"Those are the words of a child," he snapped. "Red Middle Voice well knows blood will not wash off blood."

Another chief asked Red Middle Voice whether he wanted hundreds of Sioux to die in a war just so the four young men who killed the settlers would be spared.

Big Eagle, who was also in favor of keeping the peace, spoke next.

"Dakotas who were not killed [in a war with the whites] would be driven from such land as they have. When the messenger came with word of the council and the reason for it, thirty-two of my warriors painted themselves and asked if I would lead them. I said 'Yes, and you will have all the war you want. We will almost surely be defeated at last, but we are brave Dakotas and will do the best we can.' My braves are outside, painted and carrying guns. They want war, and I have promised to lead them, but I think war would be the act of a foolish child, and I am opposed to it."

Then it was Traveling Hail's turn. He, too, favored peace.

"We should not talk about war with the Americans," he said. "Dakotas are brave and proud. They are not fools. Red Middle Voice and Shakopee talk, but what comes from their mouths is the babble of children, as empty as the wind. We have no cannon and little ammunition. There are few Dakotas and many Americans. The Americans are as many as the leaves on the trees in the Big Woods. Count your fingers all day long and white men with guns will come faster than you can count."

A very old man—no one knew how old, not even the man himself—shuffled to the center of the group, tapping the wooden floor with his long staff. The others in the room parted respectfully to let him come forward. A former chief, now almost blind and weak of voice, still, as an elder, commanded respect.

"What! Is this Little Crow?" old Tamahay asked. "Is that [Shakopee]? You, too, White Dog, are you here? I cannot see well now, but I can see with my mind's eye the stream of blood you are about to pour upon the bosom of this mother [earth] of ours. I stand before you on three legs, but the third leg has brought me wisdom. I have traveled much. I have visited among the people whom you think to defy. This means the total surrender of our beautiful land, the land of a thousand lakes and streams.

"You are about to commit an act like that of the porcupine, who climbs a tree, balances himself upon a springy bough, and then gnaws off the very bough upon which he is sitting. Hence, when it gives way, he falls upon the sharp rocks below. . . . I do not say you have no cause to complain, but to [fight] is self-destruction. I am done."

The supporters of moderation, of peace, seemed to be prevailing. As Red Middle Voice looked around the crowded room, he sensed that he was losing support for the war. In desperation, but with a measure of cunning, he took the floor again, offering his words in a measured fashion, slowly and with dramatic emphasis.

"It is not Red Middle Voice who wants to kill the whites and drive the intruders from the land of the Dakotas."

He gestured to the door and the villagers beyond it.

"Listen to the voice of the young men."

The eerie howling continued, growing like a winter gale.

"They want to kill," Red Middle Voice said. "If the chiefs stand in the way, they will be the first to die."

He glanced around the room from one man to another. None of them showed any sign of fear, but the peace chiefs clearly resented the threat. Little Crow spoke for them.

"Dakota chiefs do not fear to die. They will do what is best for their people and not what will please children and fools. What Red Middle Voice proposes is madness."

Red Middle Voice strode quickly across the room to Little Crow's bed.

"Little Crow is afraid of the white man," he shouted. "Little Crow is a coward!"

No one spoke. No one dared even to move. Little Crow leapt from his bed, snatched the eagle-feather headdress from Red Middle Voice's head, and threw it to the floor.

"Taoyateduta is not a coward," he said, "and he is not a fool. . . . Braves, you are like little children; you know not what you are doing."

As Little Crow continued to speak, the men were riveted by the cadence and rhythm of his words, mesmerized by his escalating strength and power.

"You are full of the white man's devil-water," Little Crow said. "You are like dogs in the Hot Moon when they run mad and snap at their own shadows. We are only little herds of buffalo left scattered; the great herds that once covered the prairies are no more. See!—the white men are like locusts when they fly so thick that the whole sky is a snowstorm. You may kill one—two—ten; yes, as many as the leaves in the forest yonder, and their brothers will not miss them. Kill one—two—ten, and ten times ten will come to kill you."

Little Crow knew he had them in his grasp now, like willow reeds bending in a storm. The others sensed it, too, and the peace chiefs silently rejoiced. The warriors felt their chances growing dim, and Little Crow was not yet finished. He was challenging the argument that a war fought now would be easy because the white soldiers were occupied killing each other in the government's war in the South.

"Yes; they fight among themselves," Little Crow said, "away off. Do you hear the thunder of their big guns? No; it would take you two moons to run down to where they are fighting, and all the way your path would be among white soldiers as thick as tamaracks in the swamps of the Ojibways. Yes; they fight among themselves, but if you strike at them they will all turn on you and devour you and your women and little children just as the locusts in their time fall on the trees and devour all the leaves in one day.

"You are fools. You cannot see the face of your chief; your eyes are full of smoke. You cannot hear his voice; your ears are full of roaring waters. Braves, you are little children—you are fools. You will die like the rabbits when the hungry wolves hunt them in the Hard Moon."

Little Crow had never been more forceful, more passionate, more persuasive, and if he had stopped, there might never have been a war. But he did not stop, and no one, perhaps least of all Little Crow himself, ever understood why. Perhaps he knew that if he failed his young men by refusing to take them to war, they would never again ask him to lead them. His influence, power, and popularity would be lost forever. He knew there would be no victory for the Dakotas in any war against the whites—indeed, no one had spoken so eloquently against it—but he may also have sensed from the unnatural howling of the crowd outside his white man's house that the braves would go to war that morning anyway, regardless of his words. With their small number, they would meet certain defeat sooner and more ignominiously than if the entire Sioux nation supported them. And the rest would be punished for their actions even if they did not join in the fighting.

Perhaps Little Crow also knew that the way of life he had urged on his people and had adopted himself had been extin-

guished by the events at Acton Township as quickly and as to-
tally as the camp fire is drowned by the rainstorm. There was too
much hatred to contain anymore. War was inevitable. Defeat was
inevitable. The end of the Sioux was inevitable. If they were to
die, how much better to die in battle like soldiers, not chained to
a jail floor or hanged by the neck in retribution. A death on the
field of battle was the only way for a Sioux warrior, and a Sioux
chief, to end his days. There was honor in that. There was dignity in that. There was continuity with their fathers and their fathers' fathers in that. There was freedom in that.

If Little Crow led them, all the people would join in the
fighting. At least that way, they would win more victories, until
the day they all met a glorious end together. Perhaps this fate
was better than tilling the soil, believing in the white man's harsh
and vengeful God, or living inside four walls of wood or brick.

These may have been Little Crow's thoughts on the morning of August 18, as the darkness gave way to the gray dawn
of the new day. But whatever was in his mind, he did not stop
speaking after voicing his impassioned arguments against war.
Perhaps, in truth, he could not stop.

"Taoyateduta is not a coward," Little Crow added. "He
will die with you."

The war chiefs and the four braves who had murdered the
whites at Acton Township exploded with whoops of joy, of triumph, of victory. They turned from the house, screaming,
"Kill the whites!" The chant was repeated and amplified until
it rang through the village, and from there to all the other Dakota villages like the peals of clear, strong bells. "Kill the
whites! Kill the whites!"

The settlement of the Lower Agency was only two miles
distant. Many traders had their stores and homes there, including the hated Andrew Myrick. They would be the first to feel
the fury so long held in check.

Others would die, as well—the farmers, the Germans, the
missionaries, the soldiers. Kill them all and reclaim the land.
Kill them all and no Dakota would live like a white man again.
Kill them all and the Dakotas would recapture the ways of their
fathers, the ways in which the Great Spirit intended them to

live. Kill them all and the Dakotas would never again be lied to or cheated or see their wives become prostitutes for food and their braves become drunkards.

Kill them all and the Dakotas would roam free again. Kill them all and life would be good. Kill them all.

And Little Crow would lead them.

4

THE INDIANS ARE RAISING HELL

"During the whole of the night—I shall never forget the date, August 18, 1862—a strange foreboding kept sleep away. Marie, my fair-skinned French-Sioux wife, lay still beside me, but I knew that she, too, was awake. Cistina Joe, my son, nine days old, kicked in his crib. My slender, black-eyed girls, Elizabeth, six, and Minnie, four, breathed quietly. Duta, my red setter, rumbled low growls outside the open door. Something was out of place, but what could it be?"

So wrote Joe Coursolle, a twenty-nine-year-old mixed-blood who was a teamster and fur trader at the agency. The Sioux called him Hinhankaga, "the owl." His father was French, his mother Dakota, and when they died, he was reared by the trader Henry Sibley in his palatial home at Mendota. Coursolle believed he was as much white as Indian.

"The night was hot and sticky," Coursolle told his grandson many years later. "From the village of Little Crow, two miles up the valley, I could hear tom-toms throbbing. But that often happened, and their familiar sound could not have put that anxious feeling in my stomach."

Suddenly, a hand touched his shoulder, and a woman's voice spoke to him in Dakota.

"Shh, Hinhankaga. Be still. I am a friend. Big trouble coming. Tomorrow warriors kill all whites. Go now, before too late. Tell no one I warned you or I, too, will die."

He never knew who she was. She slipped out of the house as silently as she had slipped in, without even alerting the dog. Joe immediately got his family dressed, shut the dog in the cabin—if he took him along, his barking might give them away—and led his family to his canoe on the bank of the Minnesota River. He planned to head for Fort Ridgely, thirteen miles away.

The canoe was small, and he ferried his wife and baby to the other side first, intending to come right back for the two little girls. Before he could cross, however, he heard Indians approaching. He called softly to his daughters, cautioning them to hide in the bushes. Four Indians walked single file past the bushes, but didn't spot the children. The Indians were heading for Redwood, the Lower Agency.

At six o'clock in the morning, George Spencer, a clerk at Forbes's store at the agency, saw a large number of Indians approaching the neat, well-ordered village that was the agency. They were armed and dressed and painted for war, but that was not unusual. Sioux war parties in search of Chippewas occasionally passed through. When Spencer asked the Indians what they were doing there, they replied that some of their enemies had been spotted nearby. They assured Spencer and the other white men gathered around him that there was nothing about which to be alarmed.

In one of the houses of the agency, sixty-year-old Philander Prescott watched the Indians approach. He had lived among the Sioux for forty-five years, was married to a Sioux woman, and worked as an interpreter. He knew the Indians as well as anyone. He saw Little Crow coming down the street and stopped the chief to ask why so many Sioux had come to the agency that morning.

"Go into your house and stay there," Little Crow said, possibly to save the old man who had been such a good friend to the tribe.

Prescott's wife, who overheard the conversation, also urged him to stay, arguing that in the event of any trouble, he would be safe with her because of her family connections to the Sioux. However, Prescott was frightened—he thought there was something odd in the way Little Crow had looked at him and spoken to him—and he left at once for Fort Ridgely.

The Indians streaming into the agency village broke up into small parties and congregated around every building—the stone warehouse, the boarding school, the mess hall, sawmill, stables, the houses for the agent and the superintendent of farming, and the four stores, including the one owned by Andrew Myrick. There was not a structure standing that did not have its share of warriors surrounding it.

Andrew Myrick was upstairs in his store. Downstairs, one of his clerks, James Lynd, lounged in the doorway, watching the Indians. Lynd was fascinated by Dakota history, customs, and culture. He had three mixed-blood children by two Indian women, spoke the language fluently, and spent his spare time writing a book about the Sioux. He was the first to die at Sioux hands.

At a signal from one of the braves, the Indians clustered around Myrick's store opened fire. "Now!" came the shout. "I will kill the dog who wouldn't give me credit."

Lynd fell dead. A second clerk, George Washington Divoll, ran to the door and was shot down instantly. Upstairs, Myrick took refuge under a large dry-goods box, but when he heard the Indians say they were going to torch the building, he climbed out of a back window, slid down the lightning rod, and raced toward a clump of willow trees.

A Sioux brave shot him before he reached safety. Several warriors crowded around him as he lay on the ground, and within seconds, a half dozen well-placed arrows pierced his body. Another Indian plunged a hay scythe into Myrick's chest. Then one scooped up a clump of grass and stuffed it in the trader's mouth.

"Myrick is eating grass himself," he said.

Cooks, clerks, farmers, teamsters, carpenters, blacksmiths— all fell under a hail of bullets in a matter of minutes. Few had time to reach for a weapon. George Spencer and his friends at

Forbes's store stood transfixed when the killing started, unable to react, unable even to believe what they were seeing and hearing. Before they could comprehend it, four of them fell dead, and Spencer sustained three wounds. He clambered upstairs, followed by another white clerk and a mixed-blood boy, and closed the trapdoor behind them.

The Indians yelled for the boy to come down, promising that he wouldn't be hurt. The other clerk ran downstairs and tried to escape through the rear door, but he was shot in the side and the leg. Warriors stripped off his clothing and shoes, piled logs atop his body, and warned that they would soon return to hack him to pieces. When they left, he managed to roll the logs off and hobble away.

Spencer, in pain from the three gunshot wounds and weakened by the loss of blood, could do nothing but wait in his bed. If he did not die from his injuries first, he expected the Indians eventually to come upstairs and kill him or simply burn the building down with him inside.

Philander Prescott, the old interpreter, managed to cover several miles on his way to Fort Ridgely before a roving band of Sioux found him. They knew him, of course—all the Indians did—and Prescott pleaded with them for his life.

"I am an old man," he said. "I have lived with you now forty-five years, almost half a century. My wife and children are among you, of your own blood. I have never done you any harm, and have been your true friend in all your troubles. Why should you wish to kill me?"

"We would save your life if we could," Medicine Bottle answered him, "but the white man must die. We cannot spare your life. Our orders are to kill all white men. We cannot spare you."

Prescott stood calmly as the Indians shot him.

When the shooting started, the Reverend Samuel Hinman ran to Little Crow and asked whether anything was wrong. "He was usually very polite," Hinman recalled, "but now he made no answer, and, regarding me with a savage look, went on toward the stable." The preacher wisely decided to flee. Little Crow, who had listened so attentively to Hinman's sermon just the day before, may deliberately have allowed him to escape.

Whereas others nearby were shot down, at least one on Little Crow's direct orders, Hinman was left unmolested.

Most were not so fortunate. Dr. Philander Humphrey, a physician at the agency, managed to get away, taking his wife, who was recovering from childbirth, and their three children. They stopped at an abandoned house about four miles away because Mrs. Humphrey was too weary to continue. Dr. Humphrey placed her on a bed and sent his twelve-year-old son to find a spring and fetch some water. Before the boy returned, Indians attacked, shot Dr. Humphrey outside, and set fire to the house, burning Mrs. Humphrey and the other children alive. After the Indians left, the boy ran to his father's body and found that his throat had been cut. He hid in the trees when another group of Indians came, and watched one brave chop off his father's head.

Joe Coursolle heard the sounds of gunfire coming from the agency. He slid his canoe into the water and paddled across the river to bring back his two girls, Elizabeth and Minnie. When he reached the bushes where he had told them to hide, they were not there. He searched up and down the bank, then headed inland toward his house, hoping they had found their way home. The house had been burned to the ground. Everything was gone except Duta, the red setter, who leaped on him, barking with joy. Coursolle was terrified that the barks would attract the Indians.

"I was forced to do the cruelest task of my life," he said. "I slipped off my belt and pulled it tight around Duta's neck. Tears ran from my eyes as I felt him struggle for breath. Finally he was dead. I knelt down, took his head in my lap and whispered, 'Forgive me, Duta, forgive me.'"

There was nothing more Coursolle could do there. He had to cross the river and get his wife and baby son to Fort Ridgely. At least he might be able to save part of his family.

On the top floor of Forbes's store, George Spencer was growing weaker from his wounds. He had nearly given up all hope when he heard someone call from downstairs. It was Wakinyatawa, Little Crow's head soldier. He and Spencer had been friends for ten years. He told Spencer he would take him to his lodge and try to save him. If he could not, he vowed to bury him like a white man.

Wakinyatawa helped the wounded man down the stairs. Several other Indians in the store were outraged and shouted that Spencer should be killed. No mercy could be shown; no one could be spared. Wakinyatawa grabbed a hatchet and said that he would kill anyone who tried to hurt the store clerk.

"This is my friend and comrade," he said. "We have been comrades for ten years, and if you had killed him before I got here, of course I could have said nothing. But now that I have seen him, I will protect him or die with him."

The other Indians let them pass. Outside, Wakinyatawa placed Spencer in a wagon and ordered some Indian women to take him to their village and care for him. Spencer would live.

When the killing at the agency ended, the warriors and their squaws emptied the warehouse, the stores, and the houses of everything they could pile into the settlers' wagons or carry themselves. Whatever they could not take, they destroyed. One by one, the buildings were set ablaze, and before long, only the blackened shell of the warehouse, the steam sawmill, and three small log cabins remained standing.

Those white families who escaped from the agency and from nearby houses in the first hours of daylight were the lucky ones. They had a way to cross the Minnesota River, a formidable natural barrier between the reservation and the safety of Fort Ridgely. They owed their lives to the ferry operator, a Frenchman named Hubert Millier, affectionately known as Old Mauley. He stayed on the job until he had brought everyone—more than forty people—to the other side.

After bringing the last group across, Old Mauley returned to the agency side of the river, in case any other settlers needed help. The Indians came instead. They disemboweled him, cut off his head, hands, and feet, and stuffed them inside the bloody corpse. The main escape route from the reservation to the fort was now closed.

The killing quickly spread beyond the boundary of the Lower Agency. Even as the smoke from the burning buildings at Redwood stained the morning sky, warriors roamed the woods surrounding the agency and forded the river upstream, searching for whites to kill. Some settlers escaped, but many more died, and the difference between life and death was often random circumstance and chance, the taking of one trail over another, lagging behind a few extra minutes to load a cherished possession into a wagon, or happening upon a friendly Indian in a crowd of hostiles. It was usually luck that spelled survival.

Ten miles northwest of the agency, Joseph and Valencia Reynolds, teachers at the government school near Shakopee's village, were eating breakfast when a mixed-blood came to the door with the news that Indians were attacking the agency. The breakfast table was crowded that morning. Their niece, Mattie Williams, from Painesville, Ohio, was there, along with the two hired girls—Mary Anderson, a Swedish immigrant, and German-born Mary Schwandt—and the hired hand, William Landmeier. LeGrand Davies was visiting, and Francis Patoile, a Canadian trader from the Upper Agency, had stopped by for breakfast on his way south.

On hearing the news, they decided to make for New Ulm, a town forty miles southeast. Reynolds and his wife took the buggy. The girls and Davies rode with the trader Patoile in his wagon. Landmeier left on his own and reached Fort Ridgely that night.

Reynolds decided that it would be safer to leave the main road and travel across the prairie. Not far from their house, they met Shakopee and two other Indians, with whom they had been friendly in the past. Reynolds asked the chief what the trouble was. Shakopee said he did not know, but he motioned for them to keep going across the prairie. Beyond the agency, they spotted a group of about fifty Indians no more than a half mile away, but skirted them without being seen. A lone warrior startled them, coming close enough to aim his double-barreled shotgun directly at Reynolds's face. The Indian pulled the trigger, but the gun did not fire. Reynolds urged his horse on, and they raced for the safety of Fort Ridgely, which was closer than New Ulm.

Francis Patoile, the trader, decided to stay on the main road. They passed the burning agency and by afternoon were within eight miles of New Ulm. They had seen no Indians along the way. Suddenly, several Sioux arrows hit the wagon, but no one was injured. Mattie Williams pulled them out and joked that she would take them back to Ohio as souvenirs of her trip to the wild West.

Because the horses were exhausted, the settlers got out of the wagon to walk. They considered crossing the river and making for the fort, but there was no ferry, and no one knew whether there was a place to ford it, so they continued on their way to New Ulm, feeling that by then they were safe.

Fifty Sioux clad only in breechcloths surrounded them. Most were drunk, all were shouting and had smeared their bodies with war paint. They killed Patoile and Davies instantly. Mary Anderson was shot in the back, and the Indians carried off all three girls into captivity.

Across the river from the Lower Agency, six miles northwest, twenty-eight white settlers gathered at the home of Jonathan and Amanda Earle. Indians had been roaming from one farmhouse to another looking for horses and weapons. They claimed that they needed them to fight the Chippewas, but shortly after breakfast, word reached the settlers that the agency was under attack. As they got the news, the neighbors all headed for the Earle house, which was the largest one in the vicinity.

Among the settlers in the area was nineteen-year-old Helen Carrothers and her two children. Married at fourteen to a carpenter at the agency, Helen lived in a secluded cabin, from which her husband was frequently gone. Being so isolated, she had few white people to talk to and she befriended the Indians, learning their language and their ways. Sioux visited her cabin almost every day, bringing food and helping out with the chores. Squaws chopped wood for the fire and helped her care for the infant boy and four-year-old girl. From the medicine man, who thought she was a kindred soul, she learned about the healing powers of roots, herbs, wildflowers, and barks, and how to mix them to cure various ailments. She was a good pupil, and the medicine man appeared to enjoy teaching her his secrets. Helen considered herself to be an adopted child of the Sioux, and she never had any reason to fear them.

On the day of the uprising, Helen Carrothers and her children were at the home of neighbors, Mr. and Mrs. S. R. Henderson. Mrs. Henderson was sick, so ill that Dr. Humphrey at the agency had said there was no hope of recovery. The Hendersons, in their desperation, had called on the medicine man, whom they had always ridiculed before. He despised the Hendersons but agreed to help, reluctantly, and only if Helen Carrothers would do the nursing.

Helen was confident that whatever the Indians were up to at the agency, they would not harm her or her children. Her brother-in-law, David Carrothers, insisted that she could not stay in her cabin alone at such a time, so she consented to leave with the party of her neighbors. She helped to settle the ailing Mrs. Henderson on a feather bed in one of the three wagons, and the group of nearly thirty, including twenty women and children, embarked for Fort Ridgely. Only two people had guns, and one of those weapons was loaded with pebbles.

A half mile from the Earle house, seventy-five Sioux warriors leapt from the prairie grass and surrounded the column of refugees. Helen Carrothers, the only white present who spoke the Dakota language, asked the Indians what they wanted.

"We are going to kill you all," the leader said.

Helen pleaded for their lives. "I reminded them how I had always been their good friend," she wrote more than forty years later, "how I had lived among them for four years, that my children had been born among them and had been often carried to their tepees on the backs of their women, that I and my children loved the Indian people as we did our own. 'Surely,' I said, 'you will not kill me or my children, when you all love us as if we were of your tribe. Why kill my friends? To take our lives can do you no possible good. If you shoot us down like dogs, the Great Spirit will be very angry and will avenge our blood and bring woe and trouble to your nation.'"

"All whites must die," the Indian said, but he listened as Helen argued fervently, and agreed to spare them if they surrendered their horses and wagons. The Indians' manner became conciliatory, even friendly, and they shook hands with all the whites. They consented to leave the wagon in which Mrs. Henderson rested, and led the horses and the other wagons away.

The party continued on foot, with the men pulling the

remaining wagon. They had gone no more than a mile when they heard the sound of the Indians chanting on the path behind them. Helen recognized the Dakota death song. Shots rang out. Mrs. Henderson pulled out a white slip and gave it to her husband to wave. He held it up, and in seconds, his thumb was shot off and the makeshift flag was riddled with bullets. The man standing next to him fell dead. Henderson looked at his wife in the cart, despair plain on his face, and he tore himself free from the grasp of his two-year-old daughter and ran away. He later reached Fort Ridgely.

Everyone rushed to take cover. Helen Carrothers shoved her two children in a ditch and shielded them while she witnessed sights she was never able to forget. A warrior snatched up the Henderson girl and beat her about the face and head with a violin case taken from the wagon. In moments, the child's features were obliterated. He swung her by the feet, slamming her against a wagon wheel again and again, and threw the battered body to her mother.

Helen watched as another Indian grabbed the Henderson baby and, "holding her by one foot, head downwards, deliberately hacked her body, limb from limb, with his tomahawk, throwing the pieces at the head of Mrs. Henderson. Some of the Indians made a big fire and when it was burning fiercely, they lifted the feather bed on which Mrs. Henderson lay, and tossed bed and woman and the mangled portions of her children into the flames."

Others died more quickly by the bullet and the knife. Jonathan Earle saw a group of braves carry off his wife, and he knew there was nothing he could do to save her. His seven-year-old daughter begged him to take her away, but Earle refused. He believed that the Indians would not harm the other women and children—or so he testified later—and he knew he could never escape if he had the child with him, so he told his daughter to go back and stay with her mother.

Earle fired one shot at the Indians as he ran, then he threw away his rifle. He caught up with his fifteen-year-old son, Radner, who was carrying the shotgun loaded with pebbles. As Earle ran past, he shouted at Radner to shoot at the Indians who were chasing them. The boy did as he was told. He dropped into the tall grass, waited for his father to get some distance away, and fired. Earle glanced over his shoulder and saw two Indians closing in on his son. He yelled at the boy to run, but there was no answer.

"Noble boy," Earle later wrote. "He saved my life by the sacrifice of his own."

Earle later overtook his two other sons and a third boy who had been with their party, and eventually they reached Cedar City, some forty miles away.

Helen Carrothers remained in the ditch, with her arms around her children, awaiting death. A warrior rushed toward them and she braced herself, hoping the end would come quickly. However, the Indian shook her hand, holding on to it long enough to wrench off her rings.

"Are you going to kill me?" she asked.

"No. The medicine man says we must not kill you. He says I must save you and take you and your children to my tepee, and then you will be my squaw. All the nice women we will not kill. They will be squaws for the Indian braves."

When the shooting stopped and the screams were silenced, eight were dead and thirteen women and children were prisoners. The Indians formally shook hands with each captive, placed them in the wagons, and hauled them away.

The first refugees from the Lower Agency reached Fort Ridgely at about ten o'clock that morning. Few people believed their story. The idea of the Sioux attacking the settlement and killing the whites was preposterous, but the new arrivals insisted that it was true, and they were soon followed by others, with wounds and burns as more convincing proof.

The fort's commanding officer, Capt. John Marsh, who had fought as a private at Bull Run, decided to lead a force of soldiers to the agency to crush the uprising at once. Only a small band of dissidents could be involved, he thought, and he assumed that one company would be sufficient to deal with them. He ordered a long drumroll to be sounded, and he chose forty-six men to accompany him, along with the interpreter, Peter Quinn. Each man would carry forty rounds of ammunition and one day's rations; it would surely take no longer than that to clear up the matter.

Before leaving, Marsh sent for reinforcements for the post. Lieutenant Sheehan had departed the fort only the day before with fifty men, heading for Fort Ripley on the Mississippi River. They would still be within easy reach. He dispatched a note to Sheehan: "It is absolutely necessary that you should return with your command to this post. The Indians are raising hell at the Lower Agency." Until Sheehan or Marsh returned, Fort Ridgely would be defended by a mere twenty-nine soldiers, commanded by Thomas P. Gere, a nineteen-year-old lieutenant.

Marsh's expedition saw the first gruesome evidence of the uprising within six miles of the post. Obviously, the violence was not confined to the agency alone. The column of soldiers halted beside a burning log cabin and found the remains of the agency physician, Dr. Humphrey, and his family. The twelve-year-old Humphrey boy, who had witnessed the killings, emerged from the bushes. Marsh comforted him and sent him on to the fort.

The soldiers passed other bodies by the roadside and met several panicky refugees, who advised them not to continue. The Reverend Hinman warned Marsh that if he planned to go all the way to the agency, he was heading for serious trouble, because the Sioux were killing everybody. He advised the captain not to go farther than the ferry, and to round up all the women and children he could find and escort them back to the fort.

Marsh, who may have been more brave than prudent, more courageous than cautious, told Hinman that he had enough men and enough powder and lead to whip every Indian between there and the Pacific Ocean. He said he intended to cross the river at the ferry and enter the reservation.

Hinman reminded him that he would be outnumbered by three to one and that the soldiers faced certain death. Marsh thanked the preacher politely for his advice—although he doubted that a clergyman really knew anything about fighting Indians—and said that he would push on. He remained convinced that the violence was the work of only a handful of Sioux, and that with the aid of the friendly chiefs of the villages around the Lower Agency, he would capture the guilty braves and bring them back to Fort Ridgely.

The troops reached the ferry at noon. The little boat was there, ready to take them across. Marsh displayed no apprehension, even though they were in a perfect spot for an ambush. Tall grass and scattered thickets of hazel and willow provided excellent hiding places for the enemy. On the far side of the river, a lone Indian beckoned to them. It was White Dog, a farmer Indian chief of the Upper Sioux.

"Come across," he yelled. "Everything is [all] right over here. We do not want to fight and we will hold a council."

He went on to explain that they had had trouble with the traders but that Captain Marsh could settle their differences. All the Indians were at the agency, the chief said, waiting to talk with him.

On the riverbank near the soldiers, a drunken white man wandered out from behind the trees. His words seemed to make no sense. "You are all gone up," he was saying. "The Indians are all around. That side hill is covered with Indians."

Two troopers strolled down to the water's edge to fill their canteens. As they leaned over, they spotted several Indians hiding in the brush on the other side. One soldier, Sgt. John Bishop, also noticed twigs and leaves floating down the river, and the water roiled up as though someone was crossing it not far upstream.

He alerted Captain Marsh. "I believe we are being surrounded by Indians crossing the river above us," he said. He ran up on a sandbank and spied a herd of Indian ponies on the far side. This, too, he quickly reported to Marsh.

The captain told Quinn, the interpreter, to ask White Dog what the ponies were doing there if all the Indians were at the agency waiting to hold a council, but the chief did not wait to be questioned. He raised his rifle and fired.

A volley of shots exploded from across the river. "Look out!" Quinn shouted. His warning died as he fell with a dozen bullet wounds, along with nearly half of the soldiers. Marsh ordered his men to fall back from the river, but more Indians appeared behind them, cutting off their escape route and pinning them in the cross fire. Several more troopers were shot, and Marsh corralled the survivors, urging them to head south along the bank toward a clump of trees. He and about twenty others reached it, crashing through the tangled undergrowth, with the Indians firing wildly after them.

For three hours, the dwindling band of soldiers worked their way south, never daring to leave the dense cover of bushes and trees. By four o'clock, they reached the end of their protection. Only open ground lay ahead, and a large party of Sioux braves was approaching, prepared to cut them off when they emerged. They were down to no more than four rounds of ammunition per man. Marsh realized that their only means of escape was to cross the river, which at that point was about fifty yards wide.

Marsh went first. He unbuckled his sword, held it and his revolver above his head, and waded in. About two-thirds of the way across, the water suddenly became too deep to stand in. Marsh dropped his weapons and tried to swim but was seized by a cramp. He cried out for help. Sergeant Bishop sent two strong swimmers after him, but they were too late.

"I will never forget," Bishop said, "the look that brave officer gave us just before he sank for the last time—will never forget how dark the next hour seemed to us, as we crouched underneath the bank of the Minnesota River and talked over and decided what next best to do."

Fourteen soldiers were left, two of them wounded, and they were eleven miles from Fort Ridgely, a long way from home.

For the rest of the day, the Sioux ravaged the countryside between the ferry crossing and the fort and terrorized the settlements north and west of the crossing. Several thousand whites lived in the area, most in isolated cabins. Many were German immigrants, whom the Indians hated even more than they disliked the Americans—or the traders. Some American settlers were willing to befriend the Indians, to share their food when the Sioux were hungry and to allow them into their homes to examine their wondrous possessions; not so the Germans. They seldom shared food with the Indians, not even when they caught fish or trapped game on Indian lands. And they chased the Indians away whenever they came too close to their houses, hitting at them with sticks and shouting oaths.

"The guttural speakers," Shakopee said, referring to these immigrants, "have made me so angry that I will cut off their heads while they are still breathing."

The chief made good his threat. Shakopee and his braves, along with Red Middle Voice and his band, were particularly brutal. They rode up to Johann Schwandt's cabin, where the farmer was repairing his roof, and shot him instantly. They tomahawked and slashed to death his wife, his pregnant daughter and her husband, his two sons, and a hired hand. The twelve-year-old son, August, was bludgeoned with a tomahawk and left for dead, but he remained conscious, recording in his mind the horrible deaths of his family. He watched the Indians slice open his sister's belly, snatch up the fetus, and nail it to a tree. August crawled to safety at Fort Ridgely, the only member of his clan to survive, except for his sister Mary, the hired girl at the Reynolds's house who was now a captive.

Scores of families met death in similar ways, many of them trapped in houses that were set on fire. Women and girls endured multiple rapes before being stabbed to death. Children were nailed to doors; heads, hands, and feet chopped off; bodies mutilated in the most appalling ways. Many of these atrocities were traditional ways of killing among the Sioux. Scalps were taken as proof of bravery and to count the number of kills, because a brave was entitled to add an eagle feather to his headdress for every enemy slain. Limbs and heads were severed so that enemies would be at a disadvantage if the Sioux encountered them in the hereafter. They believed that a person who died without a head or hands entered the next world in that condition and remained so for all eternity.

Whole settlements of Germans, some thirty to forty people at a time, were set upon, slaughtered, and their houses ransacked and burned. Families in flight were tracked down in their wagons and murdered. It was almost effortless. The Germans seldom carried weapons, having come from a culture in which physical violence and the use of firearms were rare. And even many American settlers were easy prey, armed with little more than shotguns.

The killings were also made easy by the skepticism that greeted the accounts of the rampage in the neighborhood of

the agency. As a result, many families did not flee, even
though they had been warned, or they left too late. Also, those
farmers who counted the Sioux as friends were not alarmed
when bands of Indians showed up. After all, they often came
to visit. The Indians smiled and shook hands, then brought out
their knives, tomahawks, and hatchets.

News of the uprising reached the Upper Agency around noon
that Monday. The Indians heard about it first, although most of
them refused to believe it was war, assuming instead that it was
the work of a few discontent, and probably drunk, braves. One
of the first whites to learn of the attack was the Upper Agency
physician, Dr. John Wakefield, who told the bearer of the report
that he would be foolish to give credence to such a story.

Yet Wakefield evidently did believe it. He had sent his
wife and two children to the Lower Agency at the beginning
of August, when large numbers of Indians were encamped at
the Upper Agency to get food. They had since returned, but
Mrs. Wakefield had already decided to take the children east
to visit her parents for a while. She was terrified of the Sioux
and of the possible violence. She said that just the thought of
an Indian uprising was enough to make her teeth chatter.

Her husband, without mentioning the news he had just
received, suggested that she and the children depart for Fort
Ridgely that afternoon, instead of waiting a few days for the
stagecoach, as planned. The storekeeper for the Lower
Agency's warehouse, George Gleason, had been visiting at the
Upper Agency and was eager to go home. He agreed to take
the Wakefield family to Fort Ridgely in return for the loan of
a wagon and two horses.

Sarah Wakefield was sad to leave. She had a premonition
that she would never again see her house. "I remember going
from room to room, taking a final look." When everything had
been loaded into the wagon, she was surprised to overhear her
husband tell Gleason to drive fast. When she asked him why,
he gave a vague reply.

They pulled away from the house and drove past the traders' stores. Stewart Garvie, manager of Myrick's store at the
Upper Agency, hailed them. He came over to the wagon to tell

them that Indians had been killing whites on the north side of the river.

Sarah Wakefield urged Gleason to take her back home, but he discounted the tale and told her that Dr. Wakefield had heard similar rumors, which was why he had wanted them to leave. Gleason himself did not believe the stories, and he tried to cheer her, but she remained anxious and fearful. "I had a strong feeling of evil," Sarah said, "and it was a presentiment of what was to happen."

By the time they had covered fifteen miles, halfway between the two agencies, they saw smoke rising in the distance. Gleason, becoming impatient with Sarah's nervousness, joked that he would never take her anywhere again. He scolded her for acting foolishly.

A little after six in the evening, they came within sight of the Reynolds house. Gleason suggested that they stop to see whether they could join the family for dinner. As they neared the house, two Indians, called Hapa and Chaska, approached their wagon on foot. Sarah Wakefield urged Gleason to draw his pistol. To her horror, he explained that he had lied about carrying a weapon and had done so only to reassure her.

He stopped the wagon to chat with the braves, and, after a moment, they all moved on. Still wary, Sarah turned to watch the Indians and saw Hapa raise his gun and fire, hitting Gleason in the shoulder.

Hapa fired again and Gleason fell out of the wagon onto the road. Chaska, a farmer Indian who dressed in white man's clothing, ran up to the wagon, shook Sarah's hand, and asked whether she was the doctor's wife. When she said she was, he cautioned her to say very little, adding that Hapa was a bad man who had drunk too much whiskey.

Hapa slowly reloaded his gun, watching Gleason writhe on the ground. His moans were drowned out by Mrs. Wakefield's shrieks as she pleaded almost incoherently to be spared for the sake of her children. She vowed to sew, wash, chop wood, or do anything else rather than die and leave her children alone. Hapa looked at her with contempt while Chaska silently urged her to be quiet.

Gleason screamed, "Oh my God, Mrs. Wakefield!"

Hapa shot him again, killing him, and stepped up to the wagon to take aim at the doctor's wife. Chaska grabbed his arm, explaining that the Wakefields were good people who had shown the Sioux many kindnesses.

"She must die," Hapa insisted. "All whites are bad. Better be dead."

Chaska continued to argue with him, however, and finally Hapa consented to take them back to their village. As they rode on, though, he changed his mind. "Those children I will kill," he said. "They will be a trouble when we go to Red River."

"No," Chaska said. "I am going to take care of them. You must kill me before you kill any of them."

As the wagon rolled on toward the Indian village, Chaska reassured Sarah that he would protect her. He sounded sincere, but Hapa had the gun.

By Monday evening, the Indians at the Upper Agency villages had received many more reports that braves of the Lower Sioux were killing whites farther south. There was no longer any reason for skepticism. The tales were accepted as true and a council was called. The Sisseton and Wahpeton bands of the Upper Sioux attended, along with a group of thirty warriors visiting from the Yanktonais. Although their home was farther west in the Dakota Territory, off the reservation, several of their spokesmen quickly became leaders of the war party, advocating the killing of all whites. Allied with them were the Sissetons and a few of the Wahpetons. The majority of the Wahpetons, however, many of whom were farmers and Christians, opposed them and argued for keeping the peace.

Three Indians from the Lower Agency joined the council, captivating and inflaming the warriors with their stories of bloodshed. They described how easy it had been to kill whites, even soldiers, and recounted the bounty they had looted from homes and stores. They boasted of killing hundreds that day at the cost of only one Sioux brave lost. The peace advocates were horrified.

Trying to be practical, peace spokesmen argued that whether or not the Sioux liked the whites, they depended on them for food, provisions, and ammunition. Where else could they get weapons and bullets for hunting or to defend themselves against the Chippewas? If the Sioux persisted in harming the whites, the Great Father would send soldiers to drive them off the reservation.

John Other Day, a Christian Indian leader, told the council that, yes, they could easily kill unarmed settlers and even small bands of soldiers, but soon so many soldiers would come that they would slaughter the Indians or banish them forever. "Some of you," he said, "say you have horses and can escape to the plains, but what, I ask you, will become of those who have no horses?"

The war leaders, and some of those still uncommitted, countered that the Lower Sioux had already gone so far that the whites would punish all of them, anyway. If they were going to take the blame, why not kill the whites and take their supplies?

The arguments raged for hours, and the council was unable to reach a consensus. Most of the Wahpetons, who supported the peace party, left to return to their villages. The Yanktonais, Sissetons, and the handful of Wahpetons remaining gathered together to prepare for war. As they all moved out to head for the Upper Agency settlement, each brave had one thought in mind, to murder every white person he could find.

John Other Day, the peace spokesman, got his gun and hurried away to try to save his white friends.

At noon that Monday, a stagecoach had arrived at Fort Ridgely, at about the time Captain Marsh and his men had reached the ferry crossing. As soon as the coach came to a halt, a civilian and four armed guards climbed down and approached Lieutenant Gere. The civilian introduced himself as Cyrus Wyckoff and explained that he had been sent by Clark Thompson, the Superintendent of Indian Affairs at St. Paul. Wyckoff carried a valuable cargo—two kegs of gold coins—the annuity payment for the Sioux reservation.

Wyckoff had intended to ride on to the Lower Agency, but when Gere explained that there was some Indian trouble there, he changed his mind. He agreed with the lieutenant that it would be best to wait until Captain Marsh returned and told them it was safe to proceed. The young officer led Wyckoff and the guards to the officers' quarters, where they could wait with the gold. Gere told no one else on the post that the payment had finally arrived.

Frightened and wounded refugees were pouring into the fort in great numbers, bringing alarming reports of other white settlers left dead or dragged off into captivity. They told an increasingly uneasy Gere of the Lower Agency left in ruins and of Indians marauding over a wider and wider region. They described attacks in the area between the fort and the ferry, where Captain Marsh was supposed to be. Gere concluded that the uprising was far larger than Marsh believed, and he hoped he would have enough men to defend the fort if the Indians decided to attack. He expected Lieutenant Sheehan and his fifty men to return by nightfall, and he believed that Captain Marsh would bring his troopers back soon after.

Many of those seeking refuge at the post had sustained bullet and knife wounds or burns. Most of the victims were women and children. As their number continued to increase throughout the afternoon, the post surgeon, Dr. Alfred Müller, and his wife, Eliza, set up cots in their living quarters. There was no longer room at the tiny hospital. Some of the women settlers volunteered to help with the nursing and cooking. Those who did not need medical care worked to prepare shelters in several large frame buildings. Gere knew that the stone barracks would be safer if the Indians attacked, but those were the quarters for Marsh's troops and had to be reserved for their return.

The post sutler, Benjamin Randall, was placed in charge of the water supply. Because there was no well on the fort's grounds, all water had to be carried from a nearby spring. Randall collected all the objects that could serve as containers—tubs, bottles, barrels, and jugs—and organized details to fill them and transport them to the post.

Sometime in the early afternoon, Randall told Lieutenant Gere that he thought he heard gunfire from the direction of the agency. They walked a short distance down the ferry road, but they did not hear anything suspicious. Gere increased the

number of pickets around the perimeter and issued a weapon
to any man who claimed he could handle a gun. Among them
was Joe Coursolle, who had arrived with his wife and baby boy.
He was worried about the child, who had become feverish during the journey, and also concerned about the fate of his missing daughters.

New arrivals at the fort brought more word about increasing numbers of Indians between the fort and the ferry. They
heightened Gere's concern about Captain Marsh. Had he
crossed and gone to the agency? Had he gone north to chase
the Indians over the prairie? Why didn't he send word to Fort
Ridgely?

By sundown, the fort contained more than two hundred
refugees, and still they kept coming. At 7:30, two troopers
from Marsh's command, sent by Sergeant Bishop, brought the
terrible news. Gere was thunderstruck. If the Sioux dared to
attack Marsh's outfit at the ferry, then they would not hesitate
to come after Gere's smaller force at a fort that did not even
have a wall around it!

The lieutenant hastily wrote a message to the commanding officer at Fort Snelling, the nearest army post, and to Minnesota's governor, Alexander Ramsey.

> Captain Marsh left this post at [10:30] this
> morning to prevent Indian depredations at the
> Lower Agency. Some of the men have returned.
> From them I learn that Captain Marsh is killed
> and only thirteen of his company remaining. The
> Indians are killing the settlers and plundering the
> country. Send reinforcements without delay.

Gere handed the note to Pvt. William Sturgis, who took
the best horse on the post and set out at once. If he met no
hostile Indians along the way, he might reach Fort Snelling in
twenty-four hours. And it would take at least that long for him
to bring back reinforcements.

The lieutenant decided to move all the refugees into the
stone barracks building. It was the only place that would be
protected from fires started by flaming arrows. The refugees

had made themselves comfortable in the frame buildings, however, piling their meager possessions around them like walls, and they were reluctant to be uprooted.

A civilian picket walking outside fired his rifle. He thought he detected some movement in the darkness and came running in from the guard post yelling that the Indians were attacking. The settlers inside panicked. In their rush to escape, they broke several windows. Gere's troops restored order and shepherded them into the stone barracks. He sent out additional pickets but was convinced that the report was a false alarm.

At ten o'clock that night, Sergeant Bishop and a few other survivors of Captain Marsh's command returned to the fort. Eight other wounded soldiers arrived sometime later. They had hidden all afternoon in the woods near the ambush site.

After midnight, Gere dispatched another message to Lieutenant Sheehan, urging him to return to Fort Ridgely as quickly as he could.

> Force your march returning. Captain Marsh and most of his command were killed yesterday at the Lower Agency. Little Crow and about 600 Sioux warriors are now approaching the fort and will undoubtedly attack us. About 250 refugees have arrived here for protection. The Indians are killing men, women, and children.

Expecting an attack at any moment, Gere kept his men on alert throughout the night. He knew that he had to hold the fort regardless of the cost, not only for the sake of the settlers huddled in the barracks but also because his was the only military post to protect the several thousand farmers along the Minnesota River. If Fort Ridgely fell, there was nothing to stop the Sioux from sweeping down the length of the valley, all the way to Fort Snelling.

5

OH GOD! OH GOD!

Helen Carrothers and her children—the baby boy and four-year-old girl—were brought by their captors to Little Crow's camp about three o'clock that afternoon. Dazed by the butchery she had witnessed—the fiery death of Mrs. Henderson and her children—wet from fording the Minnesota River on foot, frightened and hungry, she was ordered to unhitch the wagon and go out into the fields to pick corn for the Indians to eat. They did not offer her any food.

She sat on the ground, holding the children, and watched as Sioux braves returned in triumph to the village, bloody scalps dangling from their belts. The men were laden with plunder, and many dragged white women and girls behind them. Helen waited for almost two hours before Little Crow spotted her and came over to shake hands. He knew her well and had often visited her home, approving of the way she mixed barks, roots, and herbs, just as the medicine man had instructed her.

Helen asked the chief whether she could go to his house.

She knew that she and the children would be safer there than out in the open amid the crowd of returning warriors, who had already begun to drink in celebration. Little Crow agreed, and he led her to his house, taking her into the main room on the ground floor. It was jammed with goods looted from the agency stores—sugar, coffee, tea and other foodstuffs, bolts of calico, and piles of clothing.

She told Little Crow that she and the children were hungry. She had always offered him food whenever he came to her house, and she expected to be shown the same courtesy. Instead, Little Crow looked cross and gestured to a sack on the floor.

"There is flour," he said. "If you are hungry, make yourself some bread."

Little Crow stalked out of the house without another word. He was angry, but not at Helen Carrothers. Despite the apparent successes of his braves, he was not at all pleased with the events of the day. Although gratified to learn of the deaths of certain men, such as Andrew Myrick, he was saddened by the slaying of friends such as Philander Prescott. Throughout the morning at the agency, Little Crow had urged his warriors to be less indiscriminate in their killing and to take women and children prisoner instead of killing them, but few heeded his counsel.

He had also had an unpleasant encounter with Wabasha, a chief he respected. Wabasha sat proudly and regally on a snow white horse, wearing all his ceremonial finery: "a headdress of red flannel adorned with bullock horns and eagle feathers, wings of feathers over his shoulders and down his back, great strings of beads around his neck, and a belt of wampum around his waist. His lower limbs were clad in fringed buckskin, and he carried a beautiful rifle across his lap, with two pistols in their holsters."

Little Crow asked Wabasha whether he had led his braves in the attack. Wabasha's reply was curt. He declared that the uprising was not an act of war but rather a wanton slaughter of civilians, unworthy of true Indian braves. He told Little Crow that he wanted no part of it and criticized him for yielding to the mob's demands in the early-morning council at Little

Crow's home. Wabasha cast a cold stare at Little Crow, then rode past him, back to his own village.

Little Crow was left to wander through the smoldering remains of the Lower Agency buildings, but there was nothing for him to do there. He realized that there had been little for him to do anywhere. The events he had unleashed had spilled over without him, quite beyond his control. He returned to his village then, to watch his warriors haul in their captives and their stolen goods and relate their tales of killing.

The sixteen-year-old son of Wacouta, who, like Wabasha, opposed war with the whites, came to Little Crow to ask whether he could stay with him. The boy had been drinking, and he told Little Crow that his father was angry with him for joining in the fighting. Little Crow chastised him for drinking the white man's whiskey and reproached him for bragging that the Sioux had slain hundreds of whites so easily.

When the rest of the white settlers heard about the uprising, the boy claimed, they would all leave and the land would once again belong to the Sioux. It would not be so easy, Little Crow told him. The whites could no longer be taken by surprise. More soldiers would come, armed with more powerful weapons than muskets. The next time, they would bring their wagon guns. The Sioux had no weapons to equal the power of those cannon. The boy was a fool and a braggart, and Little Crow knew that there were many others just like him.

Little Crow decided then that he would have to take control of the war, to lead his braves to fight the white man's way. The Sioux could win only if they united and attacked the soldiers at Fort Ridgely. If not, if they continued to raid in small bands, killing civilians and looting their homes, they would lose the war. Despite all the plunder and the captives and the death toll, Little Crow knew that the uprising had not, so far, been satisfactory.

A mixed-blood woman prisoner, whom Little Crow later set free, recalled seeing the chief that afternoon. He looked sad, she noted, and told her that the war had been forced on him by the murders committed by the four braves at Acton Township. Despite his misgivings, however, he intended to do everything he could to win.

Victory depended on having the support of all the Sissetons and Wahpetons at the Upper Agency and the other tribes in the territory as well—the Chippewas in the north and the Winnebagos in the south. He had to succeed at what no other chief before him had ever accomplished, to persuade the various tribes and bands to set aside their jealousies and their differences and unite for the common cause. But Little Crow had not even been able to unite and lead his own band of Mdewakantons.

After Little Crow left Helen Carrothers at his house, one of his wives prepared coffee and fried bread for her and the children and offered her advice on how to stay alive. The squaw said that the white women prisoners were making the braves angry by their constant crying and that they would be killed if that behavior did not stop. Helen vowed to do nothing to upset the Sioux and to try, instead, to please them.

When she finished eating, she took the children outside to play and stood in the doorway watching them. Little Crow strode up and pushed her back inside.

"Go into the house," he ordered. "The Indians will kill you if you do not."

Pleased that the chief seemed concerned for her safety, she picked up the baby and brought the children inside. Two other white women soon joined her, Amanda Earle and Urania White and their children, who had survived attacks on their wagons when they tried to flee to Fort Ridgely. A young German girl was with them, and one of Little Crow's brothers sat beside her.

"This is my squaw," he announced, putting his arm around her. He told them that the Indian who had captured Mrs. Earle and Mrs. White—a warrior the whites called John—wanted them all brought to his tepee. He led them there, and they were treated to a meal prepared by John's wives. One squaw took Amanda and her daughter away, leaving Helen and her two children, and Urania and her baby. They were given blankets and lay down on the floor to sleep. At about ten o'clock that night, Little Crow visited them and said that if they hoped to survive, they would have to braid their hair in Indian fashion and wear Indian clothing.

Helen Carrothers asked him about the uprising, and he spoke to her at length about his feelings and his plans. He seemed to her to be more optimistic than he had been earlier in the day. Either his own mood had changed or he wanted to impress her with the power of the Sioux nation. He said that the Indians intended to kill all the whites along the Minnesota River valley as far as St. Peter and retake the land north and south of the river.

Helen asked how Little Crow expected to hold off the army that the government would send after them. The chief scoffed at the idea, arguing that there was no one left in the territory to fight except women and old men. Everyone knew that all the soldiers had been sent south to fight for the Negroes, he said. No, the Sioux did not have to be concerned about the soldiers.

A few miles downriver from Little Crow's village, the three young women captured together—Mary Schwandt, Mattie Williams, and Mary Anderson—were led to a house in Wacouta's village. Inside were twenty-nine-year-old Jannette DeCamp and her three children, who had been taken near the Lower Agency. At about 10:30 P.M., several warriors entered the house and began to annoy fourteen-year-old Mary Schwandt.

"One of them laid his hands forcibly upon me," she recalled, "when I screamed, and one of the fiends struck me on my mouth with his hand, causing the blood to flow very freely. Then they took me out by force, to an unoccupied tepee, near the house, and perpetrated the most horrible and nameless outrages upon my person." This was only the first of the rapes inflicted on Mary Schwandt during her long captivity.

More Indians arrived at the house later that night. They were carrying bloody knapsacks, which they claimed to have taken from the soldiers they had ambushed at the ferry. They shouted and brandished their tomahawks, waking the children. Jannette DeCamp's nine-year-old son began screaming.

"Are we going to be killed, Mama? Don't let them kill us with knives!"

Mary Schwandt and Mattie Williams clung to Mrs. De-

Camp for protection. Mary Anderson huddled on the floor, in grievous pain from the bullet wound in her back. The braves pranced around them, yelling and chanting. Their frenzied dance angered Jannette DeCamp, and, for a moment, it made her fearless. She knew some of these braves; in better days, they had been guests in her home. They had partaken of her food and played with her children. She resolved to remind them that they would be punished for their misdeeds.

"I told them," she wrote later, "that they would all be hanged before another moon; that if the white men had gone away, they would soon return; that the 'whispering spirit' [the telegraph] would at once bring more men than would cover the prairies; and that if they did kill us it would not be long till their hideous forms would be dangling from a rope's end."

The warriors laughed at her and threatened them, tormenting them until Wacouta arrived and ordered them out. Among the warriors were two of Wacouta's sons, including the one who had boasted to Little Crow how easy it had been to kill the whites. Wacouta was distressed by the way his braves had terrorized the white women, and he was particularly solicitous of the wounded girl, Mary Anderson. He asked what he could do to help. She pleaded with him to remove the bullet that had entered her back. The chief took an old jackknife and probed the wound gently, but her moans made him stop.

Mary took the knife from him, made an incision, and plucked the bullet out. Wacouta dressed the wound with wet cloths. The pain had made her delirious, and they bedded her down and took turns watching over her. Wacouta promised to guard the house from outside so that they would not be molested again.

Sarah Wakefield, the wife of the Upper Agency physician, was thinking about the last sight she had of George Gleason before the Indian warriors Hapa and Chaska drove her away. Gleason's body was lying in the road, his hat pulled over his face, watched over by his dog.

As soon as Sarah was brought into an Indian camp—it was Shakopee's village—she was recognized by many of the squaws and braves as a longtime friend of the Sioux. They wept at the sight of her as a prisoner and spread carpets on the ground for her to sit on. She had begun to feel a little less desperate about her situation when a mixed-blood wandered past. He told her that the braves had sworn to kill every white captive and so, within a few days, most likely she would be dead.

Chaska suggested that she and the children spend the night at his house nearby, where another white woman was staying. Although he had saved her life when Gleason was shot, she did not fully trust him. She asked the mixed-blood's advice; in her mind, he was more trustworthy than the Indian because he was half white. He advised her to go.

"Chaska is a good man," he said, "and you must trust him. You will be better treated."

"Then," Sarah Wakefield wrote later, "he gave me some very good advice; he said as long as I was with them I must try to be pleased and not mistrust them; make them think I had confidence in them, and they would soon learn to love and respect me, and that would be the only way of prolonging my life."

Resolving to heed that advice, she gathered up her children and followed Chaska through the dark woods. She was determined that they would survive.

A single shot shattered the dawn silence at Yellow Medicine, the Upper Agency settlement. More gunfire followed, interspersed with the bloodcurdling yells favored by the Sioux at the onset of an attack. To the fifty-eight whites huddled in the stone and brick warehouse building, the shots and shouts signaled the beginning of their last sane hours on earth. The men knew they faced death. For the women, the prospect of captivity and rape was more terrifying. That was the living death feared by all women on the frontier.

The whites, including almost all of the agency's residents, had passed the night in the warehouse. They had some weapons, and the building was a stout one. They resolved to hold off the savages as long as they could. Their only real hope of surviving, however, depended on an Indian, forty-two-year-old John Other Day, who had rounded them up late the previous evening and herded them inside.

Not all the white settlers trusted him. It mattered little that for six years he had been a Christian and a farmer, that he wore white man's clothing, and that he was married to a white woman. Some whites still feared him despite his hymn singing and his long pants. They had heard the tales of his violent warrior past when he had bested the brave considered to be the Sioux's fiercest fighter and had bitten off his nose. (The man had been called Cut Nose ever since.) Could the missionaries truly have tamed such a wild spirit? Would he revert to his warrior ways now that his Indian brothers were on a rampage? John Other Day bore close watching.

However, throughout the night in the Yellow Medicine warehouse, it was John Other Day who had done the watching. He and four of his relatives stood guard. Toward morning, small groups of Indians approached the building, five to ten at a time, forming a loose circle around the warehouse and its guards. They did not threaten Other Day—he was respected and feared as a fighter—but they tracked his every move. The scrutiny unnerved his relatives, however, and one by one they slipped away, leaving him alone.

The shot fired at daybreak came from the direction of the stores, a half mile away. Bands of Sioux were bent on looting them. Not wanting to miss out on their share of the plunder, the Sioux warriors around the warehouse ran off to join them. A few white tradesmen and clerks had remained in their shops, perhaps out of loyalty to their employers or to protect their property, or because they refused to believe that the Indians were a threat.

Stewart Garvie was one. He stood in the doorway of Myrick's store and took a charge of buckshot in the stomach. He staggered upstairs, jumped out the rear window, and made his way to the warehouse, leaving a path of his own blood. At Forbes's store, a Frenchman by the name of Constans was killed. Two men from a third shop raced to the warehouse for safety, passing within eight feet of a band of Indians.

At the store owned by Francis Patoile, who had been killed the previous day after escaping from the Reynoldses' house, where he had stopped for breakfast, his nephew Peter was shot in the back. The bullet passed through the boy's lungs and exited his chest. An Indian rolled him over, pronounced him dead, and went inside the store to grab what goods he could carry. Peter summoned up the strength to crawl into some bushes. He remained hidden all day, drifting in and out of consciousness.

That night he hauled himself to the Minnesota River, about two miles away, and waded across. In the morning, two mixed-bloods found him, gave him crackers, tripe, and onions to eat, and warned him to stay away from Fort Ridgely, because it was going to be attacked.

Alone and in constant pain, Peter wandered aimlessly, his circuitous path taking him more than two hundred miles. He soon used up the provisions the mixed-bloods had given him, and over the next twelve days found only two potatoes and three ears of green corn, which he wolfed down raw. He finally met up with some settlers forty miles north of St. Cloud, and they helped him get away to St. Paul.

The Sioux ransacked the stores at the Upper Agency, unconcerned for the moment about the whites taking refuge in the warehouse. They could wait.

John Other Day was not prepared to wait, however. He planned to act to save his white friends. Seeing that the Indians were occupied at the agency stores, Other Day helped the refugees hitch their horses to five wagons. They placed a mattress in one and settled the wounded Stewart Garvie on it, to cushion the rough ride. One by one, the men, women, and children in the warehouse—now sixty-two in number—exited the east door. Dr. Wakefield was among them; he remarked that he was thankful he had sent his wife away the previous day. Also in the group was the woman who had the most to fear from the Sioux—the wife of the hated Indian agent, Major Galbraith.

The women and children climbed into the wagons, clutching the few loaves of bread someone had had the presence of mind to bring from home. The men walked alongside the wagons, peering all around, examining every clump of bushes and stand of trees for signs of the Indians. The settlers did not have enough guns or ammunition to defend themselves for long. As they moved on and the day grew brighter, they could still hear the yelps of the Indians back at the settlement.

The party crossed the Minnesota River and climbed out of the valley to the bluff and the open prairie beyond. When they had covered eight miles and seen not a soul, they stopped to decide on their destination. Some wanted to head for the nearest sanctuary—Fort Ridgely. Others argued that they should get as far from the reservation as possible and head for St. Paul, even though it was 120 miles away.

John Other Day said that if they went to the fort, the Indians would massacre them all. The Sioux were likely to assume that the Upper Agency whites would head for Fort Ridgely and would be waiting along the road to ambush them. The men agreed with Other Day, and the little caravan turned northwest, proceeding slowly across the empty prairie.

After a journey of five days and four nights, they reached St. Paul, sustained by food found in deserted farmhouses and fields. No Indians had been seen. Stewart Garvie died of his gunshot wound, but the other residents of the Upper Agency survived, owing their lives to John Other Day. Major Galbraith would comment on that fact later in his official report:

> And this Other Day is a pure full-blooded Indian, and was not long since, one of the wildest and fiercest of his race. Poor, noble fellow! Must he, too, be ostracized for the sins of his nation? I commend him to the care of a just God and a liberal government; and not only him, but all others who did likewise.

The Reverend Stephen Riggs, together with his family and other members of his Christian mission, lived three miles north of the Upper Agency at Hazelwood, an Indian farmers' community he had established. Late on Monday evening, an elder of his church, Gabriel Renville, a mixed-blood, had run to the reverend's house to tell him of the uprising. Riggs thought it was probably the work of a few Indians who had had too much to drink. Soon other mixed-bloods and farmer Indians came to tell the same story.

Parents flocked to the mission boarding school to take their children away. Indians they had never seen before appeared at the stables and stole their horses. About a dozen armed farmer Indians came to Riggs and announced that they would stand guard over his house. Unconvinced that they were facing a large-scale uprising, Riggs sent an Indian to the agency to find out what the situation was. The man returned with word that the stores were surrounded by bands of Sioux warriors who planned to loot them at daybreak. The wives of the farmer Indians gathered in the mission parlor for a prayer meeting, which they concluded by singing the old hymn "God Is the Refuge of His Saints."

Riggs did not agree to leave until he was reminded of the possible danger to his three young daughters. However, it was a personally devastating decision to accept because it meant that his years of missionary work had been in vain. "What will become of our quarter-century's work among the Dakotas?" he asked his wife, Mary. "It seems to be lost." If the Sioux were carrying their murderous rampage far and wide, then the preaching and good works, the Ten Commandments and baptisms, had failed to bring God to the savages.

Sometime after midnight, Riggs and his wife woke their children and their houseguests—Mr. and Mrs. D. W. Moore, a honeymoon couple from New Jersey who had come west in the hope of seeing Indians—and prepared them to leave. They decided to spend the remainder of the night on an island in the Minnesota River, three miles away. By the time they were ready to depart, seventeen of the mission teachers and trainees had come to the house to join them.

The next afternoon, Riggs left his party and went alone to the agency. The ruins he saw there left no doubt in his mind about the need to flee the reservation. He called at the home of a fellow missionary, Dr. John P. Williamson, to tell him that they were going, but Williamson said that he and his wife would stay. They did not believe they were in any personal danger. The Sioux were their friends.

By late in the day, Riggs's group numbered thirty-three and included families from the nearby sawmill. For defense, they had a shotgun and a revolver. With a single horse-drawn buggy and a few oxcarts, the column of refugees headed east toward the town of Henderson, north of St. Peter. They had brought sacks of flour but had no way to cook or bake with them, so their only food was what they could forage along the way.

Day after day, they struggled on, skirting Fort Ridgely—where they could hear the sounds of gunfire—and past the town of New Ulm. They grew weaker with each passing hour. An oxcart overtook them, bringing Dr. and Mrs. Williamson and three others. Now there were forty-two people in the column, almost thirty of these women and children.

The rains fell, the wind blew, the nights brought bitter cold. They dared not build fires for warmth for fear they would be spotted by the Indians.

"The evening came with a slow continued rain," Riggs wrote. "The first night we were out, the smaller children had cried for home. The second night, some of the older children would have cried if it had been of any use. We had no shelter. The wagons were no protection against the continued rain, but it was rather natural to crawl under them. The drop, drop, DROP, all night long from the wagon-beds on the women and children, who had not more than half covering in that cold August rain, was not promotive of cheerfulness. Mrs. Moore looked sad and disheartened, and to my question as to how she did she replied that one might as well die as live under such circumstances."

One week after leaving home, the Riggs party reached Henderson.

Others in the vicinity of the Upper Agency were not so fortunate. A few miles southeast, on the other side of the river, thirteen German families were trying to get to Fort Ridgely. They had learned about the uprising from two neighbors, August Fross and Eckmel Groundman. The two men had been returning from a trip to the Lower Agency when they came across the bodies of a woman and two children. It appeared as though they had been running away; some of their possessions were strewn about. One man stayed with the bodies while the other hurried off to question the neighbors.

About a mile down the road, he found a couple and three children murdered in their house. Not far from there, another

man was dead and his house ransacked. And nearby, he came
upon the bodies of a man and a woman, together with two
children whose heads had been split open. Scanning the few
houses visible in the distance, he could detect no signs of life.
Convinced that the Indians were on the warpath, he returned
to his friend, and together they rushed to the house of Frederick Krieger.

Krieger had gone fishing, but his twenty-seven-year-old
wife, Justina, was home, along with nine children and step-
children. Word was passed and within the hour Justina's husband returned, and the thirteen families in the settlement
gathered at the house of Paul Kitzman, Justina's brother.

By eight o'clock Monday evening, they had made the decision to head for Fort Ridgely. They traveled throughout the
night in eleven wagons and covered some fourteen miles by
daybreak. About two hours later, eight armed and painted Indian warriors on horseback came into view. Kitzman knew
some of them—one had often dined at his home and they had
gone fishing together. Only half of the men in the wagon train
were armed. Some wanted to fire on the Indians immediately,
but others urged caution.

They were still arguing the point in German when the
Sioux drew up and lowered their weapons. The man who knew
Kitzman dismounted, shook his hand, and embraced him. He
wanted to know where they were going. To the fort, Kitzman
told him, because all their neighbors had been killed by Indians.

The Sioux did not kill them, the Indian explained. They
had been murdered by Chippewas, and now the Sioux were
going after the Chippewas to punish them. He urged the German settlers to return to their homes because the Chippewas
were probably waiting up ahead on the road to the fort to ambush them. Then he placed a hand on Kitzman's shoulder and
smiled.

"You are a good man," he said. "It [would be] too bad
that you should be killed."

He shook hands with all the whites and assured them that
the Sioux had no intention of harming them. Quite the con-
trary—they were there to save them from the Chippewas. He

gestured for the rest of the Indians to dismount, and they mingled with the families, shaking hands and urging the women to keep the children quiet. Blankets were spread on the ground, and everyone sat down to a meal of bread and milk.

The wagons were pulled around, and the settlers headed home. The Indians accompanied them, positioning themselves all around the tiny convoy. Frederick Krieger felt uneasy. Paul Kitzman was worried, too. Their shotguns were all in one wagon, piled there while the teams were being turned. Each Indian carried a double-barreled shotgun, loaded and cocked.

By midafternoon, the caravan reached the corpses that Fross and Groundman had found previously. Suddenly, the Indians drew up in a single line, aimed their weapons, and demanded money. Justina Krieger handed her husband five dollars to give to the Indians. He slipped her his pocketknife in return—to remember him by, he whispered.

The Sioux did not harm them, however. They took the money and departed, and the wagon train moved on. A mile or two from the Krieger house, they found the fresh bodies of two white men, indicating that Indians were still in the vicinity. The men retrieved their shotguns, and they all headed for the Krieger house, where they hoped to make a stand.

About one hundred yards from the house, fourteen Indians charged from behind, whooping and shouting as they opened fire. They were from the Rice Creek and Shakopee bands, led by Shakopee himself and the notorious Cut Nose. All but three of the men fell instantly. Frederick Krieger was lucky, shielded for the moment by his team of oxen. None of the settlers had a chance to return fire. The women and children, dazed and screaming, did not know what to do. The Indians called to them: any woman who came with them would live; anyone who refused would die on the spot.

Some of the women walked out from behind the wagons, agreeing to go with the Indians. Justina Krieger refused, and she told the warriors that she would die with her husband and her children. Frederick pleaded with her, urging her to go, telling her that she could probably escape after a time. Another woman moved toward the Indians, hesitated, and turned around to call to Justina. Apparently the Indians thought the woman had changed her mind, and they shot her dead instantly.

Another burst of fire killed six women and two men, leaving Krieger the only white man to survive. Several of the children sustained wounds, and the Indians, enraged, beat others with the butts of their guns. "Some [children] soon after rose up from the ground," Justina Krieger recalled, "with the blood streaming down their faces, when they were beaten again and killed. This was the most horrible scene I had yet witnessed."

Frederick begged her again to go with the Indians to save her own life, but she remained resolutely in the wagon, expecting to be shot, and knowing that her husband was doomed, as well. She watched him stand firm between his oxen as an Indian approached. He never saw the second Indian come up from behind. They fired simultaneously, and he fell to the ground. They fired again, and he was dead.

Justina gathered her skirts and prepared to jump from the wagon. The Indians shot her in the back. She fell flat in the wagon bed among her children. A Sioux brave dragged her out, dropped her on the ground, and shoved the wagon over her body. Mercifully, she fainted. The children scrambled out of the wagon and ran for the woods, but one, a four-year-old boy, knelt beside his father's body.

"Papa," he cried. "Papa, don't sleep so long."

Two Indians snatched him up and rode away. The other children hid in the woods until the rest of the Indians left. One would starve to death in the coming days, but the remaining Krieger children would eventually reach the safety of Fort Ridgely.

The survivors—one woman and several children—took refuge in the Krieger house. The woman had sustained two bullet wounds and could do little to care for the others, the oldest of whom was thirteen. The infants had been tomahawked or beaten with gun butts. The four-year-old daughter of Eckmel Groundman had lost her hand—it had been shot off. The group remained in the house for two days. They had no medical supplies or food, and were in constant fear that the Indians would return. The next day, the woman decided to leave, taking with her a baby and two older children. Within sight of the house—but hidden themselves by the tall grass—they saw Indian braves enter the house, remove the few items ignored in a previous plundering, and set it afire. It burned to the ground with seven children inside.

Justina Krieger regained consciousness sometime after dark. She tried to get to her feet but could not. She spied two Indians moving among the dead, taking their valuables. Soon they came to her. They kicked her and felt for the pulse at her wrist, while she held her breath and feigned death.

"They conversed in Sioux for a moment," she wrote later. "I shut my eyes and awaited what else was to befall me with a shudder. The next moment a sharp-pointed knife was felt at my throat, then passing downward, to the lower portion of the abdomen, cut not only the clothing entirely from my body, but actually penetrating the flesh, making but a slight wound on the chest, but at the pit of the stomach entering the body and laying it open to the intestines themselves! My arms were then taken separately out of the clothing. I was seized rudely by the hair and hurled headlong to the ground, entirely naked."

She lost consciousness again, but when she revived, she saw that the two Indians were still there. One of them picked up her niece, Wilhelmina Kitzman, who was still alive. He held the child upside down by one foot. With his free hand, he took a knife, "with which he hastily cut the flesh around one of the legs, close to the body, and then, by twisting and wrenching, broke the ligaments and bone, until the limb was entirely severed from the body, the child screaming frantically, 'Oh God! Oh God!' When the limb was off, the child, thus mutilated, was thrown down on the ground, stripped of her clothing, and left to die."

The sight of this atrocity made Justina pass out once more, and the next time she awoke, she found that the right side of her body was paralyzed. She propped herself up on her left side and felt on the ground for her clothing. She wrapped the shredded garments around her as best she could and began to inch her way along the road, crawling like a child in what she hoped was the direction of Fort Ridgely, almost forty miles away.

6
WITH THE UTMOST PROMPTITUDE

     Maj. Tom Galbraith, the Indian agent, was in the bustling town of St. Peter when the first word of the uprising reached there on Monday night, August 18. At first, neither he nor anyone else in town believed it. The messenger was J. C. Dickinson, who ran the government boarding house at the Lower Agency. When he heard the first shots, Dickinson and his family, and the hired girls who worked in the dining room and kitchen, had hitched up a wagon and fled. He had been the first to bring the news to Fort Ridgely, but he did not stop there. He pushed on all the way to St. Peter to get as far from the Sioux as possible before his horses collapsed from exhaustion.

     By the time he arrived in St. Peter about sundown, Dickinson was, according to Galbraith, "in a state of excitement bordering on insanity." The innkeeper told the townspeople about the trouble at the agency—"that the Indians had broke out"—"but so confused, conflicting, and disconnected were his statements, that at first we were in doubt what reliance to place on them."

At midnight, a more sober and believable report came from Mrs. Adolph Seiter, whose husband ran the Dacotah House, a hotel in New Ulm. As soon as she heard about the uprising, she had gathered her children in a small wagon and raced to St. Peter. She persuaded Galbraith that the trouble at the agency was real, and he decided to take the fifty men he was escorting to join the Union army—a force now called the Renville Rangers—and return with them to Fort Ridgely. It was the best place from which to assess the danger. The men agreed to return. They had left friends and loved ones at both agencies and were concerned about their safety. Galbraith issued government bonds on the spot to pay for fifty muskets for his men, along with ammunition and supplies from the state warehouse. The outfit departed before sunrise.

At four o'clock on the morning of the nineteenth, Judge Charles Flandrau was awakened in his St. Peter home by a frantic pounding on the front door. Flandrau had slept fitfully, awakened often by the sounds of horses galloping past his house on their way into town. When he answered the door, he knew the reason for the commotion. Henry Behnke had ridden from New Ulm to spread the alarm to the settlers to the east. He told Flandrau that the Sioux were killing whites throughout the countryside.

Flandrau knew the Indians well, having served as government agent to the Sioux. A highly respected, brilliant lawyer and a natural leader, he had dropped out of school at the age of thirteen and gone to sea. When he returned, he worked for two years in a lumber mill before reading law in the office of his father, a prominent New York State attorney who had once been a partner of Aaron Burr's. Looking for adventure, fame, and fortune, the restless, aggressive, and athletic Flandrau emigrated to Minnesota in 1853 at the age of twenty-five. He quickly became influential in the political life of the territory. When Minnesota became a state in 1858, Flandrau was appointed associate justice of the state supreme court.

Flandrau acted decisively that morning. He put his family in a wagon and sent them east, then gathered up all the guns, powder, and lead from his house and rode the mile into the center of St. Peter. He found the townsmen gathered in front of the courthouse, milling around, waiting for someone to tell them what to do. Flandrau took charge, and by noon he had assembled a company of 115 men ready for action. To no one's surprise, the men elected him captain.

Although many of the men had brought weapons from home, some of these were old. In addition, Flandrau's outfit had insufficient ammunition, supplies, or equipment to do battle with who knew how many Indians. Every gun in town was appropriated for distribution to the makeshift militia. Most of the arms were shotguns, with only a few rifles. Some men carried revolvers and even swords; a few had clubs and pitchforks. What they lacked in firepower, however, they made up in determination and in their hatred of the Indians.

Flandrau put the blacksmiths and gun shops to work molding bullets, and soon each of his men had full powder horns, a box of caps, and a pocketful of bullets. Wagons were commandeered, along with blankets and food. Three doctors agreed to join the expedition—William Mayo and Otis Ayer of nearby Le Sueur, and Asa Daniels of St. Peter.

The captain organized a cavalry force to send in advance of his main party—fifteen mounted men under the command of L. M. Boardman, a former sheriff. Boardman was ordered to scout the area of Fort Ridgely and New Ulm. At noon, he led his men out of town, having decided to go to New Ulm. It was the town closest to the Lower Agency and so was likely to come under attack. It was also vulnerable because its population consisted largely of newly arrived German farmers who had few weapons and no experience in fighting Indians.

Fort Ridgely, in contrast, would surely not need help. Flandrau believed that Captain Marsh had enough soldiers to defend the post should the Indians be foolhardy enough to attack it, and now Major Galbraith was on his way there with his fifty Renville Rangers. Flandrau expected to hold New Ulm, assuming he and his men got there in time. If not, they would fight the savages wherever they found them and at least keep them out of St. Peter.

As Flandrau's men were leaving St. Peter, refugees from the countryside began to flood in, soon numbering several thousand, tripling the town's population. By afternoon, every private home, hotel, church, school, warehouse, saloon, and shed was packed with people.

"All is clatter, rattle, and din," wrote a St. Paul lawyer. "Wagons, ponies, mules, oxen, cows, and calves are promiscuously distributed among groups of men, women, and children. The livestock from thousands of deserted farms surround the outskirts of the town. The lowing of strange cattle, the neighing of restless horses, the crying of lost and hungry children, the tales of horror, the tomahawk wounds undressed, the bleeding feet, the cries for food, and the loud wailing for missing friends, all combine to turn into the souls the dreadful reality that some terrible calamity was upon the country."

They arrived in an endless, pitiful stream, as though the entire western portion of the state was being drained. Exhaustion, and the promised comfort of others, led most of them to stop at St. Peter, wondering whether it would be their grave site but too weary to move on.

With most of the men in the town already gone, and few weapons available to the rest, the settlers realized that they would be helpless if the Sioux chose to attack. They barricaded the town's few stone buildings and posted sentries to watch the open prairie, scanning for the dust clouds that would signal the approach of the Indians. They saw no Indians, only more frightened refugees, sobbing and bleeding victims carrying the sum of their possessions in carts, buggies, and sacks.

At noon on Tuesday, a message from Major Galbraith was received by Governor Alexander Ramsey in the capital, St. Paul. This was the first notification the governor had of the trouble at the Lower Agency. He rode to Fort Snelling to ascertain the number of available troops, should they be needed. Like Galbraith, he believed that Captain Marsh had enough men at Fort Ridgely to contain anything short of a full-scale uprising, so he made no immediate plans to dispatch additional troops.

At three o'clock that afternoon, Pvt. William Sturgis—sent out by Lieutenant Gere at Fort Ridgely the previous night—arrived at Fort Snelling. He had made the 165-mile ride in eighteen hours, an achievement for which he was promoted to sergeant. He brought the shocking news that Captain Marsh and most of his men had been killed at the ferry crossing and that the Indians were murdering civilians in large numbers. This was not a matter of a few raiding parties. This was war.

Four companies of recruits were at Fort Snelling, part of the Sixth Minnesota Infantry, a new outfit that had not yet been mustered into the Union army. As such, it was still under the control of the governor. Its officers and men, however, were untrained and untested in battle.

To command them—and whatever additional troops might be gathered—Governor Ramsey chose a man whose reputation would calm the fears of the white populace, a man who spoke the Dakota language and knew their ways. That was his old friend and onetime political rival, Henry H. Sibley. The governor rode to Sibley's palatial house at Mendota and told him what he wanted.

Sibley agreed to accept an appointment at the rank of colonel to head the expedition against the Sioux, on the condition that command would be his alone. He would tolerate no interference, not even from the governor. He expected Ramsey's unqualified support and the freedom to conduct the campaign in his own way. Ramsey agreed to the stipulations and wrote a dispatch to the adjutant general at Fort Snelling.

> Sir. Information just received . . . leaves no doubt that the Sioux Indians, in considerable numbers, in the vicinity of the Redwood Agency, have taken the lives and property of our citizens, and that as a consequence, the people on the frontier are alarmed and excited. You will therefore immediately organize an expedition composed of four companies of the infantry now at Fort Snelling, and place them in charge of ex-Governor Sibley, to move to the scene of difficulties with the utmost promptitude.

With 225 men, Sibley was expected to move with utmost promptitude 165 miles to Fort Ridgely and subdue a much larger force of marauding Indians, but he appeared up to the challenge. At fifty-one, Sibley had a powerful, commanding presence. Six feet tall, he was stout in the manner of the day, when girth was associated with manliness, vitality, and strength. In his younger days, he had acquired a reputation as a man who would fight anyone, in self-defense, no matter how vicious the opponent. It was said that there was only one man in the territory—a trader even stouter than Sibley—who dared to stand up to him.

Few people in Minnesota in 1862 possessed a better knowledge and understanding of the Indians. He spoke their language, as well as French, which many of the mixed-bloods spoke, and had known Little Crow and the other chiefs for more than twenty years. He had often gone hunting with Little Crow and probably understood him better than any other white man did. In return, Little Crow, and many of the Sioux, liked and respected Sibley. They called him Wapetonhonska, the Long Trader, a reference to his height and profession.

Sibley's father had been a prominent attorney in Detroit. During the War of 1812, when Henry was only a year old, he became a prisoner of war. His father was serving in the army, and his mother had taken shelter at the nearest fort when the British laid siege to the city. She kept busy making cartridges for the defending troops while the fort came under continuous bombardment. Finally, the post was forced to surrender, and all of the occupants, including the Sibley infant, became prisoners for a short time.

Sibley's early years at home were dedicated to mischief making, which, as he put it later, came naturally and provided him with a great deal of pleasure. "So many were my exploits in that direction," he wrote, "that my dear mother often declared me incorrigible and the black sheep of the family." At his father's insistence, he studied Greek and Latin and started to read law, but after two years he declared it an "irksome task." He wanted to do something more adventurous, away from the routine of city life. He longed for excitement and physical challenge, and there was only one place to find them—on the frontier.

At the age of eighteen, Sibley left Detroit for the northwest wilderness. He hunted game, explored the territory, and worked for a year as a clerk in a sutler's store. He then took a job with John Jacob Astor's fabulously successful American Fur Company, which had made its fortune by trading with the Indians for a variety of furs and pelts. It was a hard and dangerous life, but Sibley excelled at the work and in only five years was made a partner, responsible for all of the company's operations throughout the northwest. He was well on his way to becoming a wealthy man.

Two years later, Sibley built the first stone house in the area and equipped it with the finest of furnishings, a large staff of servants, and a French chef. He maintained an impressive library of books in English, French, Latin, and Greek. In 1843, he married a Baltimore woman, and they began a family that eventually included nine children. Not content to rest on his success in business, Sibley turned to writing and published articles on wilderness life for eastern magazines such as *Spirit of the Times*. Using the pen name "Hal a Dakotah," he became well known for his exciting tales of hunting and survival on the edge of civilization.

At thirty-eight, he launched his political career with a successful run for a seat in the U.S. Congress. At first, he represented Wisconsin, but the following year his district was incorporated into the new territory of Minnesota. He served in Congress from 1848 to 1853, then retired from Washington to stand for election to the Minnesota legislature. Four years later, he was elected the territory's first governor and guided it to statehood the following year.

During his congressional career, Sibley became one of the most unflinching champions of the Indian cause ever to appear in the capital city. As his biographer observed, Sibley "regarded the Indians as wronged, oppressed, betrayed, and driven to desperation, and even to massacres, by the inhuman conduct of the federal government and its agents." The congressman was bitingly critical of Indian agents but not of traders; he was still a trader himself. He chastised agents on the floor of the House of Representatives for taking unfair advantage of the Indians when negotiating treaties and accused them of cheating the natives out of their rightful annuity payments.

In 1850, Sibley had introduced a bill to extend the laws

and rights enjoyed by all U.S. citizens—except slaves, of
course—to the Indians, and he spoke passionately in its support:

> During this session we have heard these halls
> ring with eloquent denunciation of the oppressor,
> with expressions of sympathy for the downtrod-
> den millions of other lands, while gentlemen
> seem not to be aware that there exists, under the
> government of this republic, a species of grinding
> and intolerable oppression of which the Indian
> tribes are the victims, and, compared with which,
> the worst form of human bondage, now existing
> in any Christian state, may be regarded as a com-
> fort and a blessing.

The federal government was faced, Sibley continued, with
only two alternatives with regard to the Indians—to civilize
them completely by giving them parity with whites, or to exterminate them to the last man, woman, and child. There could
be no middle course. Sibley declared the government's present
policy to be:

> One of injustice, cruelty, treachery, violation of
> treaties the most sacred, stipulations and prom-
> ises being regarded as convenient means of pub-
> lic robbery and private fraud, the will of the
> stronger over the rule of action . . . the red man
> forced to surrender his possessory rights in imme-
> morial tenures of country endeared by the tradi-
> tions and graves of his tribe, or bayoneted, rifled,
> shot, or driven from one so-called "reservation"
> to another, until, at last, turning enraged on his
> foe, he sought vengeance in massacre, crime, and
> deeds of brutality for which the government it-
> self, and its horde of vagabond "Indian agents,"
> worse than the Indians themselves, were alone
> responsible.

No other nation of conquerors in any age had allowed
those who were conquered to become extinct as a people, as

the Indians, who, to Sibley, possessed "noble natural virtues," were in danger of becoming. He proposed to save them with his radical proposal to extend all U.S. laws to the tribes and to endow them with full civil and political rights.

In addition, he planned to eliminate the system of reservations in favor of private ownership of land and to continue annuity payments until such time as the Indians were capable of living without them. To help the tribes achieve independence and self-sufficiency, his bill called for the establishment of schools to teach Indian children marketable skills such as carpentry, blacksmithing, and farming. This was the same type of useful training offered to white children at a time when only a minority of the population attended college or even completed high school. Sibley believed that Indians were in no way intellectually inferior to whites. All they needed to prosper were equal opportunities, which his bill was designed to provide.

Although the bill was defeated, Sibley continued to push for Indian rights and an increase in the amount of money appropriated to provide them with food. His was a rare voice, reminding Washington that if the plight of the Indian nations was not eased, they would one day rise up to take vengeance.

Now, in August of 1862, this paradoxical man who had tried at the highest levels of government to improve conditions for the Indians, and who had also made a fortune trading with them, was called on to use force against them, to quell their uprising and to fight his old friend and hunting companion Little Crow.

But to move with the utmost promptitude and to fight with what? Sibley had no army worthy of the name in size, skill, or supplies. He knew that the Sioux could field as many as fifteen hundred warriors, if all the bands on the reservation united. They were practiced, seasoned, fearless fighters. His four companies of 225 raw troops were no match for them. He needed a larger force before he could act, and the men would have to be properly trained and equipped.

Only three cannon were available. Almost all of the rifles and revolvers were obsolete and of foreign manufacture, which meant that the standard U.S. Army ammunition on hand did not fit. To fabricate bullets of the proper size, lead teapots and water pipes were confiscated and melted down, and the metal molded into bullets.

There could be no mobile cavalry force to screen the main body of soldiers or to reconnoiter ahead of it, because Sibley had access to few horses. And there were not many government wagons in which to transport the infantry, so he resorted to commandeering them from the hands of dazed refugees who suddenly found themselves deprived of their only means of transportation and holding slips of paper as receipts. Medical supplies, food, tents, cooking and camping gear—everything required for survival in the field—had to be found or borrowed or improvised.

At the same time, uprooted white settlers kept arriving in St. Peter, all of them homeless and hungry, and Sibley was ordered to provide for them while provisioning his troops. He established a huge bakery, a butcher shop, and a soup kitchen. He scrounged for spare rooms, tents, and sheds—any place with walls and a roof—to house the population that had swollen from one thousand to ten thousand. He arranged for twelve thousand meals a day to be served, eight thousand rations of beef alone.

No, Sibley could not yet move, as he had been ordered, to relieve Fort Ridgely and the countless settlers fleeing and hiding and seeking shelter. For now, they would have to fend for themselves.

At Fort Ridgely, Lieutenant Gere and his handful of men, along with 250 refugees, huddled together inside the stone barracks building. They had been awake most of the night, expecting an Indian attack. Daybreak came as a relief—the darkness had magnified the terror—and Gere set about the task of arranging to feed all the people now depending on him. His men remained on the alert, certain that the Sioux would strike that day. The Indians surely knew how poorly defended the post was, and also that reinforcements had been sent for. They would want to attack before those reinforcements arrived.

A little past eight o'clock on Tuesday morning, lookouts stationed on the roofs of several buildings spotted movement in the distance. They alerted Gere, and he raced to the top of the officers' quarters, the post's highest point. Peering through a telescope, he focused on the sight he had dreaded, a band of Indians about two miles to the west. Some were on horseback, others on foot, and they had quite a few wagons with them. Gere knew what those were for—to carry away the spoils of war, the cannon and other valuables from the fort, and the white women and children. He scanned the party, trying to estimate their number, and thought there were about three hundred. As he continued to watch them, he frowned, however. The Indians were dressed, painted, and armed for war, but they were not heading toward the fort. They were milling around, conversing with the chiefs. It looked to Gere as though they had stopped to hold a council.

Little Crow had deliberately called a council within sight of Fort Ridgely in an effort to gain control over the war he had set in motion. It was an indication of his uncertainty about the extent of his power that he assembled the council there, instead of at an Indian village. He chose the time and place to be free of the influence of Shakopee and Red Middle Voice, the two chiefs who were primarily responsible for instigating the uprising. Neither man was with Little Crow that morning, but both had spent the previous day and night with their warriors, raiding farms and settlements north of the river, overseeing the murder, rape, and capture of scores, perhaps hundreds, of whites.

Little Crow hoped that without their malevolent presence, and that of Cut Nose and other bloodthirsty members of the bands, he could direct the war his own way. His plan was to attack the fort as quickly as possible and, with it out of the way, proceed through the river valley, ridding it forever of the white man's presence. Little Crow knew, however, that if they did not attack Fort Ridgely that morning, while it was still so lightly defended, they would need more than his three hundred braves to subdue it.

At the council, Little Crow spoke first, summoning up all the eloquence and force at his command. He told the warriors that scouts reported seeing fifty soldiers marching toward the fort from the northeast. These reinforcements, Lieutenant

Sheehan's unit, which Gere had recalled, would reach it within the hour. Scouts also told of other contingents of soldiers heading that way, but they were not expected to arrive until the afternoon. Little Crow reminded his braves that now there were no more than two dozen troops at the fort, not enough even to fire all their cannon. The Indians outnumbered them ten to one.

He predicted that when the soldiers saw the size of the Indian band, they would run away, abandoning the women and children and more riches than could be found in a hundred farmhouses. The Sioux could capture the wagon guns, which would finally give them the firepower to fight all the soldiers the Great Father might send against them. And they would find more food than even the agency stores contained, plus horses, cattle, blankets, powder, and lead. Fort Ridgely was a major prize, just waiting to be claimed.

Little Crow had more to say, but he did not get the chance. He was interrupted by Mazzawamnuna, a brave from Shakopee's camp, who at first appeared to agree with Little Crow about the goods they could capture at the fort. But, he went on, there was more bounty to be had at New Ulm. For every blanket or sack of flour or bag of sugar they might find at Fort Ridgely, Mazzawamnuna contended, they would find fifty times that in the town! And for every white woman at the post, there were a dozen at New Ulm—younger, he promised, and prettier.

Also, there were no soldiers at New Ulm. Obviously, it would be easier to capture. Once the Indians held it, no soldiers could pass on the road between the town and the fort. Those few troops now on their way to Fort Ridgely would present no greater obstacle to the Sioux than those who were already there. And the Indians could handily capture the fort after they had secured the town. Both prizes were theirs, waiting to be claimed, but they should take the more valuable one first.

Most of the warriors sided with Mazzawamnuna. They whooped and shouted their approval so loudly and for so long that Mankato, the next chief waiting to speak, had to stand in silence until they quieted down. Mankato had joined the farmer movement in 1859, but he and his band had gone along with the uprising. They would do whatever the council agreed on, he said, but they would not torture women or kill children.

The braves should take heed of Little Crow's words, Mankato argued, and attack Fort Ridgely first. With the cannon they would capture there, they could keep the rest of the soldiers out of the valley. The fort also contained enough muskets to arm all of their people. They would find no cannon and few muskets at New Ulm.

Next to speak was Rdainyanka, son-in-law of the peace chief Wabasha. He disagreed with Wabasha and favored making war on the whites, but he thought that the way they had been fighting so far—attacking isolated farms and tiny settlements—was wasteful and futile. He reminded them of the courage shown by the soldiers at the ferry crossing. They had fought as the bravest of the Sioux. They were warriors, too, and they would defend their fort and their town in the same way.

Both the town and the fort had to be taken, Rdainyanka said, and both could be captured easily, but only if the Sioux acted at once. If they delayed, both objectives would be barricaded, reinforced, and defended more tenaciously. He concluded that it made little difference which they attacked first, since both were vital to the Sioux if they hoped to win the war, but they had to move immediately.

The council dragged on, however, for another two hours, with more than a dozen chiefs and braves speaking in turn. Some argued for attacking the fort and others for carrying the war to New Ulm. Finally, the speeches were at an end and it was time to put the matter to a vote. When it was tallied, the results were unambiguous: two-thirds of the council members voted to attack the town of New Ulm.

The decision was a major defeat for Little Crow, a blow to his authority, prestige, and ego. The majority of the braves had chosen to ignore his advice. It had been only a few months since he had lost the election for speaker of the Sioux. He had failed to prevent his people from embarking on this war, failed again when he urged them not to kill women and children but to take prisoners instead, and now he had failed once more to regain control of the war and lead his people in the way he knew to be best, the only way they could win. He got on his horse, turned away, and rode back to his village, unsure of what to do next.

At Fort Ridgely, while sentinels on the rooftops kept watch on the Indian council two miles away, Lieutenant Gere welcomed Lieutenant Sheehan and his fifty men and happily turned over command. The arrival of reinforcements had brought a feeling of deliverance, a release from the panic that had gripped them all since they had learned of the death of Captain Marsh and his men at the ferry crossing. Now, although the post was still inadequately defended, the extra men brought a sense of hope, even joy.

Lieutenant Sheehan had received Captain Marsh's message—"the Indians are raising hell"—on Monday night, while encamped at the town of Glencoe, forty-two miles northeast of the post. Immediately breaking camp, the men started back, re-covering the distance it had taken them two days to travel in only nine and a half hours.

Later that day, other reinforcements reached Fort Ridgely: Major Galbraith and his Renville Rangers, and some three dozen volunteers from St. Peter. Between sunup and sundown, the troop strength at Fort Ridgely increased from 29 to 180. The fort was no longer an easy prize just waiting to be claimed by the Indians.

New Ulm was a prosperous town of nine hundred inhabitants located fifteen miles downriver from Fort Ridgely. Its original settlers in 1854 were members of two German colonization societies from Chicago and Cincinnati. Almost all of the residents of New Ulm were German, and many were newly arrived immigrants who spoke no English. They did not socialize with other American settlers in the area, some of whom thought the Germans were libertines and freethinkers who refused to accept their more devout religious beliefs.

"Sad to say," wrote one American woman, "a class of infidel Germans . . . were first to build here their homes. The original proprietors had stipulated that no church edifice should ever 'disgrace its soil,' under penalty of returning to the former owners. Thus, with no religious restraints, they became strong in wickedness, defiant of the restraints of the gospel, and resolved that no minister should ever be allowed to live among them. . . . They built a dancing hall, and Sabbaths were spent in drinking and dancing."

The Germans were industrious, hardworking, and conscientious, however, and no one could deny that their farms and businesses were successful.

Their town of New Ulm was attractive and neatly laid out but highly vulnerable to attack. The land rose more than two hundred feet from the Minnesota River, forming two terraces with a bluff on top. Most of the buildings had been erected on the first terrace, with only a few on the second, and most were scattered over some distance. Deep woods along the bluff, and swamps between the bluff and the second terrace, provided plenty of cover for attackers. The Sioux were familiar with the terrain, and they also knew that some of the younger men of the town had joined the Union army. Also, few of the remaining Germans were armed.

When New Ulm's residents first learned of the Indian uprising, a few gave in to panic and fled eastward, but most stayed, taking comfort in the presence of friends and neighbors. Two men moved to initiate defensive measures—the county sheriff, Charles Roos, and Jacob Nix, who had had some military experience in Germany. Together, they organized the town militia, comprised of forty-four men with guns. One squad consisted of fourteen men armed with rifles, another of eighteen men with double-barreled shotguns, and a third of twelve with ordinary shotguns. About fifteen other men who possessed weapons of various kinds refused to join the militia force, electing instead to defend their homes and businesses personally. Roos and Nix also established a reserve unit equipped with an assortment of weapons and farm implements, including revolvers, axes, and pitchforks.

The men erected barricades around an area of several square blocks in the center of town, enclosing the sturdiest brick buildings. Streets were obstructed with wagons and barrels and anything else that might stop an arrow or a bullet.

Refugees fleeing the isolated settlements for the safety of the town had their wagons commandeered and added to the blockades. Armed men crowded behind the makeshift barriers while the women and children were herded into the Dacotah House hotel and the other brick buildings. The hotel was soon so crowded that the women had to remove their hoopskirts and pile them in the backyard.

Messengers were sent to St. Peter and the other settlements within reach to ask for help. One of the couriers was Henry Behnke, who rode to St. Peter to seek out Judge Flandrau. Sheriff Roos and others led small relief parties into the countryside to search for families who might be hiding in the woods or who had not yet heard about the uprising. One rescue party of sixteen men was ambushed close to town; only five men returned safely.

The Sioux attacked New Ulm at three o'clock in the afternoon. About one hundred of the warriors who had held the council with Little Crow decided to go south, where they raided isolated cabins, killed and captured whites, and set the grain fields on fire. The party that besieged New Ulm also numbered about one hundred, but they lacked a leader. There was no one chief to coordinate or direct the attack. The Indians dismounted on the bluff and rushed on foot past the outlying buildings toward the center of the town.

Jacob Nix, who dubbed himself Platzkommandant, saw them coming. "*Auf euer Posten!*" he shouted. "*Fertig zum Gefecht!*" "To your posts! Get ready to fight!"

The Indians charged the barricades first from the south, then from the northwest, and when these sorties proved unsuccessful, they began a series of wild charges from all directions. At no time were they able to penetrate the barriers. A few of the New Ulm men made a daring run to a house beyond the barricades to drive out the Indians who had occupied it and were using it to fire on the town's defenders.

Both sides sustained casualties; at least five whites were killed and five others wounded, but no records remain of Indian losses. Platzkommandant Nix had his ring finger shot off—the wound was so severe that he later lost the use of his hand—and a thirteen-year-old girl was killed when she defied her elders and stepped out of the front door of a building.

After an hour and a half of fighting, dark clouds from the southwest brought torrential rains, jagged shafts of lightning, and giant peals of thunder. The Indians broke off the attack. At about the same instant, the first reinforcements reached New Ulm— L. M. Boardman and his fifteen-man cavalry force, sent by Judge Flandrau in advance of his main party. Boardman and others would later claim that they saved New Ulm, that when they arrived, the Germans were in disarray and about to be slaughtered, but Nix and his German defenders maintained that they saved the town by themselves, that the Indians were already retreating when Boardman arrived. But whoever saved New Ulm, the fact remained that the Sioux had lost, beaten in what should have been an easy contest, because they lacked leadership, unity, and sufficient numbers to overwhelm the town's defenders.

At eight o'clock that night, Judge Flandrau and his relief column of some one hundred volunteers reached the ferry crossing two miles from New Ulm. Dr. Mayo had accompanied them. "They made a motley, straggly column," he recalled. "A few of them rode in buggies, some were on horseback, but most of them walked." They were soaked, having been caught in the drenching rainstorm, and they were exhausted from making the thirty-two-mile trek in seven hours. Flandrau ordered a halt at the ferry. Smoke from burning houses rose in the distance, and the men saw no signs of life.

They manned the ferry, got everyone across the river, and, to their great relief, were soon welcomed by the townspeople of New Ulm and Boardman's small mounted unit. Mayo and his two colleagues set to work to treat those wounded in the battle as well as the injured settlers who had sought refuge in the town. Guards were posted at strategic points, the barricades were strengthened and new ones mounted, and a theodolyte—a surveying instrument—was placed on the roof of one of the central buildings. With it, the countryside could be observed for a distance of three miles around to provide advance warning of another Indian attack.

Judge Flandrau was elected commander of the entire defending force and given the honorary title of colonel. New Ulm felt prepared for whatever the Sioux might try next.

*   *   *

By Tuesday night, Little Crow's village had become the headquarters of the Sioux uprising. Hundreds of tepees sprang up around the chief's solid two-story house, and by this second night of the outbreak, the camp held several thousand people, including almost all of the white and mixed-blood captives.

As the braves congregated in camp that evening, intoxicated by their tales of pillage and murder, they did not receive the accolades they expected from the chiefs and tribal elders. They were awarded no eagle feathers for bravery, no praise or congratulations, only scorn and contempt from Wabasha, Wacouta, and the other peace chiefs, as well as from Little Crow. The chiefs berated their warriors when they proudly displayed fresh scalps, reminding them that killing helpless settlers was cowardly and undeserving of eagle feathers. It was not honorable; it was not like the killing of Chippewas in battle.

"You ought not to kill women and children," Little Crow said, repeating the admonition he had voiced many times over the past two days. "Your consciences will reproach you for it and make you weak in battle. You were too hasty in going into the country. You should have killed only those who have been robbing us so long. Hereafter, make war after the manner of the white man."

Little Crow realized that even if the Indians pushed the soldiers and settlers out of the valley as far as St. Peter, they would not win the war. Eventually, even with the war between the Union and the Confederates in the South, Washington would send enough troops to overwhelm the Sioux, perhaps even to exterminate them. Their only hope lay in negotiating a new treaty, but Little Crow understood that if they committed too many atrocities against women and children, the federal government would be unwilling to meet with them in council. The Sioux needed white prisoners as hostages, as bargaining points. They did not need more scalps.

Little Crow called a council meeting that night. This time, he found the young braves more willing to listen, particularly those who had been driven from New Ulm. The warriors seemed to realize that their attack had failed because of a lack of leadership and organization. They were willing to concede that perhaps Little Crow had been correct. Perhaps they should have united to attack Fort Ridgely to dispose of the soldiers and capture the wagon guns.

However, Little Crow still had to persuade the other bands to come together under his authority to make an assault on the fort. He told the council that according to his scouts, there were now 175 soldiers at Fort Ridgely, a surprisingly accurate estimate. With the three hundred braves who had attended the earlier council within sight of the fort, plus one hundred more, they would outnumber the soldiers comfortably and could easily capture their prize.

The warriors readily agreed, but some of the chiefs proved more recalcitrant. They sat up all night, wrapped in blankets, arguing back and forth. When Little Crow emerged from the meeting, he told the waiting braves that Wabasha and Wacouta, who had opposed the uprising from the outset, refused to join any attack on Fort Ridgely, but other chiefs would go along. The most important war chiefs—Red Middle Voice and Shakopee—and their two hundred warriors were absent. Their help would have been valuable, but they were out in small bands, marauding through the countryside.

The braves daubed themselves liberally with war paint, donned breechcloths and leggings, and wrapped long sashes around their bodies in which to tote food and ammunition. They hitched teams to the wagons that they planned to use to haul back their plunder from the fort. A strategy was devised—diversionary assaults and false charges to precede a single massive frontal attack. They expected to sweep away the soldiers like so much chaff.

At sunrise, four hundred warriors left the camp, heading for Fort Ridgely. At the head of the column, mounted on a magnificent white horse, rode Little Crow.

7
THERE WAS
DEATH BEHIND

Alomina Hurd was worried about her husband, Phineas. He and another man from their tiny community on the shore of Lake Shetek, some forty miles southwest of the Lower Agency, had left more than two months before on a trip to replenish their food supplies. They were a month overdue.

The isolated group of eleven families had run low on supplies because of their generosity to the Indians over the winter. Sioux often camped along the lake in the summertime to hunt and fish. Because the white families seldom saw anyone else, they welcomed the Indians, learning their language and inviting them home for food and conversation. The Sioux always left before winter to return to the reservation, but last year they had waited too long. Severe weather prevented them from leaving for several months. The whites pooled their resources and shared their provisions with the Indians, who, without that help, would most likely have starved.

When the winter weather finally eased, the Indians returned to the reservation, leaving the white families with drastically reduced food supplies, which they rationed among themselves until early June. Then Phineas Hurd and his friend hitched up a wagon and headed west. Alomina stayed behind with her two children and a hired hand, John Voigt, who ran the farm. When the men had not returned by August 1, the community was so concerned that a search party was sent out to look for them. The group returned on Tuesday, August 19, having found no trace of the two men. They decided to send a messenger to Fort Ridgely in the morning to ask the army to send out a patrol. They had no idea that the Sioux had been on a rampage. Their village was so isolated that they rarely heard any news.

At five o'clock on Wednesday morning, while Alomina Hurd was milking her cow some distance from the house, twenty Sioux braves rode up and greeted her cordially. She was not alarmed. She knew five of the Indians by name, and they seemed as pleasant as they always were. She invited them to go up to the house and have a chat and a smoke with Mr. Voigt.

The Indians trooped off to the cabin and went inside. When she finished the milking, Alomina started toward the house, lugging the full milk pail. As she neared the spot where the Indians had left their ponies, a dog rushed out from among them and ran up to her, barking joyously. She recognized it as her husband's dog, and then she noticed his horse among the ponies.

A stab of fear ran through her. She dropped the pail and ran to the house, just as John Voigt came through the front door carrying her one-year-old son. The boy was crying. An Indian followed Voigt out of the cabin, raised his gun to his shoulder, and fired. Voigt fell dead with the baby in his arms. Alomina rushed to him and grabbed the child. Another Indian grasped her by the shoulder and shoved her away.

A dozen braves swarmed out of the woods and swept through the house and the barn. Alomina's other child, three-year-old William, rushed out of the house, calling for her. A warrior snatched him up, raised him high above his head as though he intended to smash the boy to the ground, and handed him over to her.

Inside the house, the Indians embarked on an orgy of destruction, "breaking open trunks, destroying furniture, cutting open feather beds, and scattering the contents about the house and yard. We had on hand two hundred pounds of butter and twenty-three cheeses; the latter the Indians threw into the yard and destroyed."

Clutching her children, Alomina Hurd watched, horrified, as her world was torn apart. One of the braves took her roughly by the arm and spun her around to face the prairie.

"White squaw go to her mother," he said, pointing the way.

He told her that she and the children would be spared if she gave no warning to the other settlers living around the lake, and if she left immediately by a little-used trail that led to New Ulm, sixty miles away. She knew that the path wound through wilderness and that the Indians had left her no food, no shoes, and only the clothing she wore.

She begged to be allowed to get shoes for the children and a shawl and sunbonnet for herself, but the Indians refused to let her in the house. If she did not leave that instant, they would kill her. Mrs. Hurd agreed to go. Seven Sioux on horseback escorted the family three miles along the trail, until they were too far away to warn the neighbors. And there the Sioux left them.

Alomina trudged on down the path, carrying her sleeping baby. Young William was shivering in the early-morning chill. He was crying, and he kept asking why they did not go home, but she had no answer for him. She heard two shots and suspected that the Indians had murdered her nearest neighbors, Mr. and Mrs. Koch.

"There was death behind," she wrote later, "and all the horrors of starvation before me. But there was no alternative. For my children, anything but death at the hands of the merciless savages; even starvation out on the prairie seemed preferable to this."

Around ten o'clock, the wind whipped up and a thunderstorm began, pelting them with rain for the next three hours. A light rain continued to fall most of the day. Alomina lost sight of the trail during the storm, but she knew that they had to keep moving to stay ahead of the Indians. She forded swollen streams and urged the children on across the sodden grasslands. At nightfall, she found a small knoll. She fashioned crude beds for the boys, shielding them with her own body from the cold rain and wind.

Charley Hatch lived six miles from the Hurds' house. At daybreak, about the time Alomina was milking the cow, Hatch mounted his horse and rode toward her cabin, intending to borrow a team of oxen. He rode as far as the home of Mr. and Mrs. Koch, where he left his horse, and waded on foot through the swamp to where the Hurds lived. When he reached the farm, he was stunned. There was John Voigt lying dead in a pool of blood, with debris from the cabin and barn strewn all around the yard. Hatch saw no sign of Mrs. Hurd or the children, but he noticed a great many footprints.

Believing that Indians had carried them off, he rushed back across the marsh to warn the other families. Before he reached dry land, he spied a group of Sioux braves advancing stealthily on Koch's place. Mrs. Koch was out in the cornfield firing a gun in the air to keep the birds away from the crop. Her husband was inside eating breakfast. A few of the Indians approached her, and they began to talk, as they had often done in the past. One warrior asked to see her gun. When she handed it to him—and she knew of no reason why she should refuse—he turned it on her.

"White squaw go to her mother," he said. "Big Indians kill all paleface men."

He gestured with the gun toward the woods. She understood instantly and, terrified, raced for the sanctuary of the trees, knowing that her husband was doomed.

The Indians went into the house. They sat down at the table for a smoke and to pass the time with Mr. Koch while he finished his breakfast. One of them asked for a drink of water. Koch offered to walk down to the spring to fetch some fresh water. He got no farther than the doorway before he was gunned down.

Charley Hatch saw the killing. Keeping out of sight in the safety of the swamp, he made his way to the next house, where the Eastlicks were sharing their breakfast with a friend, Mr.

Rhodes. One of the five Eastlick children burst into the room.

"Oh, Mamma," he shouted. "Charley Hatch is coming as fast as he can run."

Lavina Eastlick rushed outside to meet Hatch. He told her what he had seen, and he asked to borrow a horse so that he could warn the other families who lived around the lake. Before he rode off, he suggested to her that they all gather at the Smiths' cabin at the far end of the lake.

John Eastlick grabbed two rifles and the baby, while Lavina looked after the other children. She asked him whether she should take extra clothing, or at least some shoes, but he insisted that they leave right away. There was no time to spare. She lingered just long enough to scoop up an armful of powder, lead, and shot.

When the family reached the Smiths' home, they found it empty, and hurried on to the house of John Wright. His was a sturdy two-story structure built of thick logs, the biggest home in the community. On their way, the Eastlicks overtook the Smith family, who were also fleeing, and when they all reached Wright's house, they found several other lake families there, and Mrs. Koch.

Some Indians had gathered at the house, too—Old Pawn, who had long been a friend to the whites, and five other braves, also considered to be friendly. Pawn expressed concern about the safety of his white friends. He told them about the uprising at the Upper and Lower agencies and the killing of Captain Marsh and his troops at the ferry. Pawn said that three hundred bad Indians were prowling the area around Lake Shetek, but he and his friends would help the whites defend themselves. They offered to retrieve Mr. Koch's body if two white men would accompany them, but the whites refused. They no longer trusted any Indians, not even ones they had known for such a long time, and they turned the Indians out of the house.

As the rest of the settlement's families straggled into the yard, the men organized their defense. They armed the women and older children with clubs, axes, and knives, and sent them up to the second floor of the house. John Eastlick handed his wife a large butcher's knife and told her not to hesitate to use it if necessary. The men brought the horses into the rear of the house, knocked holes in the chinking between the logs to serve as rifle ports, and barricaded the doors and windows, turning the building into a fortress. There was enough cleared land around it to deny cover to any attackers. They had a fair supply of ammunition but only a little food and water. They expected to be able to hold out until nightfall, when they could try to slip away.

From the upstairs window, the women could see a band of Sioux ransacking the Smiths' house. One of the Indians who had been with Old Pawn joined them. They watched him speak with the group for a few minutes, then report back to Old Pawn.

Pawn went to talk with them himself, and returned to warn the whites that they were surrounded by a large contingent of warriors—maybe as many as two hundred. They planned to set fire to the house and burn them all to death. To the settlers, Pawn seemed frightened, as though his own life was in danger. He urged them to leave immediately and make for the woods, two miles away. There they could hide, he told them, but if they remained in the house, they would be killed within the hour.

No one trusted Old Pawn. Some of the men wanted to stay and take their chances, but others argued that the woods offered protection so that they might be able to get away. A few left the house on their own, and the Indians let them go on their way unmolested. The others took this as a good sign. More families decided to make a run for it. Lavina Eastlick ran outside to join her husband, cradling her baby in her arms. In her haste, she left behind her sunbonnet and the butcher's knife.

Two men hitched a team of horses to a wagon to carry the women and children. The men walked alongside and behind, glancing back from time to time to keep an eye on the Indians, who were following at a distance. Old Pawn was among them. After the whites had covered about a mile, not yet to the safety of the woods, the Sioux quickened their pace. The women in the wagon whipped the horses, trying to make them go faster, but the stubborn animals continued to plod along at a walk.

One man shouted a warning, urging the families to abandon the wagon and run for the trees.

The Sioux opened fire. Two white men, Smith and Rhodes, immediately ran away, deserting their families and friends. John Eastlick yelled at Rhodes, calling for him to come back with the rifle—it belonged to Eastlick—but the frightened men never looked back. The rest of the men returned fire at the Indians to cover the retreat of their families. The women and children rushed for the tall grass of the marsh. Its thick weeds, the clumps growing as high as seven feet, provided the only shelter in sight.

Lavina Eastlick took a bullet in her heel. One child was shot in the leg. Two of William Duley's children were also wounded by the Indians' gunfire. The men followed their families, retreating to the swamp, firing as they ran. Duley and Uncle Tommy Ireland hit their mark, killing Lean Bear, a Sisseton chief from the Upper Agency.

The whites were all screened from the Indians now, but they were also trapped. The Sioux surrounded the marsh and outnumbered them thirty to one. Each time the whites fired their weapons, which gave away their position, the shots were followed by a volley from the Indians. The men could not see where to aim unless they stood up and risked showing themselves. Even the slightest movement rustled the grasses and revealed their location.

One after another, the settlers sustained wounds. Lavina Eastlick heard someone groan and asked who it was. Charley Hatch cried out in reply. Almira Everett told him to come over so she could bind up the wound, but he preferred to stay where he was. He was afraid he would be shot again if he tried to move. A child screamed, hit in the stomach. Lavina felt blood trickling down her face. She had been caught in the side and head by buckshot.

"I told John, my husband, that I was shot," she recalled, "and thought I should die. I told him not to come to me, but if he had any chance of shooting an Indian, to stay and shoot him, for he could not do me any good."

A bullet struck Billy Everett. He yelped in pain, and his wife called out to soothe him.

"Oh, Billy, do let me come!"

"No, Mirie, stay where you are."

A moment later, she was shot in the neck. Bleeding profusely, she called to her husband again.

"We will both have to die," she told him, and asked whether they should pray.

As her voice rose in prayer, someone else was heard to groan. Lavina Eastlick thought it sounded like her husband. She spoke his name, but there was no answer. Then Mrs. Koch told her that he was dead. Lavina started to crawl through the weeds, wanting to be with him one more time, but Mrs. Koch stopped her, reminding her that it would do no good. The children clung to her, the youngest of the five an infant, the oldest eleven, but one son was missing. She cried out for him, but the others tugged at her skirts, asking whether their daddy was dead. All she could tell them was to keep quiet or the Indians would get them.

The sun was high and the day was growing oppressively hot. No breeze stirred the air, and people began to suffer from thirst. The Sioux moved closer, so near that the whites could hear them talking. They continued to fire at random. When Sophia Smith was shot, the Indians laughed at her screams. They called to the settlers to come out, promising that the women and children would be spared.

Billy Everett asked Old Pawn to come talk to him, but the Indian said that Everett would have to come out of the swamp.

"I can't," Everett said. "I'm wounded so that I cannot walk."

"You lie," Pawn said. "You can walk if you want to."

The Indians fired two shots in the direction of Everett's voice, striking him in the elbow and the foot. When Almira Everett heard her husband's moans, she stood up in full view, faced Old Pawn, and told him that he was treacherous and ungrateful. She accused him of killing her husband, a man who had always treated Pawn with kindness. She reminded the Indians that the whites had been generous, feeding the Indians when they were hungry. The Sioux, surprised, held their fire.

Pawn said that he wanted her and Julia Wright to be his

wives. If they came out of the swamp, they would be safe.
The two women discussed the proposition and agreed to take
their children and go with Old Pawn. When they reached the
edge of the grass, Pawn picked up two of the children in his
arms, to demonstrate to the other women that they would not
be harmed. He said loudly that if the other women joined
them, they, too, would be safe. If not, the Sioux would set fire
to the grass and burn them all to death. The rest of the women
agreed, and said tearful farewells to their husbands.

Before she left, Lavina Eastlick made her way to her husband's body. "He lay on his left side, with his right hand on
his face. I kissed him two or three times. I felt his face and
hands. They were cold. I could not shed a tear, although I
knew it was the last time I should ever see him."

She dragged herself out of the weeds, carrying her baby,
supported by her eleven-year-old son, Merton, and by Julia
Wright. Along with them emerged Sophia Smith, Laura Duley,
Sophia Ireland, Mrs. Koch, and their surviving children. They
all rested on the crest of a ridge beyond the swamp while the
Indians encircled them, leaning on their guns. Two Indian
women lingered off to one side, watching the white women
intently.

Rain started to fall and suddenly the Indians were in a
hurry to leave. One brave took Mrs. Koch by the arm and led
her off. Another took Mrs. Eastlick and Mrs. Ireland, and a
third grabbed the two older Ireland girls. As Lavina Eastlick
was led away, she glanced behind her to see whether the children were following. Her five-year-old son, Freddy, started
after her. One of the Indian women picked up a club and
smashed him over the head. Blood poured from his nose,
mouth, and ears. He ran toward his mother, but the squaw
caught him and hit him again. She picked him up and dashed
him to the ground.

Lavina froze with horror. She started to run, but Old Pawn
restrained her, warning her to move on. She took a few steps,
then stopped and turned back. The second squaw had attacked
young Frank Eastlick and was beating him about the head. He
screamed for his mother, but the warriors threatened her with
their rifles and forced her to move on up the ridge. Merton

helped her climb the hill, the cries of the younger boys ringing in their ears.

The Indians continued to torment them. Willie Duley was shot and fell at his mother's feet. As Laura Duley knelt to comfort him, a brave yanked her up and pulled her away. Two more shots were fired, hitting Sophia Smith and Sophia Ireland. The Indians laughed as the women fell dead. Laura Duley pleaded with the braves to spare them. She stood her ground, one child in her arms and another by her side. The Sioux taunted her and claimed that they would not harm her. She walked on a few steps and heard gunfire. Her older child and the Everett boy were the victims. Almira Everett broke free and ran toward them, but the Indians quickly cut her down.

Lavina Eastlick confronted Old Pawn.

"You aren't going to kill me, are you?" she said.

"No," he said. "Go on."

She urged her children forward and walked on, her shoulders tense, expecting to feel a gunshot wound in her back at any moment. They reached a grassy patch and began to make their way through it. Pawn raised his rifle and fired. The bullet struck Lavina just to the left of the spine and exited her right side above her hip. She thrust the baby at Merton and yelled for him to go on as long as he could. Then she sank to her knees and collapsed on the ground.

To the men left in the marsh, those moments were filled with terror. They heard the gunfire and the screams of their wives and children, the ghastly wails and moans. They checked their few weapons and waited, preparing to die. The Sioux would either burn them out when the rain stopped or pick them off, one by one, in their own time. Either way, each man knew he had seen his last sunrise.

When the last shot rang out and the last scream faded, the Indians went away. Puzzled, the whites took a count. Five men were still alive, and shortly afterward they were joined by Merton Eastlick and his baby brother, Johnny, who returned to the swamp after their mother was gunned down.

Was the silence a trick, a ruse to get them to come out?

Someone risked a glance and drew no fire. The Indians were gone.

One man instantly made the decision to leave. He snaked his way through the marsh to the edge of the clearing and ran, abandoning his injured friends. He had fought bravely and had shot Lean Bear, but with his wife and children lost and the chance to flee before him, his mind snapped. He did not even examine the bodies lying in the clearing to see whether his family was among them, perhaps still alive. In that instant, he had lost all reason, all pride and honor, and he ran to save himself. His name was William Duley, and on the day after Christmas next, he would spring the trap of the gallows at Mankato.

Of the four men remaining, Uncle Tommy Ireland, the patriarch of the Lake Shetek community, had the most severe wounds. He urged the others to leave him and save themselves before they became too weak from their own injuries to escape. They did what they could to make him comfortable and then headed off on foot, leaving the two Eastlick children with him.

By the afternoon, the three men spied a wagon in the distance. Mr. Bentley went ahead, to find out whether the driver would give Billy Everett a ride. He was growing weaker by the minute from his wounds. It took a couple of hours for Bentley to catch up with it, and when he did, he was surprised to find Mr. and Mrs. Meyers, neighbors who lived at the head of Lake Shetek.

Meyers had spotted Indians at daybreak deliberately trampling his corn crop. The sight had made him angry. They were the same Indians he had fed last winter, at great hardship to his own family, and now they were destroying the crop he was counting on to get through the winter.

He had run toward the Sioux, yelling for them to get out of his fields or he'd give them a good thrashing. The Indians shouted back, got on their horses, and rode off, mocking him with words and gestures. Meyers heard one say to another that he was "a good white man."

Although the braves had not harmed him, Meyers felt apprehensive. The Sioux had never done anything like that before. He wasted no time in analyzing the situation. He prepared the wagon, and within minutes, he and his wife were on their way to New Ulm.

When Bentley caught up with them, they were near the cabin of a German settler known as Dutch Charley. The cabin was deserted, but they rested and ate the few provisions Meyers had brought along. The other survivors from the swamp, Billy Everett and Charley Hatch, reached the cabin later that night.

In the morning, Bentley and Hatch searched around the house and the barn for any signs of the Indians. They were tired and edgy and held their rifles at the ready. In the hazy predawn light, each rounded a corner and spied a figure in front of him. They aimed and pulled the triggers at the same instant, but neither gun fired. Yesterday's rains had ruined the powder, and a moment later they realized how close they had come to killing each other. They got under way shortly after, and eventually reached New Ulm.

After a few hours of rest, Uncle Tommy Ireland felt that he was regaining strength, and he resolved to try to save the Eastlick boys. He told Merton to carry the baby on his back, and they would try to make it to Dutch Charley's place. Ireland was determined to accompany them at least that far, but he walked no more than several hundred yards before he collapsed. It was clear to Merton that the old man could not go on. He looked at Uncle Tommy with tears in his eyes, not knowing how to help him.

"What can I do, Uncle?" he asked.

"Nothing, my boy," Ireland said, "except keep on and save little Johnny."

He gave Merton directions and told him to keep walking until he found someone to take care of them. The boy gathered a pile of leaves and grass, placed them under Ireland's head as a pillow, and kissed him on the cheek. Then eleven-year-old Merton hoisted his brother on his back and started off.

Little Crow and his four hundred warriors reached Fort Ridgely at noon on Wednesday. After stopping to enjoy a leisurely lunch out of sight of the post, he dispersed his forces according to his plan of attack. He was familiar with the terrain and the layout of the fort, and he knew where the wagon guns were usually located. He planned to divert the defenders' attention to the west side of the fort while half of his braves gathered in a ravine to the northeast. They would charge down the ravine into the post itself and quickly overwhelm it. If that tactic failed, which seemed unlikely to Little Crow, he would unleash his remaining warriors from the opposite direction, the southwest, catching the soldiers by surprise.

Shortly after one o'clock, he set the operation in motion. With three braves as escort, Little Crow rode back and forth west of the fort beyond the range of the pickets' guns, signaling that he wanted to hold a council. Lieutenant Sheehan, Lieutenant Gere, and several others watched the four Indians from the roof of the officers' quarters, wondering what they were up to.

Stationed on the western edge of the post, Sgt. John Bishop, a survivor of the ferry ambush, waved for Little Crow to approach, but the chief knew that the soldiers had him in their sights and would like nothing better than to bring him down. He kept his distance. One of the warriors with him raised his hand to acknowledge Sergeant Bishop's gesture, but at the same time he shook his head.

Little Crow and his party rode along slowly, making sure to stay beyond firing range, judging the passage of time by the sun and its shadows. They were examining the post with great care. To them, Fort Ridgely looked open and vulnerable to attack. Like a buffalo trapped at the end of a canyon, it was theirs for the taking.

The fort had no stockade surrounding it, and all the buildings, each detached and unfortified, were easily seen. Lieutenant Sheehan had built temporary breastworks connecting the buildings at the center of the post, but there were no barriers around the perimeter structures. Worse, the nine-year-old fort was poorly sited for defense. It sat on an exposed plateau 150 feet above the floor of the Minnesota River valley, slightly less than a mile from the river itself.

Open prairie ranged to the northwest, but deep ravines to the east, northeast, and southwest provided excellent cover for attackers to approach unseen within rifle range. It was in the northeast ravine that half of Little Crow's men were assembling while he rode back and forth on the far side of the post. They would be in place by two o'clock.

Fort Ridgely's main buildings were grouped around a parade ground ninety yards square. The two-story stone barracks building that now housed more than three hundred settlers who had fled their homes stood on the north side of the square. Next to it was a large one-story stone building used by the quartermaster. The rest of the structures were wood-frame buildings whose walls would stop arrows but not bullets. Three officers' quarters were located on the east and west sides of the parade ground.

Behind the barracks stood the old stables and a row of log houses, quarters for the post's civilian employees and their families. The commanding officer lived in a large house on the south side of the parade ground. Some distance behind that were newer, larger stables with haystacks alongside.

West of the main buildings were the sutler's home, a warehouse and store, and the ice and root houses. The ammunition and powder magazines were out on the prairie some two hundred yards northwest of the fort, a perilous distance to travel if the men were under attack.

For all its vulnerability and poor design, Fort Ridgely had one advantage—six artillery pieces under the able command of Sgt. John Jones, an oldtime regular army ordnance expert. Jones had diligently taught his troops to load, aim, and fire the pieces, and he had drilled them repeatedly until they could perform the procedures rapidly. They were a match for any unit in the army.

Jones formed three artillery detachments and placed each in a crucial position. At the southwest corner, he and Dennis O'Shea manned a six-pound fieldpiece. The other cannon, mobile and so easily shifted from one point to another, were commanded by Sgt. James McGrew and a civilian refugee from the Lower Agency, J. C. Whipple, who had served as an artilleryman in the Mexican War. Jones and his men were determined to exact a high price from any Indians who threatened their cannon.

Little Crow knew that he and his braves could suffer heavy casualties at Fort Ridgely, but he had no doubt that they would succeed and be amply rewarded with a host of valuable supplies. The ammunition magazines alone held the largest supply of powder and lead this side of Fort Snelling. The army storehouse was packed with blankets, tents, and many other items the Sioux could use in extending their war. The sutler's store and warehouse were filled with enough flour, sugar, tea, coffee, and other foodstuffs to feed the people for many weeks. The stables contained several dozen horses, and nearby grazed oxen, cows, and mules. Fort Ridgely was indeed a rich prize for Little Crow. He was unaware, however, that it also contained $71,000 in gold coins, the overdue annuity payment that was the ultimate cause of the uprising.

By two o'clock, the two hundred warriors were in place in the northeast ravine, hidden from view in the long depression that ran only a few yards from the officers' quarters on the eastern edge of the parade ground. At the agreed-upon signal—a volley of three shots—the Sioux swarmed out of the gully whooping and yelling. They quickly drove back the surprised pickets.

Lieutenant Sheehan was stationed on the parade ground with about fifty men, ready for action wherever needed. He formed his men into a battle line, the first rank kneeling, the second rank standing behind them, as prescribed in the standard military textbook of the day. The formation was designed to present a massive volley of fire against an opposing army marching toward them in an orderly line. The Indians knew nothing of West Point doctrine, however. They charged in a ragged formation, pausing when firing to take shelter behind rocks, trees, and hummocks.

In seconds, two soldiers were dead, and the rest scattered to find shelter. They held their ground, hidden behind boxes, windows, and the corners of buildings, and from there poured deadly fire on the Indians. Lieutenant Gere reinforced the besieged corner of the post with thirty-five men.

McGrew and Whipple wheeled their cannon around to face the attackers, but the guns would not fire. Hastily, they removed the charges and discovered the problem: Some mixed-bloods at the post had stuffed rags in the guns before deserting to the Indian camp. The artillerymen pulled out the rags and had no more trouble firing.

The cannon and rifle fire broke up the Indian charge. "Two of our men were killed," a Sioux warrior wrote later, "and three hurt. . . . We did not fight like white men, with one officer; we all shot as we pleased. The plan of rushing into buildings was given up, and we shot at the windows, mostly at the big stone building [housing the refugees], as we thought many of the whites were in there. We could not see them, so were not sure we were killing any." No one inside the barracks was hit.

The warriors pulled back into the ravine and shot flaming arrows at the wood-frame buildings. The only roof to catch fire was one of the officers' quarters. Joe Coursolle, a refugee from the Lower Agency, helped to put the fire out.

"My legs felt wobbly," he recalled, "but up the ladder I went, two rungs at a time. Bullets and arrows whistled past my head. Never did an axe swing faster than mine as I whacked out the fire. The ladder was too slow; I rolled off the roof and landed with a grunt on the soft top of an earthwork wall. I thought there would be more holes in me than a sieve. But I didn't have a scratch. They were bum shots."

Having seen his first attack fail, Little Crow sent his remaining two hundred warriors into the ravine that pointed like an arrow toward the parade ground from its southwest corner. Sergeant Jones faced them with his six-pounder. Out in the open, exposed to enemy fire as the Indians burst out of the ravine, Jones maintained a continuous rain of deadly canister shot, shells that exploded on impact and spewed out hundreds of small pieces of steel. The Indians were terrified of those shells—they called them "rotten balls"—and the braves scattered each time the shrapnel showered the air.

Soldiers added their rifle fire, and in minutes the Indian advance was broken. The Sioux fled to the safety of the ravine, and from then on they willfully ignored Little Crow's carefully crafted plan of a coordinated attack.

Warriors spread out around the perimeter of the fort and kept up a heavy fire, albeit from a safe distance, for the next five hours. Some crept into the outlying buildings and took cover behind the haystacks, but Jones and the other artillerymen set those shelters ablaze in short order.

Fort Ridgely was under siege from all directions, and the cannon were running low on ammunition. Lieutenant Sheehan ordered a detail of men to cross the open fields two hundred yards to the magazines and return laden with armfuls of powder and lead. James McGrew wheeled his howitzer into position to give them covering fire, and not a man was hit on that hazardous duty. The Indians remained too far away to shoot with any accuracy.

A few braves managed to work their way closer. One slipped in among the houses behind the stone barracks. Sergeant Jones's wife was trapped inside with her children and another young girl. She saw an Indian at the window, grabbed the youngsters, and hid them all behind an iron stove. The brave stuck his rifle through the window and fired. He missed, and decided not to linger long enough to try again.

At dusk, several Indians entered the old stables at the end of the row of log houses. J. C. Whipple fired two shells at the stables, both of which exploded inside, setting the hay on fire. Joe Latour and George Dashner, two mixed-bloods who had stayed to defend the fort, saw the fire from the bakery nearby. An Indian ran out the stables' door, heading for the ravine. Dashner took aim and hit him. He fell to the ground and started to crawl away. Dashner and Latour ran to him, picked him up by the arms and legs, and threw him headlong into the flames.

The Sioux lifted the siege at sunset and retreated to Little Crow's village. The chief was disappointed and angry. The day before, they could have taken the poorly defended fort easily, but now, even outnumbering the soldiers two to one and completely surrounding the garrison, they had failed, mostly because of the cannon.

Little Crow knew they would have to try again. The Indians had to control Fort Ridgely before they could proceed down the valley to rid it of whites. He would need more men, perhaps double the number he had today. He would have to persuade Shakopee and Red Middle Voice to refrain from attacking isolated settlements for at least one day and to add their braves to his war party. The assault on the fort would have to be made soon, the following day or the day after at the latest. Every hour of delay could bring more reinforcements to the post.

It had started to rain before the Indians reached Little Crow's village, and they were soaked and uncomfortable by the time they arrived. Their spirits were sagging, too. They had not returned as victors with plunder and scalps. Their wagons were empty. They had been defeated, and they took out their shame and frustration on the mixed-blood prisoners. The braves rode sullenly through the camp, taunting them.

"We will fix you, you devils," one shouted. "You will eat your children before winter."

They told the mixed-blood captives that they were worse than whites and should all be killed, and they also felt that without the assistance of mixed-bloods at the fort, the soldiers would not have been so successful. When the braves started to drink, they became even more surly, and they swaggered along the lines of lodges, shouting threats and curses and chanting ominously. At the same time, the storm grew more intense. The wind flattened the rain against their faces. Lightning raced across the night sky, and one jagged bolt reached down—like the hand of God, said some of the farmer Indians—and struck a warrior dead.

Lieutenant Sheehan had won the battle, but he was too concerned to celebrate, too anxious about how to prepare for the next attack to even think of relaxing. The Indians would come back, of that he was certain, probably tomorrow, and with a much larger force. He had lost two men killed and nine wounded, along with some mules and horses the Indians had stampeded. He did not know how many Indian casualties there were.

Everyone at the post was ecstatic when the rain began that night. Some of the refugees ran out of the stone barracks to dance wildly in circles on the parade ground. "Rain! Rain!" they shouted, knowing that the bad weather would keep the Sioux from creeping in under cover of darkness and unleashing their flaming arrows. The steady rain soaked the shingles and the frame buildings. There would be no burning that night.

Sheehan put his men to work strengthening the defenses, erecting additional barricades out of bags of oats, rocks, and newly felled trees between buildings and at other critical locations. There was little he could do about two other major problems: food and medical supplies. With three hundred hungry civilians at the post, the military's provisions were being consumed at an alarming rate. Sheehan had to prepare for the possibility that fresh supplies would not be delivered for many days, and he decided to put everyone on half rations. There could be no rationing of medical and surgical supplies, however. The wounded from the battle had to be treated, along with the settlers who had arrived with injuries.

Lieutenant Sheehan's greatest worry was about reinforcements. Would they come before the next attack? Had Private Sturgis been able to reach the governor? Sheehan had been able to march his men forty-two miles in a single night. If the governor had dispatched reinforcements as requested, why hadn't they reached Fort Ridgely?

He decided to send another message to the capital, to impress on Governor Ramsey the urgency of their situation. He chose for the mission the mixed-blood Jack Frazer, the best scout, hunter, and trapper in the territory. To the Sioux, Frazer was known as Iron Face. Although he was in his sixties, he could outrun and outfight most men half his age. He counted Henry Sibley as an old friend and hunting companion, and Sibley had published Iron Face's biography, a tale of staggering courage and endurance. Frazer set out in the middle of the storm to ride for help.

Colonel Henry Sibley and his men were on the move, traveling in the direction of Fort Ridgely, but they did not get far. In the morning, a steamboat arrived at St. Paul to transport the force up the Minnesota River to the town of Shakopee. Sibley discovered that not all the promised supplies were on board, and he wrote to Governor Ramsey to complain.

"I have the honor to report that the steamer Pomeroy has arrived here with, however, but a portion of the fixed ammunition required, and without tents or camping equipage of any kind."

He would remain in Shakopee, he said, until all the supplies and equipment needed to mount a proper expedition were delivered.

"The men are without cooked rations, and I trust no time will be lost in having all these articles furnished, as they are necessary, not only to the comfort of the men, but to the success of the expedition."

Sibley intended to be a thorough and careful commander. His troops would move against the Indians only when they were fully prepared.

As the men disembarked at Shakopee that Wednesday night, they saw considerable evidence of the scale of the uprising. Hundreds of displaced white settlers had overrun the town, and local officials had placed guards on the outskirts, expecting the Sioux to come screaming down on them at any moment. This was not the time to move too far or too fast, Sibley decided, not with the savages likely to be around the next bend or over the next hill. Utmost caution took precedence over utmost promptitude.

Sibley's force had covered only fifteen miles that day and remained 150 miles from Fort Ridgely. Lieutenant Sheehan and his men could expect no help anytime soon.

8
OVER THE EARTH

Lavina Eastlick thought her back was broken. She lay in the grass, bleeding from the bullet wound, terrified that she might be paralyzed and that the Indian ponies behind her would trample her to death. She tried to move and found that she could crawl. The pain of her wound was excruciating, but she managed to pull herself along for a few yards before collapsing. Facedown, she lay there listening to the sounds of someone walking through the grass toward her. She placed her hands over her thick hair and waited in terror for the slash of the knife that would tear her scalp away.

An Indian stood over her for a moment—it seemed so long that Lavina almost believed that he intended to let her die in peace—but then he raised his rifle and struck her in the head. She groaned as her face was mashed into the mud. He hit her again and again, so hard that her arms and legs convulsed. When her tremors subsided, the Indian dropped his gun at her side and walked away.

Still conscious, Lavina lay still for more than two hours in

the rain, while the men hiding in the marsh left so hurriedly
that they did not take time to examine any of the bodies lying
nearby. Finally, she raised herself to a sitting position and discovered that she could stand. Slowly and unsteadily she forced
one foot in front of the other, retracing her steps to the clearing. She thought she heard a child calling for his mother. At
first, she hoped it was her Johnny, but then recognized the
voice of Willie Duley. She started to go to him but changed
her mind. In her painful and weakened condition, there was
nothing she could do to help him. It would be worse for him
to see her and think that help was at hand, only to have her
abandon him. It was a brutal decision, but she had no choice.

She found the body of Sophia Smith next. Lavina eased
off the dead woman's apron and wrapped it around her shoulders to keep from getting chilled. Sophia Ireland was dead,
too, but her two-year-old baby was alive, asleep with his head
on her breast, a gunshot wound through one leg. She turned
away and saw her son Frank, looking as peaceful in death as
in sleep. Lavina wandered on a few yards more and found her
son Freddy. She knelt beside him and heard a rattling sound
in his throat. She rubbed his arms and legs vigorously to try to
bring him around, but he died a few moments later.

A cry made her turn away, and she dragged herself on,
thinking the child might also be hers, but it was the Everetts'
six-year-old Lillie and her baby brother. The girl ran to her.

"Mrs. Eastlick!" she said. "I wish you could take care of
Charley."

"I cannot, Lillie. I must go and find Johnny."

The child's eyes filled with tears. She asked Lavina for
some water.

"My dear Lillie, I have no water and I cannot get any.
You'd better lie down and sleep."

"Is there any water in heaven?" the girl asked.

"Lillie, when you get to heaven, you will never be thirsty
again. I wish you and I were both there now."

Lillie nodded her head and walked back to her baby
brother. She lay down beside him, cuddling him in her arms.
Lavina walked on, beyond the killing ground and over a ridge,
out of sight of the children she could not help. Exhausted, she

gently lowered herself to the ground and fell asleep.

In the morning, at about ten o'clock, Lavina awoke to the sound of gunshots, followed by long and agonizing screams. The cries continued throughout the day, and she saw images in her mind of her sons being tortured, but she knew it was the children she had left beyond the ridge. Tormented by her own pain and hunger, she could not force herself to move, neither to try to help them, which would have been futile, nor to flee. "I wanted to die," she remembered, "and yet I feared to die by the hands of the Indians. Had I not feared this horrible mode of death, I should have run away out of hearing of these innocent sufferers." At four o'clock in the afternoon, she heard more shots, one for each child. There was only silence after that.

Several miles away, eleven-year-old Merton Eastlick, carrying his baby brother Johnny on his back, spotted a woman and two children sitting in the grass. Merton was near collapse. He had had no food and was chilled through by the rain. All night he had stayed awake, yelling at the wolves to keep them away while Johnny slept. As he staggered closer, he recognized Alomina Hurd. He summoned the energy to run to her, only to find that she was as exhausted as he, and even more discouraged.

Her oldest boy was ill and she had found, after two days of struggle, that she had been walking in a circle and was now no more than four miles from home. She wanted to die but willed herself to move on, carrying one child for about a quarter of a mile, setting him down, and going back for the other child. Back and forth she went, walking three miles for each one covered. With the Eastlick boys in her wake, she continued on, until they reached the deserted cabin of Dutch Charley.

"Soon I was changed from a white woman to a squaw," Sarah Wakefield recalled. "How humiliating it was to adopt such a dress, even faced by such circumstances." On Tuesday morning, August 19, the wife of the Upper Agency's physician had begun her second day as a prisoner. Her life had been saved by the Indian called Chaska. His mother and several other women were trying to protect her from hostile Indians while

Chaska was away. They rubbed dirt over her face to darken her skin and moved her from one lodge to another throughout the day.

The squaws heard various rumors about the captives—that all the whites were to be killed, or that the Sissetons from the Upper Agency were coming to take them west—and each time they bundled up Sarah and her two children and hid them in a different tepee. They tried to disguise the children but four-year-old James's blond hair gave him away. The baby girl, Nellie, had a dark complexion and, dressed in Indian garb, she easily passed for an Indian child.

That afternoon, another rumor reached them. The Indians, it was said, intended to kill Sarah Wakefield in a few days but would keep the children for years, until the Great Father in Washington paid much money to get them back. "I became nearly frantic," Sarah said, "and I determined I would kill [the children] rather than leave them with those savages. I ran to a squaw, begged her knife, caught up my little girl, and in a moment would have cut her throat, when a squaw said it was false." She thought that if only her children were dead, then she would willingly die. She was certain that her husband had been killed and she would thus have no more reason to live, to endure what lay ahead for a white woman captive.

At four o'clock that afternoon, Chaska's mother burst in and announced that an Indian was on his way to kill Mrs. Wakefield. The woman picked up Nellie, Sarah grabbed James, and together they ran off into the woods. Handing Sarah a bag of crackers and a cup, the Indian led her down the banks of a ravine. At the bottom, she hid them in underbrush and cautioned them not to move until morning, when she would return.

As the sun set, a drenching storm fell upon them, so intense that mud washed down the sides of the ravine, threatening to bury them alive. Throughout the night, the rain continued. Periodically, Sarah gave the children tiny sips of brandy from a flask she had secreted in her clothing. Sleep was impossible, and so was survival. She was convinced that this would be her last night on earth.

"I am by nature a very cowardly woman," she said. "Ev-

ery leaf that fell that night was a footstep, and every bough
that cracked was the report of a gun. My nerves were so weakened that my heartbeats would sound like someone running,
and I would frequently hold my breath to listen. Muskrats
looked like wolves, and as they crawled around me in the darkness, I thought they were wolves, and they were going to devour me. I sat all night, my feet in a running brook, and I
dared not stir for fear I might make some noise that would lead
to my discovery, for I could hear the Indians racing around,
firing guns, singing, hooting, and screaming."

Whenever James awoke, he asked why she did not take
them home and let them sleep in their own beds. She hushed
him each time, saying that the Indians were all around them
in the woods. If they made any noise, the Indians would find
them and kill them all. The children remained quiet and clung
to her, trembling, as much from fear as from the rain and cold.

The sun rose higher and higher in the sky the next morning, but the old Indian woman did not return. Sarah Wakefield
did not dare to move. All three of them were covered with
mud, and as the sun warmed the earth, thousands of mosquitoes stirred and began to attack them. In a short time, the bites
were so numerous that their faces were running with blood.

When Chaska's mother finally arrived, she took them to
her own lodge and gave them some food, urging them to eat
quickly. She led them three miles to another Indian encampment, where Sarah had a chance to bathe herself and the children and to put on dry clothes.

Another old squaw came to the door with a warning that
a bad Indian was out to kill her. She had better take to the
woods again. Sarah Wakefield refused. She could not bear to
spend another night like the last one. She got up and peered
outside, noticing a hut nearby that was constructed of green
boughs. Women were being led to it, one at a time. She heard
shrieks, and after a time saw what appeared to be bodies being
loaded onto a wagon and driven away.

The women said they would hide her and the boy. They
covered them with a pile of buffalo robes. The old squaw
strapped the baby on her back, pretending it was her own.
Without Chaska, Sarah knew there was no one else to protect

her. She whispered to her son, snuggled under the buffalo robes, urging him to remember his name and Nellie's. He must always take care of his baby sister so that one day, if their father was still alive, he would be able to find them.

After a few hours, Sarah could stand the suspense no longer. She pulled back the covers and asked the women whether Chaska had come back yet.

"Chaska dead," she was told, "and you will die soon."

Resigned to her destiny, she tried to prepare her young son.

"James," she said, "you will soon die and go to heaven."

"Oh, Mama! I'm glad, aren't you? My father is there, and I will take him this piece of bread."

Sarah asked the Indian women how she would die. She and the children would be stabbed, she was told.

A man pushed his way through the tent flap. It was Chaska. He helped her out from the pile of buffalo robes and shook her hand, promising her protection. He said he would shoot anyone who threatened her.

Sarah was awakened early by the sounds of the warriors preparing to leave for Fort Ridgely. Chaska was going with them. He said he feared for his life if he failed to join his brothers in the attack. To ensure her safety while he was away, Chaska took Sarah and the children in a wagon to his grandfather's house, a sturdy brick dwelling about a mile distant. There they found a number of Indian women they had known from their days at the agency.

The house was near enough to the fort for everyone to hear the battle. The cannon boomed, and smoke rose from the burning buildings. The women saw the Indian braves reload their weapons and regroup for another charge. By nightfall, the women received word that a chief was coming to kill the white captives. Chaska had not returned. His grandfather, who was almost eighty, said he would take the Wakefields deep into the woods for the night. Sarah carried the baby, but at the insistence of the friendly squaws, she left James with them.

Helen Carrothers, imprisoned with her two children in Little Crow's village, began her second day in captivity hard at work. She chopped wood, fetched pails of water, gathered corn from

the fields, and fed the horses. She was watched closely and was
never allowed to leave the tepee alone. An Indian woman was
always at her side. Helen's knowledge of the Dakota language
helped her get along with the hostile squaws, but she had been
unable to find her old friend the medicine man. She hoped he
would help her and would want to protect the young woman
who had become his friend and apt pupil.

At about eleven o'clock that Tuesday morning, much commotion arose in the center of the village as four braves held a
spirited discussion with Little Crow. They frequently glanced
in her direction during their council, and later an Indian woman
told her that all four wanted her for a wife. They had appealed
to the chief to resolve their dispute. He refused to say which
of the braves could claim her because they were among his
most valuable warriors and he did not want to risk trouble
among them over a white woman. It was better that she be
killed. That way, none of the four would feel that he had been
treated unfairly.

For the rest of the day she waited for the death sentence
to be carried out, anticipating the moment when the flap of the
tepee would be lifted, revealing a warrior with a knife. She
pleaded with the woman who was guarding her, appealing to
her as a mother for help in escaping with her children, but the
woman refused. As night came, however, Helen was still alive.
Perhaps Little Crow had changed his mind. She spoke to the
children calmly and prepared them for bed. A squaw beckoned, gesturing for them all to come outside with her. Helen
protested, objecting to taking the children out in the rain, but
the woman shouted at her.

The Indian led them into the middle of the cornfield and
told them to wait. The braves would be coming for them soon.
She insisted that Helen remove her Indian dress, saying that it
was too fine to wear for her execution. Helen refused. The
woman went to her tepee and brought back a ragged shift that
had belonged to another white woman. Helen put it on and
the squaw left her alone.

She waited a moment, trying to shield the children from
the rain, and decided to seize the chance to escape. The Sioux
were camped all around the field, and the cornstalks did not

even reach above her head, but she crouched on hands and knees, told the youngsters to cling to her back, and made her way toward the far end of the field.

Within minutes, she heard the Indians searching for her, thrashing through the rows of corn. She froze and whispered to the children to stay quiet, hardly daring to breathe. The men passed six rows away but did not see her. She knew, however, that once they reached the end of the field, they would turn around and come back, searching the areas they had missed before.

She hesitated, uncertain whether to go right or left. The force of the rain increased and turned to hail. The wind blew fiercely, and the men hurried back to their lodges. Helen crawled to the edge of the field and ran to the riverbank. She reasoned that once the rain stopped, the Indians would resume their search, expecting her to try to get away. She decided to outwit them and stay close to the village, so she worked her way through a stretch of tall grass along the south bank of the Minnesota River until she reached the head of a small lake. She set the children down, warned them not to make a sound, and retraced her steps through the grass. Backtracking again, she carefully brushed up the grasses, erasing her trail.

They spent the next several hours by the lake, menaced by mosquitoes. Helen covered the baby boy and four-year-old girl with her skirt to protect them, but she had no extra wrap for herself. She counted hundreds of bites on her body, but she dared not raise an arm to swat at the bugs for fear of giving away their position. By three o'clock in the morning, she could stand it no longer. She snatched up the children and ran back to the river, cutting her feet badly on the thorns and weeds. Her own house lay just across the river. If she could get there—and if it had not been ransacked—she could get some clothing and shoes, and perhaps even some food.

Helen wandered up and down the bank, searching for a place to cross. Whenever she came to a likely spot, she put the children down and waded into the river until the water reached her armpits and became too deep for her to cross, forcing her to turn back. Several times, the children cried out, thinking she had disappeared, and they ran down the bank after her.

She told them that Fort Ridgely was on the far side of the river and that they could not go home or get anything to eat until they crossed over.

"I became nearly wild at my failure to find a fording place across the river," Helen Carrothers said. She was to keep looking for a crossing for three more days.

On Monday night, Mary Anderson had taken a knife and cut the bullet out of her own body. By Tuesday morning, she was critical. Wacouta, true to his word, had remained on guard throughout the night outside the house in which she, Mary Schwandt, Mattie Williams, and Jannette DeCamp and her children were imprisoned. His presence kept the braves from molesting them further. At daybreak, the chief told the women that he had to leave. He carried the ailing Mary Anderson up to the attic and ordered the others to stay with her. He left them a single pail of water—there was no time to bring them food, he said—and told them to keep quiet until he returned.

Mary Anderson was running a high fever, and in her delirium she cried out for food, but there was nothing to give her. She flailed about, moaning in pain. The other women took turns holding her hands and trying to soothe her. By nightfall, they were all so hungry that Mary Schwandt and Mattie Williams took the risk of creeping out into the fields to bring back some green ears of corn. Mary Anderson refused to eat and in her ranting accused the others of trying to starve her to death.

The Indians who finally came for them seemed friendly. They put them in a wagon and said they would be taken to Little Crow's village. Mary Anderson's limbs had grown rigid. Jannette DeCamp cradled Mary's head in her lap, praying that the poor girl would live long enough to reach the village, where she might get some medical treatment.

The wagon wound slowly past the ruined buildings of the Lower Agency. Bodies lay in the streets where they had fallen in Monday morning's attack. "It was an awful sight," Jannette DeCamp recalled, "and I tried to screen the children from seeing the dead. When we came to where the stores had been, I saw Divoll, one of Myrick's clerks, lying extended on the burnt floor, his features looking natural as in life but the body burnt to a cinder. Myrick, Linde, and others lay outside. Some of them had been decapitated, but the Indians did not touch them or seem to notice them."

When they reached the end of the street, the Indians escorting the women gathered up some stones and threw them at the windows of the last building, which for some unknown reason had escaped destruction. The glass shattered, and the men swarmed around the building with blazing torches, finally pitching them inside.

At Little Crow's camp, the brave who had claimed Mary Anderson as his wife tried to take her out of the wagon. Jannette DeCamp told him that Mary was dying. She pleaded with him to let her stay with the women.

"She is better than two dead squaws yet," he shouted. "Get along out!"

They climbed down from the wagon and carried the wounded girl into a tepee, where they gently laid her on the floor. Mary Schwandt and Mattie Williams were allowed to stay with her, but Jannette and the children were led away. Indian women brought them some soft food, and Mary Anderson was able to take a few swallows. A rainstorm pelted the village, and water ran under the tepee walls, turning the dirt floor to mud, but there were no blankets to wrap around her to keep her dry.

"She was very thirsty," Mary Schwandt recalled, "and called often for water, but otherwise made no complaint and said but little. Before she died, she prayed in Swedish. She had a plain gold ring on one of her fingers, and she asked us to give it to her mother, but after her death her finger was so swollen we could not remove the ring, and it was buried with her. I was awake when she died, and she passed away so gently that I did not know she was dead until Mattie began to prepare the face cloths."

Mary Anderson was buried in the morning, wrapped in an old tablecloth the Sioux had looted from a settler's home. Several Indians dug a grave near Little Crow's house and placed the body in it. Mattie Williams and Mary Schwandt saved a photograph the dead girl had carried, a photograph of the young man she was to marry. Many years later, they were able to return it to him.

The death greatly affected fourteen-year-old Mary Schwandt. She had been raped and she knew she could be killed at any time. She had kept her spirits from flagging with the hope that one day the terror would end and she would be reunited with her family. That hope was dashed on the same day her friend died. As she was escorted through Little Crow's village, she recognized some of her father's cattle and various objects from her parents' home. She quickly came to believe that her parents, brothers, and sisters had all been murdered by the Indians, and she was overtaken by a depression so bleak that she spent most of the day in tears. Finally, she reached that awful stage of despair when she could no longer cry.

"The dreadful scenes I had witnessed," she wrote later, "the sufferings that I had undergone, the almost certainty that my family had all been killed and that I was alone in the world, and the belief that I was destined to witness other things as horrible as those I had seen, and that my career of suffering and misery had only begun, all came to my comprehension, and when I realized my utterly wretched, helpless, and hopeless situation, for I did not think I would ever be released, I became as one paralyzed and could hardly speak. Others of my fellow captives say they often spoke to me, but that I said but little and went about like a sleepwalker."

Little Crow added to her suffering, although apparently without intent. She was sitting outside the tepee when he approached, dressed in full regalia. In one swift gesture, he pulled a tomahawk from his belt and sprang toward her, raising the weapon above his head as though he was about to split her skull in two. He leered at her and lunged. Mary did not scream or flinch. She found she no longer cared, and she waited calmly for the fatal blow. Little Crow loomed over her, waving the tomahawk back and forth, then he tucked it back in his belt, laughed, and walked away. He had been playing a game, trying to frighten her, but she was beyond fear as completely as she was beyond hope.

On Wednesday morning, Indian agent Tom Galbraith sent an interpreter, Antoine Freniere, from Fort Ridgely to scout the area around the Lower Agency and report on the situation there. A few miles south of the agency, Freniere realized that he had run out of matches to keep his pipe going. Spying a cabin ahead that appeared to be empty, he went in, hoping to find some matches. He found instead seven young children, all German, the oldest only eight. One had been wounded in the hand. None of the others appeared injured but all seemed dazed. The cabin was Justina Krieger's, and the children were survivors of the attack on her party.

Freniere asked the oldest child where her mother was, and the girl pointed outside and down the hill. He went out, walked down the narrow path, and was struck dumb by the sight. Before him was a mound of bodies—twenty-seven by a later count—hacked to death with knives and hatchets. The corpses lay in grotesque positions, the expressions of horror clearly etched on their faces. A movement caught Freniere's eye. It was a baby trying to suck nourishment from its dead mother's breast. He watched the infant for a moment, then gazed at the surrounding forest, knowing that Indians could be hiding in the trees. He walked away, aware that he was condemning the children to death, but knowing, too, that there was no way he could take them all to Fort Ridgely.

Similar grisly scenes, and some worse, marred the countryside north and south of the reservation. Most of the dead had been killed by war parties from Shakopee's and Red Middle Voice's bands. By that Wednesday, however, the Indians were finding it hard to locate new prey, so thoroughly had they done their work. The settlers near the reservation had by then heard of the uprising and fled eastward. The Sioux had to travel greater and greater distances from their villages to find the whites. Marauding bands ransacked the western portion of the state and even invaded Iowa and the Dakota Territory, where there were still unsuspecting settlers to be found.

Fifty miles north of the reservation, a number of Norwegian and Swedish families had settled along the shores of West Lake, which they called Norway Lake. A little past noon on Wednesday, several Sioux braves rode up to the house of Andreas Broberg. They dismounted and shook hands with the two of the four Broberg children who were at home, along with an uncle who had arrived from Norway five weeks earlier. Indians often visited the Broberg home—that was nothing unusual—and the family had heard nothing of the trouble to the south. They all chatted for a moment or two, until the braves opened fire, killed the three settlers, and ransacked the house.

Mr. and Mrs. Broberg and their other children, eight-year-old Christina and sixteen-year-old Ernestina, were attending a religious meeting a few miles away at the home of the Lundborg family. A neighbor boy had mentioned seeing Indians in the area, so the two husbands, plus four of Lundborg's sons, left the house to try to find the Indians and see what they wanted. They had no fear of the Indians, but they knew that sometimes the braves took things that did not belong to them.

Sometime later, Mrs. Broberg and her daughters started home, walking part of the way with an aunt and uncle, who then took a different path. After they parted, Ernestina spotted two Indians up ahead. One came toward the girls, while the other followed the aunt and uncle. The first Indian grabbed Mrs. Broberg and tried to drag her away. She screamed and fought back, giving the girls a chance to run away. When Mrs. Broberg broke free, the Indian shot her, whacked her with his gun, and beat her to death with a hatchet.

He ran after young Christina, caught her, and struck her repeatedly with the hatchet until she died. His companion shot the uncle, set him afire, and bludgeoned the aunt to death with a club. Ernestina escaped. Making her way through the underbrush, she came upon the Lundborg party. They hid in the bushes throughout the day while the Indians searched for them. The warriors fired their weapons randomly into the bushes, hoping to flush the settlers out. At nightfall, the whites decided to strike out for the small island situated not far offshore in Norway Lake. There they found several other local settlers in hiding. They learned that twenty-two residents of their community had been murdered by the Indians that day. The attackers had set fire to the victims' clothing, burning all the bodies.

On Thursday morning, near Big Stone Lake in the Dakota Territory, 130 miles northwest of the town of New Ulm, five men hired by the Indian agent Galbraith were cutting hay. A band of fifty warriors, Yanktonais from the Upper Agency, approached them. The Indians spread out until they almost surrounded the unarmed whites. They closed to within ten paces, pulled rifles out of their rolled blankets, and started to shoot. Four of the whites were wounded, but the fifth, Anton Menderfeld, a resident of New Ulm, jumped into a ravine and fled. He made his way east, wandering over the prairie for several days. He hunted for food in every cabin he passed but found only bodies and ruined homes. Eventually, he reached St. Peter, just barely alive.

Big Stone Lake had four trading posts, one owned by Nathan Myrick, brother of Andrew, who had been murdered at his store at the Lower Agency. After the braves shot the workers in the field, they headed for the stores. They killed four clerks and took a fifth, a mixed-blood named Baptiste Gubeau, prisoner. They tied his hands behind his back with rawhide strips, danced around him, and told him that he would die when the sun set.

Gubeau remained calm. He was part Sioux and knew their ways, and he was crafty and desperate enough to try anything to save his life. He sat on the ground in the center of the circle of dancing warriors, conserving his energy and waiting for them to tire themselves out in their frenzy. When the right moment came, Gubeau bounded to his feet and dashed headlong through the ring of braves.

In seconds, the Sioux recovered and started after him, firing wildly, but Gubeau was faster, even with his hands bound behind him. He headed for a patch of reeds and tall grass along the shore of Big Stone Lake, thinking that if he could reach it, he would be safe. The Indians guessed where he was going and fanned out to the right and left to reach the lake before he did, but Gubeau outran them all.

He got to the marsh ahead of his pursuers and plunged in, wading silently away from the shore. He remained motionless, with just his face above the water, while the Indians churned through the water all around him. He could feel the ripples caused by their movements. The water softened the rawhide around his wrists, making it more pliable, and soon he was able to free his hands. After dark, the Indians gave up the search and left.

Gubeau set out across the prairie and walked for three or four days without food before he reached the safety of the town of St. Cloud. Hope surged within him as he staggered down the main street. An irate crowd gathered and seized him, however, taking him for an Indian, a spy sent to scout the town's defenses.

He tried to tell them about his escape from Big Stone Lake and about the Indians' attack on the stores, but no one believed him. Someone in the crowd got a rope, and the townspeople dragged him toward a tree, prepared to lynch him at once. One man pushed through the mob, yelling at them to stop. He identified Gubeau and said he would vouch for him, but only reluctantly did the people let him go.

Lars and Gure Anderson and their children lived on Eagle Lake, ninety miles east of Big Stone Lake and fifty miles north of the Lower Agency. At seven o'clock on Thursday morning, four Indians came to the Anderson home. One was called John, because he spoke some English, and all four had often visited there. The Andersons gave them food. These Indians kept their hair trimmed and dressed in white man's clothes. Each one carried a double-barreled shotgun, but that was not unusual. Indians were always armed when they went hunting. None of the white families around Eagle Lake knew about the uprising.

The Indians shook hands with Anderson and asked for some milk to drink. He brought them a fresh pail, and when they finished drinking, they shot him. They went out to the garden, where one of the sons was digging up potatoes, and they killed him. Another son ran to the doorway to see what was happening. The Indians shot him in the shoulder, leaving him for dead.

Gure Anderson grabbed her three-year-old daughter and rushed into the cellar, but her other daughters, a teenager and a ten-year-old, ran hand in hand into the prairie grass. The Indians caught them and dragged them away. Gure watched helplessly from the cellar door, hearing their screams. She waited in the cellar until dark, then took her child in her arms and left the house. She walked aimlessly through the night and most of the next day, dazed by the suddenness with which her life had changed. She lost her way, unable to find a road or trail that looked familiar. Continuing on through the evening and the following morning, she found herself back within sight of her own house. At first, she was afraid to go inside, but hunger changed her mind. And she decided that if she was going to die, it might as well be in her own home. When she crossed the threshold, she saw that the Indians had gone, but they had taken all the food and destroyed or stolen most of the family's possessions.

Mrs. Anderson hitched two oxen to a small sled, shed a few tears over the bodies of her husband and son, and returned to the house for a last look around. Poking behind the stove, beneath a pile of rubbish left by the Indians, she found her other son, the one who had been shot in the shoulder. He was, she said, "nearly crazy with fear and pain." She carried him outside and placed him on the sled with the three-year-old. Feeling more purposeful about what she had to do, Gure mounted the sled and made for her son-in-law's house, some five miles away.

The son-in-law, whose name was Erikson, was at home with his wife, his father, and two friends—Mr. and Mrs. Solomon Foote. On Thursday morning, they had been visited by some Indians, whom they knew and welcomed as usual. The Sioux asked for some potatoes, and when Erikson went into the garden to dig them up, they shot and scalped him. They also shot his father and cut his throat. Solomon Foote was caught in the cabin doorway by buckshot. As he fell, his wife grabbed him and dragged him inside. She fetched his rifle and propped him up at a window. Foote fired at the Indians, killing one with his first shot. He wounded another but took a bullet through the lungs. As he collapsed on the floor, he passed the rifle to his wife and urged her to keep firing. Mrs. Foote kept up a steady fire at the Indians for the remainder of the day, and prevented them from storming the house.

After the braves left at dusk, Mrs. Foote and Mrs. Erikson went outside and found that Erikson was still alive in the potato field. They carried him into the house and up the stairs and placed him on a bed. He was bleeding so heavily that drops of blood seeped through the floorboards to the room below, where Foote was resting on blankets on the floor. The women did their best for their husbands, but both appeared to be beyond help. By noon on Friday, they decided that neither man was strong enough to survive, and that they had better leave if they hoped to save themselves. They headed for Forest City, ten miles away, arriving two days later.

Solomon Foote lay on the floor, in great pain from his wounds and afraid the Indians would return. He decided to kill himself to avoid capture or torture. In a moment of delirium, he thought he heard Indians prowling around outside. He put a cap on his rifle, placed the barrel in his mouth, and pulled the trigger with his toe. The gun failed to fire. He tried a second time and failed. He attempted to cut his arm with a razor but was too weak to draw blood.

When Gure Anderson and her two children reached the house on Saturday, she found the men still alive. She hitched her team to Erikson's wagon, hefted him on her back, and carried him down the stairs and outside. Foote was too heavy for her to lift, but she helped him to his feet and supported him while he walked to the wagon. Gathering all the food she could carry, she drove her party toward Forest City.

The two Anderson girls captured at the house by the Indians had managed to escape, and they, too, reached Forest City safely. Along their route they had passed the naked corpses of two of their neighbors. The heads had been severed from the bodies. The skin had been stripped from one of the faces, and long lengthwise gashes covered the torso. Two knives protruded from the stomach.

Panic spread rapidly throughout much of Minnesota and spilled over beyond the state's borders. Governor Alexander Ramsey issued a proclamation designed to calm the people's fears and urging every able-bodied man to join Sibley's expedition against the Indians. The governor needed to persuade the citizens that he was doing all he could to protect them.

To the People of Minnesota:
The Sioux Indians upon our western frontier

have risen in large bodies, attacked the settlements, and are murdering men, women, and
children. The rising appears concerted and ex-
tends from Fort Ripley to the southern bound-
aries of the state.

   In this extremity I call upon the militia of
the valley of the Minnesota and the counties adjoining the frontier to take horses and arm and
equip themselves, taking with them subsistence
for a few days, and at once report, separately or
in squads, to the officer commanding the expedition now moving up the Minnesota River to the
scene of hostilities. The officer commanding the
expedition has been clothed with full power to
provide for all exigencies that may arise. . . .

   This outbreak must be suppressed, and in
such manner as will forever prevent its repe-
tition.

   I earnestly urge upon the settlers on the
frontier that, while taking all proper precautions
for the safety of their families and homes, they
will not give way to unnecessary alarm. A regiment of infantry, together with three hundred
cavalry, have been ordered to their defense, and
with the voluntary troops now being raised, the
frontier settlements will speedily be placed beyond danger.

   Despite the governor's assurances, the settlements were
not being placed beyond danger, speedily or at all. Sibley was
still proceeding with exquisite caution, and did not reach St.
Peter until Thursday night.

   "I arrived with three companies today," he wrote to Ramsey, "after a very fatiguing march through the Big Woods,
where the roads are execrable." In truth, the roads were considered among the best in the state. Wagons and stagecoaches
easily traveled the distance in one day. It had taken Sibley and
his forces two and a half days, and having reached St. Peter,
he decided not to go farther, despite reports that Fort Ridgely

had been attacked and burned. The latter report was untrue. Only some haystacks and a few perimeter buildings had been set afire, and those by the fort's own cannon. Yet there was no denying that Ridgely and its more than three hundred refugees were in grave peril. The Indians were expected to attack again at any moment, and the only reinforcements available were Sibley's troops.

Sibley was not willing to leave St. Peter yet, however. The day before, he had sent a company of troops under Capt. Hiram Grant to Fort Ridgely, but on Thursday he countermanded the order and warned Grant to avoid the fort and come on to St. Peter instead. What had brought Sibley to a halt was information received from his old friend Jack Frazer, the scout and hunter, whom Lieutenant Sheehan had dispatched from Fort Ridgely.

Frazer, for reasons of his own, exaggerated the size of the Sioux force, telling Sibley that the Indians had at least fifteen hundred mounted warriors at the Lower Agency alone. He said that the entire Sioux nation was involved in the uprising and that overall they probably had up to five thousand armed braves. Frazer added that he could not guarantee that Fort Ridgely was still in army hands. It might already have been overwhelmed. And if the fort were already lost, then there was no point in Sibley risking his troops by hurrying toward it.

Faced with such odds—and there was no reason for Sibley to doubt Frazer's report—Sibley chose to stay put. His force of 225 men was largely untrained and equipped only with outdated muskets, improvised ammunition, and little extra food or supplies. He believed that he needed additional men and equipment before he could move against the Sioux, and he sent several urgent appeals to the governor for more of everything.

"I would respectfully suggest," he told Ramsey, "that if red tape is in the way in this emergency, that you cut it with the bayonets of a corporal's guard. This is no emergency of a common nature, to be dallied with in the circumlocutions office."

Sibley's outfit camped at St. Peter for four days before undertaking any action in relief of Fort Ridgely and New Ulm.

To his wife, Sibley wrote that he intended to "clean out the scoundrels with the utmost possible expedition. . . . My preparations are nearly completed to begin my work upon them with fire and sword, and my heart is hardened against them beyond any touch of mercy."

Colonel Sibley was not the only person interested in obtaining reinforcements. So, too, was Little Crow. He planned to attack the rich prize that was Fort Ridgely on Friday. His scouts had told him that no new troops had reached the fort, but he knew that reinforcements must surely be on their way. He was certain that Friday would be his last opportunity. If he did not capture the fort then, the war would be lost.

To take it, however, he needed more braves. His four hundred warriors had not been enough. He wanted the men of Shakopee and Red Middle Voice. They were the ones who had wanted the war in the first place, the ones who had argued for it with such passion at his house only the previous Monday morning. They were the ones who had shamed Little Crow into leading it. Yet once Shakopee and Red Middle Voice had instigated the war, they had taken no part in it in the one way that might have assured victory. Instead, they had unleashed their braves in small bands to terrorize the settlers. They had spurned Little Crow's strategy, his plan to fight in the white man's way by attacking the soldiers. They had wasted the chance for an early victory, and now Little Crow did not even know where they were.

Little Crow summoned the members of the Rice Creek Soldiers' Lodge to his village and complained to them about the lack of support from the two war chiefs. The Soldiers' Lodge, he argued, must join in the attack on Fort Ridgely, and he asked them to find the war chiefs and tell them to send their braves. He sent out runners to the other chiefs of the Wahpetons and the Sissetons to inform them of the time for the assault on the fort.

Come, he urged them, and bring your warriors. Kill the soldiers and open up the valley. Kill the soldiers and share in the rich harvest of the goods to be had at the fort. Kill the soldiers and the other whites will run so far away that the Sioux

will once again reign over the lands that were stolen from
them. Kill the soldiers and the whites will not dare to come
back. Kill the soldiers and live as Dakota warriors were meant
to live, free to roam as their fathers and their fathers' fathers
lived. Kill the soldiers, but it must be done tomorrow. The
fate of the Sioux for all time depends on it. Kill the soldiers
and sing the Dakota chant of defiance.

> Over the earth I come,
> Over the earth I come,
> A soldier I come.
> Over the earth I am a ghost.

9
THERE WAS NO TIME FOR MOURNING

Little Crow got his reinforcements. On Friday morning, he climbed into an elegant horse-drawn buggy driven by David Faribault, a mixed-blood prisoner, and led the procession toward Fort Ridgely. The column of Indians in their war garb, some eight hundred strong, appeared invincible. It was twice the size of the force that had tried to capture the fort before. Little Crow's appeal had borne fruit. The braves had listened to his words and answered his call. Shakopee and Red Middle Voice were not among them, but as many as half their warriors were riding with Little Crow, along with three hundred from the Sissetons and Wahpetons of the Upper Sioux.

Large numbers of mixed-bloods and farmer Indians, their trousers and shirts exchanged for breechcloths, came to join the fight. Although some had been coerced into doing so, their presence nonetheless added to the elation and confidence of the Indian nation. Nothing could stop such an army, united in strength and purpose in greater numbers than any Sioux had ever seen before. It was a thrilling day for a Dakota warrior to be alive.

Rolling along after the braves was a long chain of empty wagons, ready to be filled to overflowing with the white man's treasures from the fort. Scores of Indian women and boys walked alongside the creaking wagons, leading spare ponies for the warriors. They were as excited as the braves and did not show their weariness, even though they had spent much of the previous night making bullets. The prospect of so much food and coffee and sugar, dresses and beads and hats, and all the other wonders they expected to find at the fort kept them eager and alert.

The braves, intoxicated by their victories over the settlers—half of the braves had not yet tasted defeat at the hands of the soldiers—shouted and chanted as the sun grew higher. They had smeared their bodies with bright colors—reds, blues, and yellows—with lines of white snaking in between. Most of them were armed with muskets, and many carried bows and arrows, tomahawks, and knives. They sang and joked and laughed as they neared the fort. War was the greatest hunt, the greatest game, the greatest test of strength. It was what Dakota men trained for. They were not meant to dig holes in the ground and plant seeds, to live in wooden houses and sing hymns.

The warriors pulled up clumps of grass and fistfuls of goldenrod and tore leaves off the trees, and used them to decorate their headbands in celebration. Today was a festival of life, a day of which they would tell and retell around camp fires for many years to come.

Little Crow's plan of attack for Fort Ridgely was simpler and more straightforward than the last time. No diversion, no coordinated and staggered assaults from one side and then another. This time, because the Indians outnumbered the soldiers four to one, they would encircle the fort and rush it from all sides at once. If they did not immediately overwhelm the defenders, they would stop the charge and pour sustained fire on the fort while Mankato prepared for a final assault from the southwest. By the time Mankato was ready to launch his attack, the soldiers would have expended most of their ammunition.

As for the wagon guns, Little Crow had said there was no

need for concern. With so many warriors, the soldiers who fired the guns would be cut down in minutes, dead before they could fire even one rotten ball. And besides, a wagon gun could point in only one direction at a time. The Sioux would ride at them from all points. Soon we will own those cannon, Little Crow promised, and no soldiers will ever dare return to the valley. Every warrior who killed a man at the wagon guns would be given an eagle's tail feather to wear in his headband as a sign of bravery. Little Crow would award the feathers himself.

The soldiers at Fort Ridgely spotted the Indians around noon, some time before they were in position to attack. The Sioux made no effort to conceal themselves. There was no need for stealth, not when they had such superior numbers. The troops filed quickly to their posts behind barricades of feed bags and rocks, around the corners of buildings, and behind windows.

Sgt. John Jones, the old army artilleryman, had all six of his guns spotted and ready. He positioned himself in the southeast corner facing the ravine the Indians had used for cover during the last attack. Sgt. James McGrew had his cannon facing northwest, and J. C. Whipple was in the northeast corner of the fort. Jones placed the largest gun, a massive twenty-four-pounder, facing west, in the gap between one of the officers' quarters and the commissary. Two twelve-pound fieldpieces, light and mobile, stood on the parade ground, ready to be wheeled to wherever they might be needed.

Joe Coursolle, the refugee from the Lower Agency who had helped put out the fire during the previous attack, had rushed to the stone barracks building as soon as the Indians were sighted to check on the condition of his son. The boy was not thriving, and the post surgeon said that all they could do was wait. As soon as Coursolle pushed his way into the crowded barracks, he knew that the waiting was over. He saw it on the face of his wife, Marie. She took him by the hand, led him over to the corner, and pulled back the blanket. Little Cistina Joe was dead.

"There was no time for mourning," Coursolle said. "I ran to the carpenter shop where I picked up a small box with a

A farmer Indian identified as Chaska poses with his family in front of a new brick house at the Upper Agency. *Courtesy Whitney's Gallery, Minnesota Historical Society*

Susan Brown, mixed-blood wife of Indian agent Joseph R. Brown, was related to Little Crow and was the occasional recipient of confidences from the chief. *Courtesy Minnesota Historical Society*

Mdewakanton and Wahpekute delegation to Washington, D.C., 1858. Standing (left to right): Indian agent Joseph R. Brown, Antoine (Joe) Campbell, Tomahawk, Andrew Robertson, Red Owl, Thomas A. Robertson, Nathaniel R. Brown. Sitting (left to right): Mankato, Wabasha, Henry Belland. *Photo by Fredericks, Washington, D.C., courtesy Minnesota Historical Society*

Indians gather at the home of Dr. Thomas Williamson at the Upper Agency (Yellow Medicine), August 17, 1862. Williamson, a missionary, is wearing a light-colored hat. *Courtesy Minnesota Historical Society*

cover. I hurried with the box to the post cemetery, dug a little grave, and fitted the tiny coffin in the opening. Then I wrapped my son in a blanket and carried him in my arms to the grave. Marie and the chaplain walked with me. Gently I lay my baby boy to sleep while the chaplain said a prayer. Marie and I wept as I held her in my arms." It was one o'clock in the afternoon.

At that moment, the attack began. Coursolle took his place on the barricades. As Lieutenant Sheehan described it, the fighting started with the Indians' "demoniac yells" and a shower of bullets and arrows that thudded and pinged against the barricades. Overhead, scores of flaming arrows arched gracefully against a bright blue afternoon sky. Some found their mark on rooftops, but no fires took hold. The shingles were still wet from the rain.

The defenders returned the gunfire, and within moments a thick, choking pall of smoke covered the fort. Through it, the Indians charged. Coursolle spotted a brave running toward him. He took aim and pulled the trigger but later could not remember whether he had hit him. A group of braves closed to within twenty feet of the soldiers. The men made ready to fight them off with bayonets, but with a clatter of wheels unheard over the noise of battle, Lieutenant Sheehan pulled a twelve-pounder into place and fired at the Sioux at almost point-blank range.

The Indians were being stopped on all sides, unable to reach the buildings or penetrate the barricades. Only minutes after their initial charge, the warriors withdrew to the tree line. Over the sounds of the guns, the soldiers could hear the loud, angry voices of Little Crow and his chiefs, haranguing the braves to stand firm and keep up their fire on the fort. The fighting settled into a prolonged, steady duel. The forces rarely saw one another, only quick glimpses of a rifle and a head peeking over a boulder or around a tree.

Little Crow kept his men in position in a ring around the fort, but he shifted as many as he could spare to the southwest corner to join Mankato's charge. The Indians easily took over and occupied the outbuildings in that region of the post—the ice and root houses, the granary, and the sutler's warehouse and home. Mankato's men set fire to the woodpiles and the long racks of hay. Yellowish smoke clung to the ground, providing cover for the braves to move within three hundred feet of the parade ground. Lieutenant Sheehan ordered cannon fire directed against the outbuildings, reducing them to flames and kindling. The warriors scattered to find other hiding places.

The beat of the Indians' musket fire from the trees remained steady, and the return fire from the defenders matched it, but Sheehan was soon informed that the supply of musket balls was running low. He asked Sergeant Jones for advice. The ordnance man offered to take charge of the resupply. He sent one group of men over the grounds to retrieve spent balls fired by the Sioux. He put several noncombatants—older men and the ambulatory wounded—to work cutting nails into short pieces to serve as bullets. They would kill just as effectively as musket balls, and they made a fiendish whistling noise as they hurtled through the air, a sound that terrified the Indians. Then Jones had his troops bring some spherical-case shot to the barracks, where he instructed the women on how to take the canisters apart and remove the shot. All of these improvised efforts worked, and none of Fort Ridgely's defenders ran out of ammunition.

Eliza Müller, the wife of the post surgeon, organized the women into ammunition details. She put others to work making coffee, and took it herself to the men on the barricades, running from place to place, dodging bullets and arrows. She helped Sergeant Jones wheel a cannon around and assisted her husband in the makeshift hospital set up in the stone barracks. Someone dubbed her Fort Ridgely's "Florence Nightingale." When Eliza died, fourteen years later, she was buried at the post.

Late in the afternoon, Mankato was ready to send his braves forward from the southwest ravine in a final glorious charge through the fort's defenses and onto the parade ground. Once the Indians reached that broad open square, they would be behind the soldiers and could pick them off one by one. Jones had placed the two twelve-pounders and the twenty-four-pounder in position to meet the assault, and he loaded the big gun with a double charge of canister shot.

Indian agent Joseph R. Brown worked to make the Sioux become self-sufficient farmers. *Courtesy Minnesota Historical Society*

Philander Prescott, a trader and interpreter who had lived among the Sioux for many years, was killed in the initial attack on the Lower Agency. *Courtesy Minnesota Historical Society*

Alexander Ramsey, Governor of Minnesota, mobilized his scarce resources to counter the Sioux raids. *Courtesy Minnesota Historical Society*

Colonel Henry H. Sibley, former fur trader and congressional delegate, led Minnesota's volunteer militias against the Sioux. *Courtesy Minnesota Historical Society*

Little Crow, leader of the Mdewakanton Sioux, desired to maintain the peace with the whites but was forced to lead his people to war. *Photo by J. E. Whitney, courtesy Minnesota Historical Society*

A drawing of the second battle at Fort Ridgely shows at lower left and in the background the ravines that offered cover for the Indians. *Courtesy Minnesota Historical Society*

Shakopee, a traditional blanket Indian, was one of the most vocal promoters of the uprising. *Courtesy Whitney's Gallery, Minnesota Historical Society*

John Other Day led a party of white settlers to safety and fought with Sibley's troops during the uprising. After the war, the government awarded him $2,500 for his bravery. *Courtesy Minnesota Historical Society*

Eleven-year-old Merton Eastlick carried his baby brother, Johnny, some fifty miles to escape the Sioux. Their mother, Lavina, who had been wounded and left for dead, was reunited with them on the road to New Ulm. *Photo by J. E. Whitney, courtesy Minnesota Historical Society*

Refugees from the Riggs and Williamson missions near the Upper Agency rest during their flight on August 21, 1862. *Photo by Adrian Bell, courtesy Minnesota Historical Society*

Judge Charles Flandrau commanded the volunteers at New Ulm who twice repelled the Sioux attackers. *Courtesy Minnesota Historical Society*

New Ulm in 1860, showing the terraced terrain along the Minnesota River.
Courtesy Minnesota Historical Society

Flandrau leads the evacuation of New Ulm on August 25, 1862. *Courtesy Minnesota Historical Society*

Major General John Pope, sent by President Lincoln in September 1862 to command the troops fighting the Sioux Indians. *Courtesy Minnesota Historical Society*

The liberation of more than 250 white and mixed-blood prisoners at Camp Release. *Courtesy Minnesota Historical Society*

A log house at the Lower Agency used as the courtroom where many of the trials of the Sioux warriors were held. *Courtesy Whitney's Gallery, Minnesota Historical Society*

Executive Mansion,

Washington, December 6th 1862.

Brigadier General H. H. Sibley
St Paul
Minnesota.

Ordered that of the Indians and Half-breeds sentenced to be hanged by the Military Commission, composed of Colonel Crooks, Lt. Colonel Marshall, Captain Grant, Captain Bailey, and Lieutenant Olin, and lately sitting in Minnesota, you cause to be executed on Friday the nineteenth day of December, instant, the following named, to wit

"Te-he-hdo-ne-cha"   No. 2.   by the record.
"Tazoo" alias "Plan-doo-ta."   No. 4.   by the record.
"Wy-a-teh-to-wah"   No 5   by the record.
"Hin-han-shoon-ko-yag."   No. 6   by the record
"Muz-za-bom-a-du."   No. 10.   by the record.
"Wah-pay-du-ta."   No. 11.   by the record.
"Wa-he-hua."   No. 12.   by the record.
"Sna-ma-ni."   No. 14.   by the record.
"Ta-te-mi-na."   No. 15.   by the record.
"Rda-in-yan-kna."   No. 19.   by the record.
"Do-wan-sa."   No. 22.   by the record.
"Ha-pan."   No. 24.   by the record.

A facsimile of the beginning and ending of the order for the execution of the Sioux prisoners, signed by Abraham Lincoln (omitted are the additional thirty-four names). *Courtesy Minnesota Historical Society*

A copy of the $500 check paid to Nathan Lamson as bounty for the killing of Little Crow. Note the Indian decoration on the check. *Courtesy Minnesota Historical Society*

A drawing of the hanging of the thirty-eight Sioux at Mankato, Minnesota, December 26, 1862. *Courtesy Minnesota Historical Society*

Shakopee (left) and Medicine Bottle, who were kidnapped in Canada in 1864 and later hanged.
Courtesy Minnesota Historical Society

The *Davenport*, one of the Mississippi River packet boats that transported the Sioux from their camp near Fort Snelling to St. Louis, where other steamers took them to Crow Creek.
Courtesy Minnesota Historical Society

All afternoon, the defenders had watched the Indians file into the ravine and suspected that several hundred warriors were massed and ready. "My scalp tightened," Joe Coursolle said, "and the palms of my hands were wet with sweat." And throughout the long day, the hail of musket fire continued from all sides, so dense that every foot of timber atop the barricade that shielded Sergeant Jones's big gun had been splintered, chipped away to nothing.

The Sioux poured out of the ravine in wave after wave. Jones and his men never faltered. They directed cannon fire at the Indians as they headed across the open field toward the square of buildings at the center of the post. Jones reduced the angle of the guns and fired into the mass of attackers, breaking up the charge. The Indians scattered, retreating to the safety of the ravine.

Seeing Mankato's assault fail, Little Crow ordered out a band of warriors from the northeast, hoping that a fresh assault from a different direction would divide the attention of the soldiers. Whipple's cannon made quick work of the Indians, however, and they quickly withdrew. One shell from Whipple's gun skimmed across the terrain, bursting near Little Crow's position. Pieces of shrapnel struck him about the head but drew no blood. Stunned by the blows, however, he had to be helped to a safer position.

Another Indian offensive began at the northwest corner of the fort, although no one is sure who ordered it. A large band of warriors swung around in a wide arc to join those in the southwest ravine. Sergeant McGrew followed the movement with an eager sense of anticipation, imagining what a few canister rounds from the twenty-four-pounder would do to such a tempting target. He loaded a double canister charge and waited until the maneuver was almost complete. Then his big gun and the twelve-pounders fired at the same instant.

"The shells tore great holes in the ranks of the warriors," Joe Coursolle recalled, "and the crashing boom of the twenty-four-pounder rumbled and echoed up and down the river bluffs. The Indians skedaddled and the fighting was over."

Little Crow had lost his best opportunity to win the war. If he could not capture Fort Ridgely with eight hundred braves, then the fight was hopeless. He could never assemble such a large force again, and by the following day or the day after, the post's reinforcements would surely arrive. Even at four-to-one odds, the Sioux had not been able to win. His dream of reclaiming Dakota lands was over. Fort Ridgely had been the key. Some buildings were burning, others lay in ruins, but the post was still held by the army, at a cost to the soldiers of only three dead and thirteen wounded in six hours of fighting. The flag of the Great Father waved above the smoke.

Little Crow led his beaten warriors away from the fort in a silent and joyless procession. There was no laughing or joking, no boasting of killing the soldiers and winning eagle feathers. Behind them, the women walked beside the still-empty wagons, mourning the dead. Nearly one hundred braves had been buried in the woods, one hundred faces never to be seen again. The women would mourn them in proper Dakota fashion when they returned to their village. For now, all they could do was remember them.

The forlorn column stopped at dusk and made camp along the banks of Three Mile Creek. While the women cooked beef for dinner, the warriors held a council with Little Crow. The chief was angry, but for a time he said nothing, allowing the others the chance to express their views. Some argued for returning to the fort in the morning and renewing the attack. Little Crow knew that was wounded pride talking. After Ridgely, they could take New Ulm, another boasted. That town had only frightened Germans, not soldiers, and could be captured easily.

Others called for an assault on New Ulm first, before returning to the fort. They pointed out that reinforcements from the east would have to pass through New Ulm. If the Indians held the town, they could keep the soldiers from ever reaching Fort Ridgely.

Everyone fell silent when Little Crow rose to speak. He had decided, he said, to attack New Ulm early in the morning. If the Indians could capture the town and take the several hundred refugees there as hostages, then perhaps they could win this war, after all. He would leave that night, to reach the town before sunrise, and he was prepared to lead all who wanted to come with him. Those warriors who did not want to follow him, he said, were free to do what they wished.

When Little Crow left for New Ulm a few hours later, he had about half of the warriors with him. In the morning, they would fight the whites again.

Judge Charles Flandrau, now honorary colonel in command of New Ulm, prepared the town to defend itself against the Indian attack everyone knew was coming. He barricaded the central business district with everything on which he could lay hands. Earthen walls were erected and strengthened across streets. Wagons loaded with odd bits of lumber, firewood, and rocks were placed behind the houses that fronted on the business district. The refugees, now totaling more than one thousand, were confined within the barricades and ordered to stay inside the brick and stone buildings during the attack.

In the days since Flandrau's arrival, about three hundred men had come from communities located east of New Ulm to help defend the town. Their presence was welcome and good for morale, but the men were poorly armed. Over one-third had no firearms, and Flandrau had no spares to issue them. There was also a shortage of ammunition for those weapons the defenders did have. Most of these were old muzzle-loading shotguns the settlers had brought with them from Germany. No more than thirty men had modern, efficient rifles. "A worse equipped army probably never waited an attack," Flandrau said.

The colonel drilled and trained his men, but they remained an unimpressive lot. On Friday, he inspected one of the volunteer companies. There had been an accident the night before when a man on guard duty had been sprayed in the face with bird shot by another guard. Flandrau looked over the assembled company, then took the gun of a man in the front rank. It was a German small-bore single-barreled shotgun of limited range and dependability. He asked the man whether he had any ammunition to fire at the Indians. "Oh yes, I am all ready," he said proudly. Flandrau asked to see it. The man "thrust his hand into his pocket," Flandrau said, "and produced a handful of percussion caps, bird shot, cheese, tobacco, buttons, and a variety of other things that would not have been effective in a fight with Indians. All I could do was to read the company a severe lecture, and have a general inspection."

In addition to preparing New Ulm's defenses and training its militia, Flandrau dispatched patrols to search for any settlers who might still be hiding out and bring them into town. One party had ventured eight miles distant that Thursday and had found no one alive, only more bodies to bury. On Friday, Flandrau learned from a newly arrived refugee that eleven women and children were hiding in a ravine in the direction of Leavenworth. He decided to commit 140 men, almost half of his defensive force, to the rescue mission. Three of his four doctors—Ayer, Daniels, and Mayo—decided to accompany them.

Not far from town, they heard the rumble of cannon fire coming from Fort Ridgely, eighteen miles away. The men of the expedition found the sounds disturbing and chilling because they meant that the Sioux were sufficiently confident and well organized to attempt to capture the fort. New Ulm would be next.

They found the party of women and children unhurt but weak from fear and hunger. After the doctors comforted them, the men met to consider what to do next. Like all volunteer militia outfits, they debated all courses of action and put the issue to a vote. Dr. Daniels urged them to return to New Ulm right away, but the majority voted to continue on a few miles to search for more survivors. They planned to camp out overnight and return to town the next day. They pushed on, always within earshot of the gunfire from Fort Ridgely, but at sundown it suddenly stopped, and they did not know whether the silence meant victory for the Sioux or for the soldiers.

When they stopped to rest, Daniels had another chance to present his case for returning home as soon as possible. Surely the Indians knew where they were, he said, and their absence left fewer than two hundred men to guard New Ulm. If Little Crow moved downriver from the fort, he could capture the town and cut them off. The men took another vote, and this time Daniels won. The column turned around and headed back to town, reaching home at about one o'clock in the morning, the same time Little Crow and his warriors were breaking camp, ready to march on New Ulm.

While the expedition was still out, Flandrau had sent an urgent message to Colonel Sibley.

> I have large expeditions out all day, which weakens me, but I think I can hold the town until you come, if not attacked by a very large force. I hear of Indians all around me, but see none. I am making some entrenchments, etc. I am sure that everything above [the town] is lost, and all the people killed. . . .
>
> I wish you would leave the same evening you get to St. Peter, if possible. The roads are good, and you can get here by morning. . . .
>
> Bring powder, lead, and caps. We are short.

Saturday morning dawned clear, bright, and still. Shortly after sunup, Flandrau's lookouts spotted columns of smoke to the northwest, rising over Fort Ridgely. Presently, more spirals of smoke rose in the air, each one nearer to New Ulm than the one before. The Indians were burning farmhouses, barns, haystacks, even fields of grain as they marched toward the town. Before long, the northwest sky was almost black.

Flandrau and his men decided that Fort Ridgely must have fallen and that the Indians were approaching them from the south side of the Minnesota River. Flandrau sent a group of seventy-five men, a significant portion of his garrison, across the river to reconnoiter and report back on the size of the war party. However, once the detachment crossed on the ferry, it was cut off by the Indian force and had to withdraw toward St. Peter. It would be of no help to New Ulm.

Setting fire to the fields had been a ruse on Little Crow's part to induce Flandrau to send his men across the river, where the Indians could easily prevent them from returning to town. Flandrau, unwisely, had been taken in. The main Indian force was advancing toward the town on the north bank, and now

Flandrau had seventy-five fewer defenders on whom to count.

He realized his mistake at about 9:30 A.M. when a large Indian force was spotted only two miles away. Little Crow, taking his time, deployed his warriors near the foot of the bluff that overlooked New Ulm. They formed a long semicircle, encompassing the entire breadth of the settlement. A second Indian contingent assembled on the bluff on the far side of the river, capturing the ferry and cutting off any possibility of escape. New Ulm was surrounded.

Colonel Flandrau ordered all the men he could spare from the barricades to take up position on the prairie about a quarter of a mile from the center of town. He hoped to keep the outlying buildings out of Indian hands and to stop the Indians before they could reach the buildings that housed the refugees.

At ten o'clock, the braves advanced. Flandrau rode up and down behind his perimeter line, exhorting his men to remain calm and make every shot count. He tried to sound confident of victory, but he later admitted to being concerned that the line would not hold. If his men fell back in disarray, it would surely be the end of them all.

Few of Flandrau's men had fought Indians before, and he expected them to be afraid when the Sioux charged. "White men," Flandrau wrote, "fight under a great disadvantage the first time they engage Indians. There is something so fiendish in their yells and terrifying in their appearance when in battle, that it takes a great deal of time to overcome the unpleasant sensation it inspires. Then there is a snakelike stealth in all their movements that excites distrust and uncertainty which unsteadies the nerves at first."

The line of Indians moved steadily closer, never wavering, like some great unrelenting crest of water set free by a broken levee. The nerves of New Ulm's defenders were about to be put to the test.

"Their advance upon the sloping prairie in the bright sunlight was a very fine spectacle," Flandrau recalled, "and to such inexperienced soldiers as we all were, intensely exciting. When within about one mile and a half of us the mass began to expand like a fan, and increase in the velocity of its approach, and continued this movement until within about double rifle-shot, when it had covered our entire front. Then the savages uttered a terrific yell and came down upon us like the wind."

The Indians opened fire, wounding several of the defenders, and the entire line wavered. Despite Flandrau's shouts of encouragement, his men broke and ran for the safety of the buildings at the edge of town. He tried to rally them, to get them to occupy the buildings and make a stand, but they retreated all the way to the barricades at the center of town.

Had the Indians pursued them, they would have taken the town easily, but fearing that the retreat was a feint to draw them into a trap, the Sioux stopped at the edge of town. Using the outlying buildings for cover, they began to fire on the defenders from windows and doorways. They claimed one building after another and quickly consolidated their position, overlooking the fortified town center.

They missed one building. Three blocks from the barricades stood a narrow wooden four-story windmill with sail arms seventy-five feet long. A company of thirty men calling themselves the Le Sueur Tigers, after their hometown, had stopped in their retreat and clambered inside. The Tigers were excellent shots and had the best rifles of all the defenders.

They barricaded the first floor with sacks of flour and wheat, knocked loopholes in the walls to serve as rifle ports, and from there poured highly accurate fire on the Indians, stopping their advance. When the rest of Flandrau's men saw that the Indians were no longer following them, they rallied and regrouped to form strong points in the brick structures in front of the barricades. The fighting raged from point to point, thirty men in one building, three at a window, seven around a corner, twelve over there. The defenders set fire to several unoccupied buildings around town to prevent the Indians from taking possession.

In the first hour, New Ulm's defenders lost sixty men—ten killed and fifty wounded. With the seventy-five men cut off on the far side of the river, Flandrau's force was now down to fewer than two hundred.

The crackling of flames, the smoke, the acrid smell of gunpowder fueled confusion and fear. The screams of the wounded, the anxious cries of the refugees huddled in the basements, and the shouts of the Indians added to the bedlam. Some of the defenders became crazed and ran away to take shelter with the women and children in the cellars. Dr. Mayo recalled yelling at them, thrusting pitchforks into their trembling hands, urging them to get back on the barricades and run the Indians through.

Mayo and the other surgeons treated the wounded as rapidly as they could in their makeshift hospital. Doors had been ripped off hinges to serve as stretchers. While amputating a man's leg, Mayo spied two white men sneaking past the window. Taking them for shirkers, he leapt through the door, waving his bloody scalpel. Faced with the furious doctor, the men chose to return to the barricades.

By noon, the battle had become a stalemate, with neither side able to advance. A strong wind was blowing up from the south, whipping through town from the river. Little Crow saw it as an opportunity. If he could shift some of his men to that side of town, they could set fires and advance under cover of the smoke that would be blowing in the defenders' faces, effectively blinding them.

He sent a group of warriors to carry out his plan. The wooden structures near the riverbank caught fire easily, and the wind forced the smoke along the streets, around corners, through windows and cracks in walls until there was no escaping its thick, choking presence. Colonel Flandrau transferred some of his men to meet the new threat, sending them beyond the barricades to fortify the houses. The whites held their ground—three hours of fighting had made veterans of them, along with the growing realization that there were few places left to hide. The Indians were only two blocks away.

More buildings went up in flames, more men fell wounded or killed, and by midafternoon, in house-to-house fighting, the Sioux were moving up Main Street toward the center of New Ulm. Little Crow himself dashed from one burning structure to the next, urging his braves on. He ran out into the street to leave his personal totem—a piece of crow's skin—on the body of a fallen white man, an act that earned him another eagle feather for his headband.

Fighting was particularly fierce around a small brick house south of the town's center. Flandrau thought that a personal visit from him might help stiffen his troops' morale. As he started toward the house across an open patch of ground, the door opened and Jacob Nix, who had been in command at the house, began running toward him.

"We met in the middle of the space," Flandrau said, "and foolishly stopped to speak to each other. We had hardly become stationary when an Indian sent a bullet at us which hit Nix in the large muscle of his arm, jerking him nearly off his feet. He shook himself, finding that he was still alive, showed me his right hand from which one of his fingers had been shot in the first attack on Tuesday, and laughingly said, 'Colonel, that makes two.' We separated, going in opposite directions and making time [that] would amaze a professional sprinter."

By three o'clock, Little Crow was growing concerned about the outcome. It would be dark in a few hours, and they would have to break off contact. Most Indians hated to fight at night, to try to kill an enemy they could not see. He assembled sixty warriors by the river to make a massed assault up Main Street. They were to stop for nothing until they reached the barricades.

Flandrau and his men saw the braves gather and guessed what they were up to. Asa White and Newell Houghton, both experienced in Indian matters and respected by Flandrau, offered their opinion.

"Colonel, these Indians will bag us in about an hour and a half," one said.

"It looks that way," Flandrau said. "What remedy have you to suggest?"

"We must make for the cottonwood timber. It is our last hope."

The timber was three miles away, across the prairie, and Flandrau rejected the idea as foolhardy. "They would slaughter us like sheep," he said. His two hundred fighting men could never cross the open terrain safely with the Indians surrounding them, much less the thousand or more refugees. And what was he to do about the wounded? No, Flandrau decided, they could not leave the town. They would have to stand their ground against Little Crow's attack. Then a new idea occurred to Flandrau. What if he attacked first?

"Our strongest hold is in this town," he told White and Houghton. "Get me forty or fifty handpicked volunteers and help me lead them, and we will drive the enemy out of the lower town or die trying."

In a matter of minutes, they had rounded up close to sixty volunteers. Flandrau pointed to Little Crow's warriors, who were milling about in a grove of oak trees a few hundred yards away. He told the men that this was their last chance to save themselves and New Ulm. They were ready. With Flandrau in the lead, they set off at a run, yelling as fiercely as any Indian and firing as they went.

Flandrau expected to meet up with the Indians in a sunken road a few blocks away, but the warriors moved quickly when they saw the settlers bearing down on them. They advanced up the street, and when Flandrau's men closed on them, they were nearer than expected. The Indians opened fire, killing four settlers, including Newell Houghton, but the charge had so much momentum, so much desperation and fury, that it was impossible to stop.

The town's defenders never faltered. Shouting wildly, they laid down a thick curtain of fire, and when they got within fifty feet, the Sioux broke and ran. Flandrau had to stop his eager men from pursuing the Indians too far, because they would soon outrun their covering fire. He called a halt beside a woodpile near the road. The men hid behind the logs and continued to snipe at the Indians. The braves tried one more advance, but Flandrau's defenders kept them pinned down.

Then he spotted a new danger—all the houses between his force and the barricades. If the Indians got behind their line and in among the buildings, he and his men could be trapped in the cross fire. He formed a squad and sent them back with orders to set fire to every structure, fence, or stack of lumber, anything the Indians could use for shelter.

It took two hours to burn the forty houses that stood between Flandrau and the center of New Ulm, but once that was accomplished, the path to the barricades was clear and no longer offered the possibility of cover to the Indians. Little

Crow knew he had been beaten again. As the sun set, he called off the battle and led his men away.

The tired, hungry, but proud defenders of New Ulm congratulated themselves on their victory. Then they counted the cost. Thirty-two people were dead and more than sixty wounded. Over one-third of the town lay in ruins—190 houses had been torched and most of the other buildings bore signs of battle damage in broken windows and bullet-scarred walls.

There was no time for either celebration or mourning. They expected a fresh attack at sunrise, or even a surprise raid in the dark. They knew that the Indians did not like to fight at night, but who knew what their desperation or hurt pride would lead them to do? Flandrau ordered his men to dig deep rifle pits about twenty-five yards in front of the barricades, all around the center of town. He kept the pits and the barricades manned throughout the night. Only every third man was allowed to sleep.

The defenders waited in the darkness, but no Indians came that night, and when the sun appeared in the morning, the surrounding hills, bluffs, and prairie were empty. The Sioux had left. Never again would they venture so far east of their reservation. At New Ulm and Fort Ridgely, they had lost their war.

10
A HEARTRENDING PROCESSION

On Friday morning, Lavina Eastlick discovered that she had been wandering in a circle. She was back at Lake Shetek, where her nightmare had begun. In the distance, she recognized the cabin belonging to Uncle Tommy Ireland and she could hear the familiar sound of roosters crowing. It looked so peaceful, so normal, but those routine sights and sounds were dispiriting. She had lost her husband and two children, and had no idea whether the children—Merton and the baby—were dead or alive. Lavina had little strength or spirit left, and she slumped down in the grass, ready to give up.

At noon, driven by hunger, she headed for the Ireland house. Despite her injuries, she waded through hip-deep water in a slough but found that she lacked the energy to pull herself up the bank on the far side. She tried several times, only to slide back into the water. Resigning herself to drowning or starving less than a hundred feet from the Irelands' cornfield, she no longer cared. She welcomed the prospect of death.

"But after lying there a long time," she wrote later, "I

found I could not die when I pleased. I then took a cloth and wrapped around my feet, for they were very sore, the flesh being almost all worn off my toes, which gave me great pain. I then crawled to the top of the hill and lay down again, rested a few moments, arose, and went on again."

She stumbled into the cornfield, tore off the first ear she could reach, and wolfed it down raw. It instantly made her sick, so cramped with pain that she moaned aloud. When she reached the house, she found that the Indians had destroyed or stolen everything of value. There was not a crumb of food left. A rancid odor made her gag. The stench came from the bloated bodies of pigs, rotting in the sun for two days. She discovered the mangled remains of a dog, which added to the smell. Lavina staggered away from the house and collapsed in a thicket of plum trees.

After sundown, she crossed to the henhouse and found it untouched. She grabbed a chicken, wrung its neck, and tore the raw meat off the bones. She gnawed on a bit of it right away and packed the rest in a bucket, along with three ears of corn. Then she rummaged through the shed, found an old coat, and put it on.

Guided by the North Star, Lavina headed east, stopping to rest every quarter of a mile. She covered only two and a half miles that night but kept going until she reached a lake. It was Saturday morning, seemingly a lifetime since the Sioux had massacred her Lake Shetek neighbors, yet it had been only four days. She cleared a spot in some bushes and settled down to sleep. When she awoke, she was startled to see a horse-drawn sulky coming toward her. Sure that the driver was an Indian who had likely stolen the little two-wheeled buggy from a settler, she watched the figure carefully. Then she recognized August Garzene, the mail carrier, taking his regular route between New Ulm and Sioux Falls, which was just over the border in the Dakota Territory.

For a moment, Lavina thought she was hallucinating. Garzene was ambling along, making no attempt to conceal himself or to hurry. He acted as though he had nothing to fear from the Indians. She stepped from her hiding place and called to him. He pulled on the reins and stopped, gaping in surprise as she ran to him and started babbling about a massacre. He had been away for more than a week and knew nothing about an uprising, and he was hardly inclined to believe this dirty, ranting creature who herself looked like an old Indian.

"Who are you?" he asked. "Are you not a squaw?"

"No, no! I am Mrs. Eastlick from Lake Shetek and am trying to get away from the Indians. They have murdered nearly all the Shetek settlers."

She told him her story and he offered to take her in the buggy as far as Dutch Charley's cabin, eleven miles away. When they reached it, around four o'clock that afternoon, they found Uncle Tommy Ireland inside. The old man refused to die, even though he had been shot eight times. Twice he had been abandoned, once by the men of Lake Shetek at the site of the massacre, and again by young Merton Eastlick, who was trying to save his baby brother. Each time, Uncle Tommy had lain down, prepared to meet his Maker, but then decided, probably out of cussed obstinacy, that maybe he could get up that hill or into the next grove of trees. He had pulled himself along to Dutch Charley's place and was again prepared to die.

"He looked more like a ghost than anything else," Lavina Eastlick said. "He was very pale, his eyes sunk in his head, and his voice was very weak." He was also discouraged because he was thirsty and had been unable to reach the well. Garzene fetched some water, and after Uncle Tommy gulped it down, he told them about Merton and Johnny. The last time he had seen them, they were heading for the cabin with about two days' head start and should be some miles beyond it by now, provided, he added, that the Indians had not captured them.

The three spent the night in the cabin and set off toward New Ulm early Sunday morning. During the night, it had rained, and by daybreak a strong wind was blowing over the prairie. Garzene wrapped Lavina in a blanket and settled her in the sulky. He led the horse, and old Tommy Ireland walked beside him. At about ten o'clock, they crested a hill and Lavina spotted three figures, which she took to be white men. The others shaded their eyes, squinted, and pronounced them to be Indians.

Garzene hid the sulky in some bushes and they crept up

to the top of the hill for another look. After a while, they agreed that they had better push on. As they drew near, they could see that the figures were a white woman and two children—Alomina Hurd, Lavina's neighbor from Lake Shetek, with two of her children. And Alomina had good news for Lavina. Merton and Johnny Eastlick had been with her for a while and had then gone on ahead.

About a mile away, they came upon the boys resting by the roadside. Merton had carried his brother on his back for more than fifty miles. Lavina hugged him and drew back to look at him. He was "almost a skeleton," she said, "and Johnny was so ill with the cholera that he did not know his mother, and his face was so disfigured by the bites of insects that there was no semblance to his real self."

The party journeyed on another few miles to a farmhouse. It was deserted, but they found ample food. They feasted on pork, chicken, bread, potatoes, and other assorted vegetables. After the meal, Garzene set out in his buggy for New Ulm, promising to send soldiers back to get them. No one came for three days. By Wednesday, the food supply was running out.

When Garzene finally returned, he brought the news that New Ulm was under attack. No soldiers could be spared to rescue them. Unable to get help from that end of his route, he planned to ride to Sioux Falls, about one hundred miles away, where about fifty soldiers were quartered. The two women, four children, and old Uncle Tommy would be on their own. Garzene kissed Lavina and Alomina goodbye and headed west.

Lavina despaired once again, believing that with Garzene's departure, their last hope for survival was gone. They decided that it was too risky to stay in the farmhouse, so they took shelter in a thicket. The mosquitoes ravaged them, making it impossible to rest or sleep. Weakened by exhaustion and hunger, they returned to the house. Lavina had to crawl on her hands and knees to get there.

Nine days passed and no one came. Tommy Ireland announced that he was determined to go to New Ulm or die trying.

At midnight on the second day after Ireland left, the women were awakened by the sound of dogs barking. Lavina was sure it was Indians. "I thought certain our time had come," she recalled. "I could see my little ones tortured in the most cruel manner. It seemed to me that I could hear the hatchet cleave their skulls. I prayed the Lord to give me strength to die without a groan. I had forgotten everything, only that myself and children must die."

The door opened and two men entered. The women recognized them at once. They were neighbors from Lake Shetek, men who had been away from the village when the Indians came. With them were fifteen soldiers from New Ulm. Uncle Tommy had sent them, just as he had promised.

Justina Krieger inched her way to the creek some five hundred yards from her home and washed the blood from her body. It was Tuesday night. The events of the day flashed through her mind in a series of grisly pictures: the thirteen German families fleeing their homes and traveling all night; the Indians surrounding them in the morning, pretending to be friends, persuading them to return home; those same Indians torturing the children, murdering her husband, her brother, her friends within sight of the house; the bullet in her back; and the sight of the warrior standing over her, slicing open her abdomen with his knife.

She drank from the creek and pushed herself to her feet. Although weak, she found that she was not paralyzed, as she feared when she first regained consciousness. It hurt to move, but she knew she had to get as far away as possible before dawn. She covered six miles and stopped beside a stream. She had lost a great deal of blood and had not eaten in two days.

Justina camped by the stream until Saturday, preserving her remaining strength. Several times, she fell unconscious, and believed it was due to hunger. When she thought she saw Indians in the distance, she forced herself to move on, sustained by handfuls of prairie grass and water from brackish puddles. In the morning, she gathered dew from the grass and drank it from her cupped hands. When her clothes became wet, she sucked the moisture from them.

Saturday became Sunday and Justina kept moving, stumbling, falling, crawling, fainting, but always fleeing the awful pictures of the past. On Sunday night, she reached another creek, whose banks were littered with bodies. She retched from the smell and left quickly, flailing her way through heaps of furniture, piles of torn books, scattered and dented pots and pans, the debris the dead had tried to take with them.

She waded across creeks, forded shallow rivers, in water so cold that it set her teeth chattering. She shouldered her way through cane grass that grew taller than her head. It cut her skin like hundreds of tiny razor blades. She stumbled over mutilated bodies, and saw a child who had been torn apart by the legs. She forced herself to touch the corpses, to examine their possessions for food, but she found nothing. Monday came, a week since she had left home, a week since she had eaten.

That morning, she found a road, which at least provided her with a clear sense of direction. She had not had a drink of water in many hours and her throat was parched. "This road I followed," she recalled, "and in a low place found some water standing in puddles in the mud, and tried to get it in my clothes, but the water was too shallow. I then got down and sucked up and eagerly drank the water from the mud. My tongue and lips were now cracked open from thirst. After this, I went on and found two bodies on the road, and, a few steps further, a number of men, women, and children, all dead!" Was she the only survivor in the whole county?

Taking one painful step after another, plagued by one hellish memory after another, Justina Krieger walked along the road to Fort Ridgely.

Helen Carrothers spent three days trying to find a place to cross the Minnesota River. By Saturday, she abandoned the attempt. She had found no food for herself and the children since escaping from Little Crow's camp. Carrying the girl on her back and the boy in her arms, she made her way to the ruined buildings of the Lower Agency.

She reached the town after dark, dug up a few potatoes from a garden plot, and sought shelter in the largest government building still standing. She searched the rooms, but there was no food. She came across a feather-bed comforter and stumbled over a trapdoor leading to the cellar. Helen tossed the feather bed down the opening, helped the children down the ladder, and pulled the door shut after her. The cellar contained some water jugs, and they settled down for the night, relieved to be where the mosquitoes could not reach them. They remained hidden for two days, nibbling on the raw potatoes. Several times, they heard footsteps upstairs and assumed the visitors were Indians, but no one pulled up their trapdoor.

On Monday, Helen decided it was time to leave. Their food had run out. Gathering up the children, she made for the ferry crossing, but the Sioux had cut the ferry rope and the boat had drifted downriver. She could see on the far side the scalped and mutilated bodies of Captain Marsh's men, their remains festering in the summer sun. She wandered along the bank for a while and spied a large wooden waterlogged box. The bloated body of a soldier lay across it.

Gagging from the stench, Helen shoved the corpse into the river and began to bail out the box with a cup she had carried away with her from the agency building. Intending to use the crate as a boat, she lifted her children into it, climbed in after them, and pushed away from the bank. Without an oar or a pole, bailing continuously, she floated seven miles downstream, counting the bodies of six more soldiers of Captain Marsh's command. She hoped to float all the way to Fort Ridgely, but the box was taking on water faster than she could empty it. When her makeshift boat grazed the north bank, she grabbed some overhanging willow branches and scrambled ashore. It was close to sundown, one week since she had fled her home, and she had finally managed to cross the river.

"My way now lay through a dense jungle in the Minnesota bottom land of prickly ash, grapevines, and underbrush so thick that in places I had to set down the children and open a pathway and then return for them. The poor little dears had become so weak that they were unable to walk, even for a short distance, and my own strength was so exhausted that I could not carry both of them at once, so that I had to carry one forward and lay it down and return for the other."

Helen's hands and feet were cut and bleeding from the sharp vines and branches, and when she finally emerged into a clearing, she collapsed and slept for several hours, until the cries of her children woke her. She found a road, the one to Fort Ridgely, but was so weary that she could only crawl along, dragging the children behind her. She came to a house, deserted and plundered like so many others, but there were cucumbers in the garden.

As night came, the mosquitoes grew more active. Faces, arms, and legs quickly turned black from the bites and the drawn blood. Helen pushed on in the darkness until she passed out, and when she awoke, the sun was shining. Shielding her eyes, she turned her head slowly, and in the distance she saw the American flag flying over Fort Ridgely.

"Oh, the ecstasy of delight which thrilled me at the gladsome sight! That flag meant hope, liberty, life, the salvation of myself and children. Hunger, pain, bruises, danger were all forgotten and I stumbled forward in an effort to walk."

At an abandoned house only three miles from the fort, she searched again for food. She climbed down the steps to the cellar, and when she looked up, she saw through the doorway a man's face peering down at her. She gasped. Then she realized that the man was not an Indian.

He spoke to her in German, asking for food. She said she had none. Where had he come from? He told her that he had seen the Indians murder his wife and three children and that he had run away, unable to help them. He had been hiding in a haystack for three days, afraid to go near the fort. He had heard much gunfire—a big battle, he said—and he was convinced that the Indians had captured it. They had left the American flag, he believed, to fool the refugees. He had also seen Indians around this house.

Helen knew she had to leave at once, and she tried to persuade the German to come with her. He resisted at first, saying it was too dangerous, but he finally consented. She believed it was more dangerous to stay in the house. If they did not starve first, they were likely to be scalped—or worse.

The man offered to carry one of the children, and they struck out boldly, walking in the open down the road instead of through the woods. The path was the shortest and easiest way to the fort. Although Helen expected to feel a bullet in the back from the Indians she imagined around every bend and behind every bush, she was determined to reach the safety of Fort Ridgely.

When they got within a half mile of the post, four soldiers came out to meet them. Warren DeCamp, a civilian, was with them. He had spotted the group through the fort's telescope and was hoping the woman was his lost wife. A soldier gave Helen a gray blanket, which she wrapped around her tattered clothing, and she made a triumphant entry into the fort, feeling as though she had been raised from the dead. In more than eight days, she had shepherded her children over sixty miles, with only a few potatoes and a cucumber to sustain them.

Helen Carrothers's joy was short-lived. Her daughter became ill, apparently from gorging on too much food after arriving at the fort. Her wasted body had rejected the nourishment. The post surgeon, Dr. Müller, said there was no hope. She would live only a day or two more. Helen refused to accept his diagnosis. She scoured the grounds around the fort and collected roots, herbs, and plants that the Sioux medicine man had taught her about. Dr. Müller scoffed at her.

The next day, the child showed a noticeable improvement, and in three days she was up and running about the grounds. In a week, Müller pronounced her cured. A miracle, he said. Helen nodded. The medicine man had taught her well.

Sarah Wakefield felt she could not take another step. When the sun rose on Friday, they finally stopped to rest. Chaska's eighty-year-old grandfather had led Sarah and the baby on a nonstop march throughout the night to keep them away from the camp, where it was rumored that a chief was coming to kill all the white women. Periodically, they heard Indian voices behind them, and they plunged deeper into the forest. Sarah regretted that she had left her son, James, with a friendly squaw in her haste to flee. In her panic, she had convinced herself that she would never see the child again.

At dawn, the old man told her that he would return to the village to see whether the danger had passed. He scooped out a hole in the middle of a haystack, just big enough for Sarah and the baby. They had no food or water, and as the sun rose, the heat became oppressive. Once or twice, she attempted to nurse Nellie, but she had little milk to offer.

It was around noon that she heard Indians nearby. The baby started to cry. "I clasped my hands around her throat," Sarah said, "until she was black in the face." The continuing heat, thirst, and hunger heightened her fears as she waited for the old man to return. Cramped inside the haystack, Sarah sat with her feet drawn up under her, clinging to the baby, for almost eighteen hours. When Chaska's grandfather finally arrived and pulled her from her hiding place, she could not straighten her legs. She struggled painfully to her feet, tied the baby on her back, and followed him back to the Indian camp. She asked about her son, but the old man had no answer.

They walked for four miles, stopping only to sip some muddy water from a puddle. When they reached the tepee where Sarah had left the boy the night before, he was not there, but moments later an Indian woman came to tell her that he was all right. James ran into her arms, crying.

"Oh, Mama. I thought you was dead and I was left alone with the Indians. I have cried until I am sick."

James clung to her throughout the night. Whenever she tried to leave the tepee, he started screaming, but eventually he calmed down and slept. Sarah held him close, gazing at the stars through the tepee's open flap, wondering whether her husband was looking down on them from heaven.

Saturday passed uneventfully until just after dinner. Chaska returned, troubled and angry. He took Sarah aside and told her that he sometimes wished he could kill all the Indians. A warrior in the neighboring lodge was drunk and was menacing the white women. They heard a shot and a shrill scream.

It was not safe to remain there. They would have to take to the woods again. Chaska's mother led Sarah and the children a good distance away and bedded them down under a tree, covering their hiding place with boughs and vines. After an hour, she returned and took them back to the village. The danger had passed, she said. Around midnight, however, when they were all asleep, Hapa barged in, drunk, yelling for the white woman. He was the Indian Sarah feared more than any other, the one who had killed George Gleason. She pretended to be asleep, but he spotted her.

"Come here!" Hapa shouted. "I wish to talk with you."

Sarah kept her eyes closed and lay rigid. She whispered to Chaska's mother, asking what she should do.

"Lie still," the old woman said. "Chaska will not let him hurt you. [Hapa] will go to sleep soon."

The drunken Hapa did not go to sleep. He staggered toward Sarah, his knife drawn.

"You must be my wife or die," he said, waving the knife.

Chaska jumped up and confronted him. ·

"You are a bad man," Chaska said, reminding Hapa that he already had a wife, who happened to be Chaska's own sister. "I have no [other] wife," Chaska added.

Sarah interrupted them. If Hapa intended to kill her, she said, then he must kill the children first. She could not bear the thought of leaving them behind. Chaska told her to be quiet. He could see that Hapa was unsteady on his feet, about to collapse in a stupor.

"You go lie down," he told Hapa in a quiet, soothing voice.

Hapa nodded.

"That is right," he said, slurring his words. "You take her and I will not kill her."

Chaska said that as soon as he could confirm that Mrs. Wakefield's husband was dead, he would marry her; but Hapa grew suspicious. That was not good enough. Chaska must marry her now, tonight.

Sarah gasped and reached out to grab Chaska's mother's hand.

"Don't be afraid," the old woman said. "Chaska is a good man. He will not injure you."

Chaska knelt next to Sarah and spoke to her gently.

"You must let me lie down beside you," he said, "or [Hapa] will kill you, he is so drunk. I am a good man, and my wife is in the spirit world and can see me, and I will not harm you."

He stretched out next to Sarah and they waited to see what Hapa would do. The drunken Indian dropped his knife, sank down on the floor on the far side of the tepee, and fell asleep. Chaska watched him for a few minutes, to make sure he was not faking, then slipped out of Sarah's bed and went back to his own blanket.

"My father," Sarah wrote later, "could not have done differently, or acted more respectable or honorable, and if there was ever an honest, upright man, Chaska was one."

The next morning, word spread throughout the village that the white woman Sarah Wakefield had married an Indian. Several of the white women prisoners made their way to Chaska's lodge to ask her whether the story was true. They could not believe that any white woman would willingly give herself to an Indian. Because there were always Indians around, some of whom understood English, Sarah had to be careful in her replies. If she denied that she was Chaska's wife, Hapa would hear of it and come after her. Deliberately being guarded, then, she told the women that she supposed her husband was dead, and she turned the conversation to something else.

The deception worked. Hapa never learned the truth. The outraged white prisoners ostracized her, however, and the story haunted her life for many years to come. To the whites, she would always be considered, contemptuously, as no better than a squaw.

Snana was a beautiful Sioux woman of twenty-three. Her name meant "tinkling sound," but the white settlers, to whom she had always been a good friend, affectionately called her Maggie. She was unusually well educated, having attended the Reverend Williamson's mission school in her childhood. She spoke English fluently and was rarely seen without her Bible. She and her husband, Good Thunder, were married in the Episcopal Church and were among the first Indians to become Christians, a decision that brought considerable ridicule from other Indians. Snana and Good Thunder were farmer Indians and were opposed to the uprising.

Snana was despondent, however. Eight days before the fighting began, her seven-year-old daughter, Snana's oldest child, had died. When two of Snana's uncles announced that they were going to join the war party, she asked them to bring back a child to take the place of her lost daughter. They returned empty-handed but told her that they knew of a warrior who now owned a nice-looking white girl.

Snana asked her mother to try to purchase the girl, and she gave her a pony to offer in exchange. At first, the warrior was reluctant to part with his prize, but the pony was swift and worth much. He could easily find another white girl, he reasoned, but ponies like that were scarce. When the mother brought the child home, Snana was disappointed—she was much older and larger than her own daughter. "But my heart was so sad," Snana said, "that I was willing to take any girl at that time. The reason why I wished to keep this girl was to have her in place of the one I lost. So I loved her and pitied her, and she was dear to me just the same as my own daughter."

The girl was Mary Schwandt. Her family was dead, she had been raped and enslaved by the Indians, and she had witnessed the death of her friend Mary Anderson. Her world had collapsed, and she had retreated into her own mind and was barely capable of speaking. Snana—Maggie to the whites— took her in and restored her sanity.

"Maggie and her mother were both very kind to me," Mary Schwandt recalled, "and Maggie could not have treated me more tenderly if I had been her daughter. Often and often she preserved me from danger, and sometimes, I think, she saved my life."

Snana dressed her in Indian clothing and stayed by her side day and night. Whenever the white captives in the village were threatened by the warriors, Snana hid the child under a stack of buffalo robes and told anyone who inquired that the white girl had run away.

Other white prisoners were killed—one was shot in broad daylight and another had her throat cut in the dark of night—and several times drunken braves came for Mary. Snana risked her own life to protect the girl, telling a warrior that he would have to kill her first. Once some men forced their way into the tent before she had a chance to hide the child, and she sprang at them like a tiger, driving them out.

Mary Schwandt's will to survive and her hope for the future were revived by the young Indian woman she came to call Mother. "Wherever you are, Maggie," she wrote more than thirty years later, "I want you to know that the little captive

German girl you so often befriended and shielded from harm
loves you still for your kindness and care, and she prays God
to bless you and reward you in this life and that to come."

In New Ulm, fewer than twenty-five houses remained intact
in what had been, just a few days before, a prosperous, thriving
community. Supplies of food and ammunition were low, and an
outbreak of disease was feared with twelve hundred refugees
crowded into cellars and storehouses. Reinforcements had
arrived on Sunday, the day after the battle, some 150 volunteers from neighboring counties under the command of Capt.
E. St. Julien Cox. About fifty of the men had good Austrian
military rifles. The rest were armed with shotguns and hunting rifles. They brought only a limited stock of ammunition
and food and were soon just that many more mouths to
feed.

Colonel Flandrau held a meeting with the officers and
town leaders on Sunday afternoon to discuss their precarious
situation. If the Indians attacked again, the town would not be
able to hold out very long. He suggested that it was time to
consider evacuating everyone to the east. Flandrau warned
them, however, that if the Sioux returned while the people of
New Ulm were crossing the open prairie in a line of wagons,
they would be easy prey. They could all be massacred. However, the alternative was to stay in town and risk death there,
whether from Indians, starvation, or typhus. The men agreed.
They would take their chances on the prairie and head east for
the town of Mankato. Flandrau wrote out the order.

> August 24. The Provost Guard will enforce strict
> orders. Keep all women and children out of the
> streets and all men at their posts. The barricades
> will be maintained until further orders. When the
> teams are ready to be hitched up, they will be
> in the street and loaded and filed out. First the
> wounded. Second the children. The men will
> maintain their posts until the train is ready, and
> will then be formed in position and move. . . .
> The entire command will start for Mankato

tomorrow morning at daylight or as soon after as
necessary transportation can be obtained. No
baggage will be allowed to go. Sufficient bedding
for the wounded and small children will be
placed in the wagons with provisions, and all
men and women will march if teams sufficient
cannot be obtained for the women. All teams will
be harnessed during the night.

At sunup on Monday, all of the wagons, which had been
tipped over in the streets to serve as barricades, were righted
and lined up, ready to be loaded. Many of the refugees and
townspeople disregarded the order about baggage and showed
up with boxes, suitcases, chicken coops, crates, stoves, and
other bulky possessions. To make matters worse, New Ulm's
shopkeepers decided to open their stores and allow the settlers
to take whatever goods they could carry. That was better, they
said, than letting the stuff fall into the hands of the Indians.
When Flandrau and his men tried to enforce the ban, the result
was chaos. Soldiers climbed aboard the wagons and began tossing out the luggage and household goods people had tried to
stow away. Some fought back. Others abandoned their newly
acquired goods in the street.

"Thus the street soon resembled a county fair," wrote the
schoolteacher Rudolph Leonhart, "almost as if a whirlwind had
raced through and left all in the wildest disorder. Here lay half-
opened packages of knives and forks, there spoons of every
sort and size. An upturned coffee grinder and next to it combs,
brushes, shoe polish, currycombs, and many heterogeneous articles lay here and there. Even foodstuffs, which at the moment were not usable, were thrown aside with haughty disdain.
Here we saw cartons of starch, there packages of ground mus-
tard, pepper, and other spices. The only article which found
favor were shoes, and that morning many a family carried a
goodly supply of these with them."

While the officers tried to restore order and get the women
and children in the wagons, someone—it is not known
who—suggested to Flandrau that the men lay a trap for the Indians. Although Flandrau initially approved of the idea, he did not

reveal it until thirty-six years later, at which time he characterized it as "disgraceful" and "diabolical." The plan called for leaving a barrel of whiskey laced with strychnine in a conspicuous place where the Indians could not help noticing it.

They labeled the barrel POISON in English, German, Swedish, and every other language they knew—every language except, of course, Dakota. The barrel was rolled out into the street, but Flandrau had second thoughts. Suppose some settlers found it and ignored the warning label, thinking it was a joke? He felt ashamed of the whole idea, he said. It was a cowardly and immoral way to fight. That they even considered it, he wrote later, "proves how deeply the savage instinct is imbedded in human nature, whatever the color of the skin." Flandrau grabbed an ax and smashed the barrel, letting the poisoned whiskey leach into the ground.

By nine o'clock that Monday morning, the caravan of more than fifteen hundred people was ready to move out. The eighty wounded, along with the elderly and the very young, were placed on mattresses in the wagons, while the rest prepared to walk. Captain Cox was put in command of the escort, groups of mounted armed men stationed the length of the wagon train, and at the head and rear.

"A more heartrending procession was never witnessed in America," Colonel Flandrau wrote. "Here was the population of one of the most flourishing towns in the state abandoning their homes and property, starting on a journey of thirty odd miles, through hostile country, with a possibility of being massacred on the way, and no hope or prospect but the hospitality of strangers and ultimate beggary."

The column of 153 wagons, some pulled by horses, others by oxen, creaked its way over the prairie at the pace of a slow walk. Everyone feared an attack, but no Indians were sighted. At three o'clock in the afternoon, a rumor spread that a party of warriors was heading toward them. The wagons stopped and the armed men spread out in the knee-high grass with orders to hold their fire until they had a clear shot; there was no ammunition to waste. Someone shouted, "Indians!" as a group of figures on horseback appeared in the distance. The women and children in the New Ulm party flattened themselves in the grass, and the men drew a bead on the riders. Luckily, they held their fire as ordered. The approaching horsemen turned out to be their own advance guard. They had ridden ahead to scout the terrain and were returning with word that there were no Indians around.

The wagons continued to roll even after sundown. Flandrau's plan was to travel straight on to Mankato with no stops. When they reached the halfway point, he halted with the 150 men of the volunteer militia and established a rearguard camp, in case the Indians had been trailing the wagon train. The caravan reached Mankato safely later that night.

In the morning, Flandrau tried to persuade his guard to return to New Ulm to try to keep the Indians from occupying the town. Also, they could set up defensive positions as barriers to keep the Indians from roaming farther east. The volunteers vetoed both ideas. They had been away from their families for more than a week and were concerned about their safety. They had traveled to New Ulm from the neighboring counties to save the townspeople and the refugees, and they felt they had accomplished their mission. Now they wanted to go home. Flandrau said he understood. They rode on to Mankato, and Flandrau continued to St. Peter to report to Colonel Sibley about conditions in Indian country.

He found that Sibley was still in camp. The Indian uprising was already more than eight days old.

Colonel Sibley was fighting the war on paper, in bellicose and stirring messages to Governor Ramsey, requests for additional men and supplies, and forthright promises to depart at any moment for the relief of Fort Ridgely. On Sunday, August 24, he wrote to the governor about the desolation wrought by the uprising.

> There is no use to disguise the fact that unless we can now, and very effectually, crush this rising, the state is ruined, and some of its fairest portions will revert for years into the possession of these miserable wretches, who, among all devils in human shape, are among the most cruel and

ferocious. To appreciate this, one must see, as I have, the mutilated bodies of their victims. My heart is steeled against them, and if I have the means, and can catch them, I will sweep them with the [broom] of death.

Don't think there is exaggeration in the terrible pictures given by individuals. They fall short of the dreadful reality. This very moment the work of destruction is going on within ten miles, and yet we have not mounted force enough to spare for chasing and destroying the rascals. A family was fired upon last night within four miles of here, and a boy killed. You will hear of stirring events very soon. . . . Tomorrow we shall move toward the fort.

Two days later, still encamped at St. Peter, Sibley wrote again to Governor Ramsey.

We move this morning in the direction of the fort, and will reach there tomorrow. . . . Oh, that I had the means to pursue and crush these wretches, without being obliged at every moment to halt and calculate how far I can go, and how long I can get along without the veriest necessities. We are here without a solitary ration except of pork, and of that but little. . . .

The war of races has begun again, and renewed its old and simplest form, and one must go to the wall.

It was apparent, however, that Sibley was not quite ready to go to the wall to pursue and crush the wretches or to move with the utmost promptitude, even though he now had 1,340 troops, about 400 of whom were volunteer cavalry. It was true, as Sibley so frequently complained, that these were not well-trained troops, nor were they equipped with the latest in weaponry or supplied as an army prefers to be in the field. However, neither were the defenders of New Ulm and Fort Ridgely, and they fought with determination, improvised when necessary, and made do without what they could not get and still they bested superior numbers of Indians.

While these defenders of New Ulm and Fort Ridgely hung on, and while isolated settlements throughout the territory were being devastated, Sibley was complaining that his muskets were old, his food supply meager, and the roads full of ruts and potholes. He finally moved his troops out of St. Peter late on the twenty-sixth, but it was to take him an additional eight days to reach Fort Snelling, the distance a band of missionaries from the Upper Agency had walked in seven, the distance a dispatch rider—Private Sturgis—had covered in eighteen hours. Sibley was unperturbed, though. "We are gradually closing in upon the miserable hounds," he wrote to his wife.

Sibley's inordinate delays, his procrastination in pursuing the "war of races" that he claimed had begun, was not easily forgiven. Newspaper editors criticized him for his failure to move faster. One described him as "a snail who falls back on his authority and assumes dignity and refuses to march." Protests poured into the governor's office demanding the appointment of a new commander. "Send a young earnest man to take command," wrote Sheriff Roos, a defender of New Ulm. "He will do more with the present force than Colonel Sibley will ever do with 10 or 15,000 men. He is, in my mind, a coward and a rascal."

At daybreak on Wednesday, August 27, a sentinel on the roof of the officers' quarters at Fort Ridgely cried out an alarm.

"Horsemen coming on the St. Peter road, across the ravine!"

Weary men raced to their places on the barricades. Refugee families crammed into the stone barracks building. Lieutenant Sheehan prepared to meet the Sioux for the third time, asking himself how long their luck would hold, how long before Sibley arrived with reinforcements.

The riders advanced slowly, making no effort to conceal themselves. Tired eyes followed their progress, but it was not yet light enough to see them clearly. Indians, some claimed.

Whites, said others—the soldiers come to save us at last. The horsemen disappeared into the ravine northeast of the camp, and the thunder of approaching hoofbeats drummed into the expectant silence.

And suddenly, they came streaming out of the ravine, not more Indian attackers but 150 citizen–cavalrymen. Fort Ridgely's defenders welcomed them with whoops and cheers, screaming themselves hoarse while Col. Samuel McPhail marched his men onto the parade ground. The outfit, which had ridden all night from St. Peter, forty-five miles away, had been sent ahead by Colonel Sibley. He was expected to arrive with the main force the following day.

McPhail and his men were surprised by the condition of the fort. So many buildings had been reduced to charred timbers, and the walls of the houses that remained standing were so shot full of holes that they looked "like the lid of a pepper-box."

Much relieved, Lieutenant Sheehan turned over command of the garrison to Colonel McPhail, who set his men to work to strengthen the defenses. Entrenchments were dug around the perimeter and on a hill that overlooked the fort. The cannon were repositioned to sweep the surrounding terrain, and a reinforced guard was posted.

When Sibley arrived with the bulk of his troops, they bivouacked on the grounds, setting up a small village of neatly arrayed tents. He drilled the men every day, just as he had at St. Peter, and set the companies to practice skirmishing. "Dress parade, as usual," noted one of Sibley's men in his diary. Sibley gave no sign, however, that he was prepared to move out against the Indians, to take the war to the Sioux.

The men grew restless and bored, in the way of all soldiers in all wars, and they took to rambling through the woods to look for souvenirs, or for mischief. When a party of soldiers spotted a fresh grave and dug up the body of an Indian, they cut out one of its ribs for a memento and propped the corpse up against a tree to use for target practice. Clearly Sibley's men were ready to go and kill some Indians.

11

LAY ON YOUR BELLIES AND SHOOT!

"I wish it was within my power," Sarah Wakefield wrote, "to describe that procession as it moved over that prairie. I think it was five miles in length and one mile wide."

On Tuesday, August 26, the entire Lower Sioux nation was on the move, more than three thousand Indian residents of the Lower Agency—men, women, and children—together with almost 250 white and mixed-blood prisoners. Little Crow's scouts had told him that his old friend and hunting companion, Henry Sibley—the Long Trader—was coming after him with more soldiers than the scouts had been able to count. The soldiers were moving slowly, but the chief knew that eventually they would reach his village and all the other camps clustered around the ruins of the Lower Agency headquarters.

The Dakotas could no longer stay there; they could not fight such a large force. They would go upriver to the Upper Agency and join forces with the Sissetons and the Wahpetons of the Upper Sioux. Although the Upper Sioux warriors had not joined Little Crow in the numbers he had anticipated, maybe now they would all band together to fight Sibley's army.

The Sioux carried with them everything they owned—tents, clothing, food, horses, oxen, cattle, and whatever they had looted from the houses and stores of the white settlements. Most of the women walked, with their possessions strapped on their backs. Even old women carried packs that weighed up to eighty pounds. Larger items were piled into all manner of wheeled vehicle—fine buggies and stately carriages, oxcarts and bakers' carts, sulkies, peddlers' wagons, chaises, and even a few of the ungainly prairie schooners that had brought the whites west.

The men drove the wagons and carts or rode their ponies. They were "dressed in all kinds of finery," Mrs. Wakefield remembered. She continued:

> The more ridiculous, the better they were pleased. White women's bonnets were considered great ornaments but were worn by men altogether. White crepe shawls were wound around their black heads; gold watches tied around their ankles, the watches clattering as they rode. The squaws were dressed in silk short gowns, with earrings and breastpins taken from the whites. It made my heart ache to see all this. Still, I could not keep from smiling at times to see how ridiculously [these objects] were used by these poor savage creatures. . . .
>
> Everything was ornamented with green boughs: horses, men, women, and children. United States flags were numerous, and many times it looked like "Uncle Sam's" camp. The noise of that [wagon] train was deafening: mules braying, cows (poor animals) lowing, horses neighing, dogs barking and yelping as they were run over or trodden upon, children crying, kittens mewing, for a squaw always takes her pets with her; and then, to increase the confusion, were musical instruments played by not very scientific performers, accompanied with the Indians

singing the everlasting "Hi! Hi!" All these
noises, together with the racket made by Little
Crow's soldiers, who tried, but in vain, to keep
things in order, was like the confusion of Babel.

It all made a giant parade, a festival, a celebration, as
though the Sioux were marching to victory instead of creeping
away in retreat.

Sarah Wakefield and the other captives trotted barefoot
with the convoy through the tall, razor-sharp grass. Her feet
and legs were badly lacerated, and when they stopped for
lunch—some crackers and maple sugar—Chaska's mother
washed her wounds and wrapped them with roots. Chaska secured a seat for her and the children in a wagon, but she had
to drive for the rest of the day to pay for the privilege.

In midafternoon, Sarah guided her wagon past the spot
where she had been captured the week before. She averted her
eyes when she spied George Gleason's body beside the road.
It had been stripped of all clothing except a shirt and drawers,
and the skull had been crushed by a rock.

News raced along the five-mile length of the procession
that soldiers were coming their way. The group halted, and
everyone scurried for shelter in the grasses and thickets. Powder flasks were filled, weapons readied, and the men stood prepared to fight, but after a time, when no soldiers appeared, the
wagon train moved out again. More rumors spread. Now it was
said that the whites would be killed as soon as they all reached
Yellow Medicine. Sarah Wakefield wondered whether she had
endured the agonies of the past several days only to die back
where she had started, near her house at the Upper Agency.

The Indians and their captives camped beneath their wagons that night and resumed the journey the next morning. They
passed within sight of the Upper Agency's buildings, which, unlike those of the Lower Agency, had not been burned. From a
distance, the settlement looked disconcertingly normal, even
peaceful, as though the uprising had been only a bad dream.
They moved on a few miles past the agency and slept out in the
open again, and in the morning set up a more permanent camp.

* * *

Paul Mazakutemani had been a Christian Indian, a farmer Indian, for many years. Since the whites fled, he and several other farmer Indians had been staying at the Upper Agency. They occupied the houses—Dr. Wakefield's among them—to protect the properties from further depredations by the Sioux warriors. Paul was a cousin of Little Crow's; indeed, most of the Sioux staying at the agency were related to the chief in some way.

Shortly after the caravan of Lower Sioux arrived at Yellow Medicine, Little Crow was told of the presence of the farmer Indians and he went at once to Dr. Wakefield's house. He told Paul that the farmer Indians would have to leave.

"These houses are large and strong," Little Crow said, "and must be burned. If they are not burned, the soldiers will come and get into them. Therefore, get out, and if you do not, you will be burned with the buildings."

The farmer Indians agreed to go. They packed their belongings into wagons and left, heading north to join the camp of the Upper Sioux near the mission station. Little Crow's men wasted no time in applying torches to every structure still standing.

Paul Mazakutemani and the other Christian Indians rode through the camp being established by the newly arrived Lower Sioux. They were surprised to see so many white women and children, barefoot and bareheaded in the hot sun. The captives appeared to be tired and sickly. Gabriel Renville, one of the farmer Indians, expressed their shock and sadness. "If these prisoners were only men instead of women and children, it would be all right, but it is hard that this terrible suffering should be brought upon women and children." Paul Mazakutemani was also disturbed. "My heart was sad," he recalled, "and I became almost sick. I considered what I could do to save these captives."

Little Crow was becoming increasingly angry at the failure of the Upper Sioux Indians to support him in the war, and he did not hesitate to make his feelings known to his warriors. A band of several hundred of his braves rode into the main encampment of the Upper Sioux, swooping down on them with shouts and war chants, firing their rifles in the air. Confronting the Upper Sioux leaders, Little Crow's men demanded that the Upper Sioux join them and move to the new village the Lower Sioux were constructing near the agency. It was only a mile away, across the creek. It was the will of the Soldiers' Lodge, they said, and as such, it had to be obeyed. If not, the warriors intended to destroy the lodges of the Upper Sioux and punish them severely.

The Upper Sioux chiefs refused, accusing the newcomers of insolence and arrogance. The Lower Sioux had started the war, they charged, and had invaded their land without being invited. The Upper Sioux would prefer to fight Little Crow's band, even if they died on the spot, rather than move to the camp of the crazy people who followed him. The argument turned bitter. Shouts, wild gestures, and threats erupted on both sides before the Lower Sioux turned away and rode back to their camp. They vowed to return the next day with a larger force.

With that, the Dakota nation became divided. The Lower Sioux, who became known as the "hostiles," wanted to continue the war and kill their white captives. The Upper Sioux, the "friendlies," opposed the war and thought that the captives should be freed. At the time the Indians faced the gravest threat to their survival—the advance of Sibley's army—when their only hope, slim though it might be, was to unite their forces, the ill-conceived actions of Little Crow's warriors brought the two groups into conflict.

Yet the friendlies hoped to persuade the hostiles to accept their way of thinking. They wanted to reason with the Lower Sioux, to appeal to their sense of duty toward their brothers, the Upper Sioux. They decided to prepare a feast for the head chiefs of Little Crow's group, but before runners could be sent with invitations, a large band of Lower Sioux braves rode into camp, intending to force the friendlies out. They were surprised to be greeted politely and calmly by Iron Walker.

"We were about to send for you," he said. "Get down and eat with us and tell us why you come."

After a moment of confusion and indecision, and some disappointment as well, the Lower Sioux warriors dismounted and joined in feasting on a whole roasted calf. Toward the end of the meal, Iron Walker rose to speak.

"We think that you are fighting only the men, so you can let the women and children go back to their people. This is what we ask."

One of the hostiles was quick to answer him. He said that the Lower Sioux understood that the soldiers were so strong that they would drive the Indians out of the country. Nevertheless, the white captives must remain with them to suffer during the dark days that inevitably would follow. Other warriors spoke up in support of keeping the prisoners and continuing to wage war against the whites. One suggested that if the Indians could kill all the American settlers, they could then make friends with the British to the north.

Paul Mazakutemani of the Christian Indians spoke more eloquently.

> I want to speak to you now of what is in my own heart. Give me all these white captives. I will deliver them up to their friends. You Dakotas are numerous—you can afford to give these captives to me, and I will go with them to the white people. Then, if you want to fight, when you see the white soldiers coming to fight, fight with them, but don't fight with women and children. Or stop fighting.
>
> The Americans are a great people. They have much lead, powder, guns, and provisions. Stop fighting, and now gather up all the captives and give them to me. No one who fights with the white people ever becomes rich, or remains two days in one place, but is always fleeing and starving. You have said that whoever talks in this way shall not live—that you will kill him. Stop talking in that way, and if anyone says what is good, listen to it.

Little Crow's braves were not ready to listen to it; they were not prepared to abandon the war they had begun, not willing to give up their prisoners. One after another, they leapt to their feet to oppose Mazakutemani.

"If we are to die, these captives shall die with us," said one.

"The braves say they will not give up the captives," said another. "The Mdewakantons are men, and, therefore, as long as one of them lives, they will not stop pointing their guns at the Americans."

"Although we shall die bravely, and though the captives die in the way, I don't care. Don't mention the captives anymore."

Each time one of the hostiles spoke, the Lower Sioux warriors shouted their approval until, finally, they had said all there was to say. Repeating their threat to return and force the Upper Sioux to join them, Little Crow's men mounted their ponies and rode away.

The Upper Sioux leaders now realized that talk and reason would not work. They would have to take up arms to protect themselves—not from Sibley's army but from their brothers.

"Call together those who are Wahpetons and Sissetons," a chief ordered, "and we will prepare to defend ourselves."

Runners were sent to the outlying camps and villages of the Upper Sioux, and within a short time some three hundred braves arrived. More followed. They painted their faces and bodies for war and collected their weapons—rifles, bows and arrows, knives, pitchforks. A large tepee was erected in the center of the camp to house a hastily established Soldiers' Lodge, to direct the campaign against the Lower Sioux. The Upper Sioux vowed never to submit to Little Crow's demand that they join forces against the whites. If necessary, the Upper Sioux would drive Little Crow and his intruders off the land. Better to die in battle than become slaves, even of their own people.

The next morning, Friday, August 29, about three hundred Lower Sioux braves, painted and brandishing their weapons, advanced on the Upper Sioux encampment. As they drew near and saw the large Soldiers' Lodge in the center of the camp, they knew they would be in for a fight if they tried to destroy the tepees. Furious, they turned and rode away.

As soon as they left, some one hundred Upper Sioux braves, also painted and armed, followed them back toward Little Crow's village, intending to demand the return of the property that had been taken from Wahpeton and Sisseton mixed-bloods. They charged into Little Crow's camp, yelling and chanting, firing their guns in the air. They rode among the tepees, raising great clouds of dust, and surrounded the Soldiers' Lodge. Dismounting, they arrayed themselves in a circle around it. Paul Mazakutemani, the spokesman, told the Lower Sioux warriors why they had come. After a prolonged argument, the Lower Sioux agreed to allow them to go through the camp to gather the wagons and horses that belonged to the Upper Sioux mixed-bloods. Little Crow watched but did nothing to stop them, perhaps realizing that he could not fight his brothers and the whites, as well.

Paul Mazakutemani called on his men to form a line facing the Lower Sioux braves. He walked forward alone, stopping midway between the two forces. He spoke first to his own people, then turned to the others.

> The Mdewakantons have made war upon the white people and have now fled up here. I have asked them why they did this, but I do not yet understand it. I have asked them to do me a favor, but they have refused. Now I will ask them again in your hearing. Mdewakantons, why have you made war on the white people? The Americans have given us money, food, clothing, plows, powder, tobacco, guns, knives, and all things by which we might live well; and they have nourished us even like a father his children. Why then have you made war upon them?
>
> You did not tell me you were going to fight with the white people; and how then should I approve it? No, I will go over to the white people. If they wish it they may kill me. If they don't wish to kill me, I shall live. So, all of you who do not want to fight with the white people, come over to me. I have now one hundred men. We are going over to the white people. Deliver up to me the captives. And as many of you as don't wish to fight with the whites, gather yourselves together today and come to me.

First one, then another, and another of the Lower Sioux braves crossed over to the friendlies, and they brought a few captives with them. The total number was small, but the fact that any of Little Crow's warriors chose to join the Upper Sioux was painful for him to see. It was hard for him to accept that his people were no longer united.

When Little Crow replied to the friendlies, his voice was weary and resigned, like a man who had abandoned the hope not only of victory but of survival, as well. He told the Upper Sioux band that he had no intention of giving up the war, of abandoning the noble cause of reclaiming Dakota lands. That was their heritage, their birthright. Yet his tone and his words clearly suggested that the cause was already lost. He made no attempt to defend the actions of his followers, nor did he try to persuade the friendlies to join in his war. He seemed to have only one dream left, a very personal one—that he not be taken alive. The whites would put him on display, he said, showing him like an animal in a cage. He swore to all those within hearing—more than a thousand Indians from both sides—that no white hand would touch him so long as he lived.

With that vow, the council broke up, and the Upper Sioux returned to their camp. Although discouraged, Paul Mazakutemani remained determined to free the white prisoners, if Little Crow's people did not murder them first.

At Fort Ridgely, while the troops continued to drill and parade, and Sibley continued to fire off requests for additional men and supplies, the survivors of the uprising urged the colonel to send out parties to bury their dead. Many of the victims of the Sioux raids still lay where they had fallen nearly two weeks ago. Sibley consulted with his scouts, who assured him that the area around the Lower Agency appeared to be clear of Indians, and he agreed to send out a burial detail accompanied by a sizable military escort. The patrol was instructed to search for any settlers who might still be alive, and to try to determine where the Lower Sioux had gone.

On Sunday morning, August 31, thirty-four-year-old Capt. Hiram Grant was placed in command of the burial party, which consisted of twenty men, seventeen teamsters to drive the wagons, fifty horsemen of the Cullen Guards (a militia outfit under the command of Capt. Joseph Anderson), and a seventy-five-man company from the Sixth Minnesota Volunteers—more than 160 men in all. Captain Grant was ordered to supply each man with forty rounds of ammunition and to carry an extra three thousand rounds, plus two days' rations for each man. They were expected to return the next day.

Several civilians, whose relatives were among the missing, were permitted to accompany the burial detail, including the former Indian agent Joe Brown, who knew the Sioux and the territory better than anyone else in the group. Tom Galbraith also joined the expedition, hoping to find his family. Like Brown, he was unaware of their fate.

Nathan Myrick went along to bury the body of his brother Andrew. Warren DeCamp and Helen Carrothers's husband, both of whom had been away from home when the uprising began, were looking for their families. S. R. Henderson already knew that his wife and children were dead. Joe Coursolle, who enlisted in the Cullen Guards, was looking for his two daughters. He assured his wife that he would find them and bring them back.

At 9:30 A.M., the command left Fort Ridgely and headed toward the ferry crossing at the Lower Agency, fourteen miles away. It was a slow, sad march for the men, haunted by the horrors they had witnessed, by the scenes of destruction, and by growing fear that they, too, could end their days lying in a ditch like the corpses they were finding.

"A fatality seemed to hang over us from the moment we started," one of the Cullen Guards recalled. "Here along the roadside were burnt houses and bones of human beings. Among the grasses lay men in eternal sleep, mutilated and marred; to the limb of a tree hung a fair young boy; and when one of the men jumped from his horse and embracing the lifeless form of a man, cried out in the wild agony of grief, 'My God, my God! My brother!' we sickened at heart."

The detail buried fifty bodies, mostly men and boys, before they reached the ferry crossing and found thirty-three soldiers of Captain Marsh's command. Most of them were arrayed in two neat ranks where they had fallen in the ambush. All had been scalped and stripped of their uniforms. The men dug trenches at a furious pace to bury the remains as quickly as they could.

They rode back a few miles, in the direction of the fort, and made camp. In the morning, the command split up. Captain Grant and his men remained on the north side of the river while Captain Anderson and his Cullen Guards crossed to the south side to explore the ruins of the Lower Agency.

Anderson's men went about their grisly work in silence. Nathan Myrick worked alone to dig a grave for his brother, then he and several of the civilians returned to Fort Ridgely. The Cullen Guards left the agency and rode to Little Crow's deserted village. They wandered through the chief's house and the few lodges still standing, scrounging for souvenirs. "One man had an Indian drum," a soldier recalled, "another a flag, others feathers, and a small molasses keg was proudly tied to the pommel of a saddle, to tell the story in after years that Little Crow had been bearded in his lair."

Captain Grant and his detail on the north side of the river found themselves burying entire families. Before the morning was half over, they had dug graves for thirty bodies. A mile from the ruins of Helen Carrothers's home, her husband found a dead boy, and Henderson discovered his wife and daughter, their bodies half-charred by fire.

At about ten o'clock, Grant thought he saw an Indian moving through the grass several hundred yards away. He sent twenty men forward with orders to kill—or to rescue, if the person turned out to be white. It was Justina Krieger, who had wandered nearly two weeks without food, a bullet wound in her back and a knife wound in her stomach. She was weak and delirious, with no idea which way to turn and no strength to go anywhere. She had lain in the grass for two days, hoping that the Indians would come back and end her misery.

"Here I felt sure I must die," she recalled, "and that I should never leave this place alive. The cold sweat was on my forehead. With great effort I raised up to take one more look around me, and, to my surprise, I saw two persons with guns, but could not tell whether they were white men or Indians. I rejoiced, however, because I thought they would put an end to my sufferings. But as they came near, I saw the bayonets, and knew that they were white soldiers, and made signs for them to come to me."

The soldiers washed her face with water from a canteen, wrapped her in a blanket, and placed her in a wagon, where Dr. Daniels treated her wounds.

Captain Grant moved the patrol out, and they continued west, interring fifty more bodies before sunset. They turned east again to head home—that was the plan, and they had carried only two days' rations—but they had covered twenty-two miles and were too far from Fort Ridgely to get back that night. They were, however, only six miles from the nearest site with water, a ravine called Birch Coulee, just south of Beaver Creek.

On the day the burial party left Fort Ridgely, Little Crow held a council with some two dozen members of the Lower Sioux Soldiers' Lodge. They walked a little distance away from their camp, out on the prairie, and settled down in a circle around a kettle hung over an open fire. Dog stew boiled in the kettle. Someone hung an American flag on a pole nearby. One after another, each man rose and had his say, ladled out a portion of the stew, and sat down to eat while the next man spoke.

When each brave had spoken and eaten, a decision was reached. Little Crow would leave on September 2, two days hence, with a war party of 110 men. He would lead them northeast toward the towns of Hutchinson and Forest City, a distance of seventy miles. That would put them in position to prevent reinforcements from reaching Fort Ridgely and to attack settlements that so far had gone untouched. A group of more than two hundred braves, led by Big Eagle, Mankato, and Gray Bird, would follow the river on the south side as far as New Ulm, which their scouts reported was now deserted. There would be much loot to be had, so a goodly number of Indian women with wagons would accompany the braves.

The men broke camp, and by the early evening of the second, Big Eagle's party had reached Little Crow's old village near the Lower Agency. From the bluff on which Little Crow's house sat, the Indians looked across the river to the bluff that formed the valley's north rim. There, in the fading daylight, they saw a column of men and wagons moving slowly to the southeast. It was Capt. Hiram Grant with about seventy-five men. Big Eagle sent several scouts across the river to follow the whites. They returned after sundown to report that the soldiers had set up camp near the head of Birch Coulee.

Grant's campsite was directly across the river from the Lower Agency. He had chosen a spot near water to drink and trees to use as firewood. The site was flat and open and seemed a comfortable place to spend the night, but it could not have been a worse place to defend. It was within easy gunshot range of a wooded ravine on one side, and a rise in the prairie of four to five feet on the other side. Anyone could advance, sight unseen even in daylight, on both sides of the camp.

Around sundown, Captain Anderson and his men of the Cullen Guards arrived at Birch Coulee. Joe Brown, the former Indian agent, who, it was said, could smell an Indian a mile away, was with them. They had ventured several miles farther than Grant's outfit that day and had seen no sign of the Sioux. Brown said it looked to him as if the Lower Sioux had gone north about four days ago. Grant had the men place the wagons end to end to form a semicircle around the tents and tie ropes between the wagons to tether the horses.

If Brown, who had more experience with Indians than either Grant or Anderson, objected to the Birch Coulee campsite as being vulnerable to attack, there is no record of it. They apparently believed they were in no danger from the Indians. "From all reports," Captain Grant wrote later, "I did not think there were any Indians within twenty miles of us; however, I detached thirty men besides noncommissioned officers and an officer of the guard, and established ten picket posts at equal distances around the camp, with three men at each post."

Not everyone agreed that there was no danger from the Indians. Joe Coursolle had seen fresh footprints in the sand and little piles of newly shaved kinnikinnick bark, which the Indians mixed with tobacco leaves and smoked. Coursolle told his sergeant and asked that he inform Captain Grant. The sergeant went to Joe Brown instead, who insisted that Coursolle was mistaken.

"Don't worry about Indians," Brown told him. "There are none within a hundred miles. You're just as safe as if you were home in your own bed."

"We were dog tired," Coursolle recalled, "but in spite of

Brown's assurance, many of us, mostly those with Sioux blood, dug shallow holes to lie in."

On the far side of the river, the three Sioux chiefs—Big Eagle, Mankato, and Gray Bird—planned their attack with care. Their scouts had returned before the arrival of Captain Anderson and the Cullen Guards, so the chiefs believed they were dealing with no more than seventy-five soldiers. They planned to surround the camp during the night with their two hundred warriors and attack at daybreak. Most of the braves were armed with double-barreled shotguns loaded with standard buckshot as well as with the large bullets they called "traders' balls."

"After dark we started," Big Eagle said, "crossed the river and valley, went up the bluffs and on the prairie, and soon we saw the white tents and the wagons of the camp. We had no difficulty in surrounding the camp. The pickets were only a little way from it. I led my men up from the west through the grass and took up a position two hundred yards from the camp, behind a small knoll or elevation."

One group of warriors passed their guns to others to hold. Armed with bows and arrows, they began crawling toward the ten picket posts. Their mission was to kill the guards silently. Then the rest of the war party would close in from all sides and slaughter the whites while they slept. It should all be over in a matter of minutes.

At four o'clock in the morning, just before daylight, Pvt. Bill Hart scanned the area around his picket post. He gazed out to the prairie ahead of him and turned back to glance at the ring of wagons. He saw something move, perhaps a dog or a wolf, but he couldn't be sure. He decided not to take any chances, and so, risking a reprimand for waking the camp unnecessarily, he fired his rifle. An Indian carrying a bow and arrow leapt to his feet, then another and still more. Other soldiers fired, some because they saw the Indians, some out of fear.

The pickets raced for the cover of the wagons, shooting blindly as they stumbled over the hard ground. The Sioux rose up with bone-chilling war whoops and poured a hail of shot into the camp. From their tents and their berths beneath the wagons, men roused themselves, grabbed their weapons, and waited for a moment, still groggy with sleep. Captain Anderson shouted a command at the Cullen Guards.

"Lay on your bellies and shoot, goddamn you!"

Captain Grant's men responded automatically, as they had been drilled, and they started to form a line to return fire, but many fell dead from Indian gunfire before they could raise their rifles. Grant yelled at them to break right and left, take cover behind the wagons, and commence firing. Wounded soldiers screamed in pain; others shouted to give themselves courage. Indians whooped and chanted. Horses fell in crumpled heaps and men threw themselves on the ground behind them.

Lieutenant Gilham rallied thirty men and they ran through the hail of gunfire to take up positions on the east side of the camp. Lieutenant Baldwin led his men to the northeast, while Captain Grant deployed soldiers to the northwest and west. Captain Anderson led the Cullen Guards to the south side. The officers ordered the wagons tipped over to form barricades. A half dozen men ran from one wagon to the next, heaving each one over with a crash.

Justina Krieger, whom the soldiers had rescued after she had wandered outdoors for two weeks, was lying in one of the wagons. A soldier remembered her just in time, and he cautioned the others to leave that wagon alone. So one wagon remained upright throughout the fighting, its white canvas top gleaming in the early light. Justina huddled inside, too petrified to move. Bullets shattered the wooden frame and ripped the canvas all around her.

For an hour, Big Eagle's Sioux braves tried to overrun the Birch Coulee camp, but the defending fire was so heavy that they were driven back. They continued to pump bullets into the camp without letup, however, from hiding places in the woods, the ravine, and the bluff. By the time the sun came up, the cost of the attack to the whites was clear: twenty-two soldiers dead, sixty seriously wounded, many more slightly wounded. All of the eighty-seven horses tied to the ropes between the wagons were lost. The soldiers were surrounded. They had no transportation back to Fort Ridgely, no way even to send a message. The Indians could pick them off at their leisure.

"Never for an instant did the firing on us cease," a soldier wrote later. "Suddenly someone would drop his musket and roll over to die. Individual instances of bravery were many and some few of cowardice. A fine-looking man near me was unnerved; he did not shoot once, but kept crying out, 'Oh my God, my God!' George Turnbull, first lieutenant, pulled a revolver on him, cocked it, and said if he did not stop, he would blow his brains out. He stopped."

Captain Grant ordered men out to dig holes and throw up breastworks, using saddles, rocks, the carcasses of the horses, and even the bodies of their comrades to form barricades. The command had one pick, three shovels, and a couple of axes to do the job, but with those and knives, bayonets, tin pans, and sharpened sticks, the men burrowed into the tough prairie sod and built mounds of earth to hide behind. One company scooped out a trench two hundred feet long and settled in it to return the continuing fire of the Indians.

A sniper perched in a tree cut down several soldiers before Joe Coursolle spotted him. Waiting until the next time he saw the rifle barrel poke through the leaves, Joe fired, and the body of an Indian crashed down through the branches. Suddenly, a voice near the tree line addressed him in Dakota.

"Hear me, Hinhankaga," someone said, using Coursolle's Indian name. "We saw you shoot. You killed the son of Chief Traveling Hail. Now we will kill your little girls."

For an instant, Coursolle remembered, he was elated to learn that his children were still alive, but then he was overcome by fear. He had no time to dwell on the thought that he might have condemned them to death, however, because the Indians concentrated their fire on his position. Bullets thudded into the spokes of the wagon wheels he was hiding behind. The deadly splinters shattered the face of the man beside him. Another man nearby died instantly from a bullet in the head, but Coursolle remained unhurt.

The troops were down to the last of their cartridges. Captain Grant ordered a party to retrieve the reserve ammunition from the wagons. One man in the detail took a bullet through the leg, but none of the others was hit. They found the heavy ammo boxes and in a crouch dragged them back behind the barricades. Each soldier gathered enough rounds for himself and shoved the box on to the next man. In time, the cartridge boxes made their way through the entire command.

"Then we discovered a terrible mistake," Joe Coursolle recalled. "All the bullets were for larger bore rifles."

Fort Ridgely's ordnance officer had mistakenly loaded .62-caliber shot for their .58-caliber rifles. Grant ordered them to improvise, to work with their knives whittling down the balls until they fit. He warned them not to fire until they were certain of a clear shot. There was no ammunition to waste.

The day grew hotter and smoke from the battle hovered over the campsite. Their thirst became intense, especially for the wounded. They had one bucket of water left and had no way to reach the creek safely to get more. Grant passed the bucket from man to man, with orders to take no more than one swallow. The only food was a head of cabbage. For some reason, the wagon containing the remaining provisions had been left outside the defensive perimeter. Each man was given a tiny piece of cabbage leaf.

The Sioux, by contrast, were well provisioned and supplied. "We had an easy time of it," Big Eagle said. "We could crawl through the grass into the coulee and get water when we wanted it, and after a few hours our women crossed the river and came up near the bluff and cooked for us, and we could go back and eat and then return to the fight." The Indians feasted on roast corn and boiled beef and stretched out in the tall grass for a nap. They had more than enough men to spare, having sustained fewer than a half dozen casualties, only two of whom had been killed.

In early afternoon, the soldiers heard an explosion off to the east that sounded like cannon. Captain Grant wondered whether the Indians had brought up a howitzer. They heard the noise again, deep and booming, audible over the lighter popping sounds of the rifles and shotguns. Maybe it was a relief column from Fort Ridgely. The men waited to hear whether the cannon came closer, but it did not, and after a time they thought they had only imagined it. After all, the command at Fort Ridgely had no way of knowing that they were under siege at Birch Coulee. There could be no relief column coming to their aid.

* * *

In their desperation, the men at Birch Coulee had reached the wrong conclusion. Relief was indeed on the way, but it was taking its time getting there. Because of the contours of the valley and the direction of the prevailing winds, the sounds of battle from Birch Coulee had carried the fifteen or so miles to Fort Ridgely. The noises were muffled, but when a few soldiers at the post put their ears to the ground, they said that there could be no mistaking the sounds. Somewhere upriver, a lot of shooting was going on and that could mean only one thing: Captain Grant's command was in trouble. The battle was estimated to be no more than eight miles away.

A detachment was sent out, but it returned within the hour, reporting that the sounds had stopped soon after they left the fort. Those troops believed that the gunfire had been nothing more than a skirmish that apparently had ended. At Fort Ridgely men claimed they could still hear it, and the firing kept up throughout the morning. Small knots of soldiers, at first puzzled and then increasingly angry, hiked out of camp and up into the hills. They knelt down to listen, their ears to the dirt, and nodded to one another. Something was going on out there. Grant and his men might be dying. Why didn't Sibley send them out to find what the trouble was?

Sibley now commanded a force of almost fifteen hundred men. Their restlessness and eagerness to do battle were obvious. Criticism of Sibley spread quickly through the ranks, some of it highly insubordinate. Fort Ridgely veterans finally prevailed on Sibley and two of his senior officers—Cols. William Crook and Sam McPhail—to ride out to a hilltop and listen for themselves. Sibley agreed that the noise sounded like gunfire, but if it was, then why hadn't the detachment he sent out earlier heard it once they got away from the post? McPhail suggested that because the men had ridden down the ravine, the surrounding bluffs had cut off the sound. Out there on the prairie, however, there could no longer be any doubt.

Sibley ordered Colonel McPhail to take an expedition upriver with 240 men and two howitzers. It was noon by the time the men were mustered and the equipment packed. Their progress across the prairie was slow. Most of the troops were infantry, and McPhail was reluctant to send his fifty cavalry too far ahead. The closer they got to the Lower Agency, the louder the sounds of battle became.

Three miles from Birch Coulee, McPhail and his men saw some Indians. He halted the column and retreated to a spot where he could set up a defensive position. He believed he was surrounded by a great many warriors, and he was not sure exactly where Grant's command was. He sent Lieutenant Sheehan back to the fort for reinforcements. Twice, McPhail ordered the howitzers fired at the Indians; these were the deep, booming sounds heard by the besieged soldiers at Birch Coulee.

McPhail's outfit was actually surrounded by fewer than fifty braves. When Mankato's scouts reported McPhail's approach, the chief withdrew men from the Birch Coulee fight and deployed them over a wide area to taunt McPhail's soldiers by shouting and firing their rifles in the air. According to Big Eagle, the Indians "all yelled and made such a noise that the whites must have thought there were a great many more, and they stopped on the prairie and began fighting. They had a cannon and used it, but it did no harm."

Mankato followed the soldiers as they retreated, and he left about thirty warriors to watch them. He sent the rest back to Birch Coulee. The Indians were "laughing when they came back at the way they had deceived the white man."

When Sibley learned about the situation, he assembled more than one thousand troops and led them out of Fort Ridgely, intending to rescue both McPhail and Grant. It was after midnight when they reached McPhail's position. There would be no relief for the men at Birch Coulee that night.

During the night, Capt. Hiram Grant ordered that the weapons be collected from the dead and severely wounded, to be distributed to those troops still fit to fight. Each man on the firing line now had two guns but not much ammunition. At sunrise, an Indian waving a white flag rode slowly toward the ring of wagons. He stopped and shouted something in the Dakota language. Grant summoned his interpreter, Sgt. Jim Auge, a mixed-blood from Canada, and asked him what the warrior had said.

"We are as many as the leaves on trees," translated Auge.

"Soon we come and kill every soldier. We do not want to kill our brothers. All in camp who have Dakota blood come out. We will not harm you."

When they heard this, Joe Coursolle and eight other mixed-bloods left their places on the line and gathered around Auge. Grant told them they were free to go if they wished. Each man must make his own decision. Sergeant Auge hesitated only a moment and spoke for them all.

"We are going to stay with you, Captain."

Grant nodded. He told Auge to inform the Indian messenger that "they did not have Indians enough to take our camp; that we were still two hundred men; that each had two rifles loaded, and all the Indians that wanted to die should come at once; that we defied them."

Auge embellished the captain's words in his translation.

"Fah!" he yelled at the Sioux warrior. "Cowards! You do not dare. Every man in camp has five guns to shoot. You fight like Chippewas! Go back and stay with the squaws."

Then he spat, delivering the ultimate insult.

Grant told Auge to warn the Indian to get out of the way fast. His men would not respect a flag of truce for such an offer as he had made. As the brave wheeled around and trotted back to the Indian line, Grant gave the order to fire. The horse went down, but the man made it back safely.

The action enraged the Sioux. They began to close in on the soldiers, circling nearer to the wagons, keeping up a steady rate of fire. Grant and his officers ordered his men to hold their fire and to keep low until the braves came closer, then to fire one rifle after another. The captain roamed among the men, trying to bolster their morale, assuring them that the Indians could not take their position. Everyone was tense, expecting a massed charge. Suddenly, a lone Indian ran out of the woods.

Grant asked Sergeant Auge what the man was shouting. The interpreter said that he was telling the Indians that "three miles of white men" were on the way. The Sioux broke off the attack and vanished. The men who had survived the thirty-one-hour siege of Birch Coulee would be spared.

"From behind and between the shattered wagons and bloated carcasses crawled pallid, blood-streaked men," wrote a

Minnesota historian. "Some croaked feeble cheers when the relief party arrived. Most of them were coated with a thick crust of caked dust. Many found they could not stand upright and sank to the ground before they had emerged. Some faced away and vomited uncontrollably. Others staggered, fell, and needed help to crawl to the buckets of water the rescuers had brought from the ravine."

Sibley and his troops were appalled at what they found. The stench from eighty-seven dead horses, the carcasses bursting open, hung over the camp like a miasma. Dazed men stared with vacant eyes. The parched and starving wounded seemed more dead than alive, and twenty-two bodies, black from the sun, lay propped against the barricades, along with piles of dirt and saddles and rocks. "The scene was sickening," Sibley wrote to his wife. The defenders had fewer than five rounds of ammunition per man.

Shortly after Sibley's relief column arrived, Dr. Daniels remembered Justina Krieger, who had been left in the only upright wagon—and forgotten—throughout the siege. The wagon itself was a wreck, its wooden sides shattered and reduced to splinters. The white canvas cover was riddled with more than two hundred bullet holes. Some of the spokes in the wheels had been shot off. Daniels and an officer peered inside and were astonished to find her alive. She had been grazed by five bullets. A tin cup from which she had been sipping water had been shot out of her hand, but she had survived.

The troops buried the dead, placed the wounded in wagons, and set out for home, reaching Fort Ridgely around midnight.

Henry Sibley's first foray into Indian country had been a costly failure and a personal embarrassment. Already under attack for moving too slowly, he now faced ridicule for sending out an understrength force—Grant's—and for taking too long to relieve it. People were already asking why it had taken him a day and a half, from the time gunfire was heard at Fort Ridgely, to travel a distance that could easily have been covered in five hours. And why had it taken him six hours that morning to cover the few miles from McPhail's camp to Birch Coulee?

Sibley wrote a detailed report for the adjutant general in

St. Paul, noting his progress against determined Indian resistance. He also offered his resignation.

> I have learned, with pain, that much dissatisfaction exists below in consequence of the unavoidable delays in fitting the expedition for field service. I am therefore anxious to relieve your administration of any embarrassment connected with the affair. I hereby place my commission at your disposal, and shall be glad to turn over my command to some person to be selected by the commander-in-chief, in whose military training and experience the people of the state will perhaps feel more confidence.

The adjutant general decided not to relieve Sibley of his command. There was no one else available with his knowledge of the Sioux. To his wife, Sibley complained about his armchair critics. "Let them come and fight these Indians themselves," he wrote, "and they will [have] something to do besides grumbling."

Sibley tried to put the fiasco at Birch Coulee behind him and to disassociate himself from all responsibility for it. He claimed that it was not a military operation at all but, rather, a civilian rescue mission led by the former Indian agent Joe Brown.

Captain Grant became aware of this bit of subterfuge when he submitted to Sibley his own report on the Birch Coulee siege.

"It was handed back to me," Grant recalled, "and I was coolly informed that I should make my report to 'Major' Joseph R. Brown, who was in command of the expedition. This was the first I had heard of it. We had been gone for four days, two of which we had been engaged in deadly fight; no order had been given me by [honorary] Major Brown, not an intimation that he considered himself in command. To say that I was angry, when told to make my report to him, would only express half what I felt. I then and there destroyed my report and never made another."

Grant, unlike Sibley, was prepared to accept responsibility. Indeed, he insisted on it. "If any blame rests on anyone,"

Grant added, "for selection of camps, or in carrying out any of
the details of the expedition, it rests upon me. All officers,
soldiers, and citizens obeyed my orders. I had the full charge."

Sibley continued to insist in his reports and press dis-
patches that the battle of Birch Coulee involved an attack on
"J. R. Brown's party," which had no connection with his command. He also maintained that he had told Brown to "avoid
any pass or defile where they might be waylaid or ambushed."

Sibley's attempt at deception was refuted by many of his
officers and men, in addition to Captain Grant. Lieutenant
Sheehan recalled that he had overheard Sibley telling his second in command to place Grant in charge. Captain Anderson
of the Cullen Guards, as well as Colonel McPhail, characterized the men at Birch Coulee as being under Grant's command. No participant in that action, military or civilian,
including Joe Brown, ever suggested that anyone other than
Grant had been in charge of the expedition.

As far as Sibley was concerned, however, the issue was
closed. Brown was responsible and that was that. He had more
important matters to deal with—how to rescue the white captives and how to defeat his old friend Little Crow. After Birch
Coulee, however, winning a decisive military victory seemed
all the more difficult. The war could drag on for months in a
bloody series of Birch Coulees. Sibley knew that the Sioux
were fierce fighters. They could live off the land, harassing and
sniping at even the largest military force. He would need more
troops, more supplies, more time.

There was an alternative. If he could not defeat Little
Crow on the field of battle, Sibley thought, perhaps he could
negotiate a settlement with him. The war might end in a council, with the two of them smoking a pipe together. Sibley wrote
a note to Little Crow and left it on a split stake stuck in the
ground at Birch Coulee.

"If Little Crow has any proposition to make," Sibley
wrote, "let him send a half-breed to me, and he shall be protected in and out of camp."

Satisfied, Sibley settled back in at Fort Ridgely to wait for
additional troops and for a reply from Little Crow.

12

WE MUST ALL DIE IN BATTLE

Sibley was not alone in wondering whether the war could be settled. Little Crow pondered the same point as he rode in a wagon at the head of his force of 110 warriors, far to the northeast of the Minnesota River, in an attempt to cut off any reinforcements that might be trying to reach Sibley. At the reins was a thirty-seven-year-old mixed-blood, Antoine J. Campbell, called Joe, who, with his family, had been captured by the Sioux sometime before the uprising. Little Crow liked Joe Campbell. The man had special talents the chief lacked— he could read and write in English—and Little Crow had chosen him to be his driver and personal secretary. Joe's job was to record in a book Little Crow's thoughts and actions during the war.

Little Crow talked to Campbell about how badly the campaign was going for the Indians. It seemed to Joe that the chief was really talking aloud to himself, using Campbell as a mirror to reflect his own confused thoughts and to help him reach a decision about what to do next. Little Crow rambled on about their quick victory over the soldiers at the ferry crossing the day the uprising began. He knew, however, that the Indians had been successful there only because they had been able to surprise the whites.

They had not been able to count on surprise at Fort Ridgely and New Ulm, and they had lost, even with superior numbers. Little Crow realized why they had failed, he told Campbell. It was because of the shortsightedness of the younger warriors, the ones who preferred robbery, rape, murder, and the easy pickings that came from attacks on isolated settlements. That was more attractive to them than planning, organizing, and uniting with their brothers for a concerted attack on the forts. Little Crow had never been able to persuade enough braves to join him, to become an army, a force that could fight like the whites.

Little Crow also blamed the Upper Sioux. Only a few of the Wahpeton and Sisseton warriors had joined the uprising, not the hundreds he needed to win. Their attitude was to wait while the Lower Sioux took all the risk to prove that the soldiers and settlers could be beaten. Without the Upper Sioux, Little Crow could not defeat the whites. And now that the Upper Sioux knew about his failures at New Ulm and Fort Ridgely, and with Sibley amassing so many soldiers, the Upper Sioux had turned against him, threatening his people and demanding that the white prisoners be set free. Little Crow could not even count on his own people anymore.

Sibley's presence at Fort Ridgely had forced the Lower Sioux to leave their portion of the reservation. Little Crow understood that if the war continued, he would have to lead his people still farther from their homeland, perhaps out of Minnesota altogether.

As he talked on and on to Joe Campbell, it became clear that he had lost all hope of a military victory. He thought that perhaps he and his old friend Sibley could sit down and negotiate a treaty. Maybe the war could end in a council and they could smoke a pipe together.

That night, after the Indians made camp, Little Crow dictated a note. He instructed Campbell to make two copies in English, one for Colonel Sibley and one for Governor Ramsey.

The letter asked for a truce, and for a council to discuss the terms of a peace settlement. When Campbell finished putting Little Crow's thoughts into English, the chief asked him to explain it to the warriors. It was only right that they be told—that was the Sioux way.

But when the men heard Little Crow's message, they hooted and jeered. They would not be a party to surrender, they told him. They would never give in to the whites, and they vowed to fight to the death. Threats were uttered against Little Crow, in case he had any idea of pursuing the matter over their objections. Sadly, Little Crow told Campbell to tear up the notes.

In the morning, still scornful of what they considered to be an act of cowardice on Little Crow's part, seventy-five of the men refused to follow him. The chief pleaded with them, stressing the importance of his plan to sweep north and east of the fort to keep reinforcements and provisions from reaching it. He hoped that when Sibley learned that a large party of Sioux was threatening from that direction, he would be reluctant to leave the fort and venture into Indian territory.

The plan made sense strategically, but the braves saw it as fighting the white man's way. They wanted to attack the towns of Forest City and Hutchinson. Those settlements were closer and offered the prospect of swift victories, loot, and women. Let Little Crow fight the soldiers—the settlers were easier prey. The seventy-five warriors, led by old Walker Among Sacred Stones, moved out, leaving Little Crow and his three dozen men behind.

Little Crow was devastated. This was another blow to his prestige and authority. He had been challenged again by the younger warriors and he had lost. When men no longer follow a chief, he is no longer a chief, and therefore Little Crow refused to lead even the few who remained loyal to him. Turning over command to White Spider, his thirty-one-year-old half brother, Little Crow accompanied the party as an ordinary brave.

The group headed northeast, traveling parallel to the road taken by the larger, dissident group. The two bands camped a few miles apart that evening, not far from the home of Robinson Jones, where a taunt from one Indian to another about stealing some eggs had led to Jones's death and precipitated a war.

Camped nearby were fifty-five recruits of the Tenth Minnesota, under the command of Capt. Richard Strout. An infantry outfit, they were on their way to Forest City to protect the settlements. Neither the soldiers nor the Indians knew of the presence of the other. Indeed, Strout was so certain he was safe that he had not even posted guards. At three o'clock in the morning, he was awakened by a messenger from Forest City bearing the news that Indians had been spotted in the area the day before. Strout alerted his troops.

The regiment's ammunition, minié balls, did not fit their Belgian-made muskets. This had been only a minor annoyance, one they expected to correct as soon as they reached Forest City. Suddenly, it had become a matter of life or death. The men set to work whittling the balls down until they fit their guns, and by daybreak they were ready to break camp.

Although they moved out as rapidly as they could on foot, they were not fast enough. Scouts from Little Crow's party spotted them. White Spider deployed his men in a line across their path, and soon after sunrise Strout's scouts saw them. The captain ordered his untrained and untested men forward in a skirmish line. The Indians fired. The recruits held their ground and even began to advance. Walker Among Sacred Stones quickly sized up the situation and had his braves attack the soldiers from the rear.

Strout sent a detail to try to counter the new threat, and it held the larger Indian force in check until the two Sioux bands merged, surrounding the soldiers' position. The captain realized that his only option was to fight his way out of the trap. Ordering his men to fix bayonets, he charged White Spider's line. The troops broke through, leaving behind their casualties and most of their supplies. For several hours, they were pursued by Indians approaching from the rear and the flanks. Six soldiers were killed and twenty-three wounded, but the survivors eventually reached the town of Hutchinson, eight miles away.

After routing Strout's outfit, the two rival Indian bands

agreed to coordinate their raids. They took a few hours to rest and regroup, then half of the men headed north on a night march covering the twenty miles to Forest City. The rest, including Little Crow, camped overnight, then left for Hutchinson, timing their arrival for between eight and nine o'clock in the morning, when the men of the town were expected to be working in the fields.

At three o'clock on Thursday morning, September 4, some twenty Sioux warriors charged into Forest City, whooping and firing their guns. They were the advance party, intending to spread alarm and chaos before riding out of town. The main force of Walker Among Sacred Stones's men would attack a few minutes later, catching the townspeople milling about in confusion. It was a good plan, but it did not work. The Indians triggered no panic because the residents of Forest City expected them. Alerted the previous day to the presence of Indians nearby, the settlers had, in less than twenty-four hours, erected a stockade more than ten feet tall and approximately one hundred feet square. They built it of stout logs with loopholes chopped out for their guns.

When the first Indian band rode into town, almost everyone from Forest City and the surrounding countryside was crammed inside the stockade, more than two hundred settlers plus forty armed men. As soon as Walker Among Sacred Stones saw it, he decided to withdraw. He knew that his force was too small to take a walled-in fortress.

The Indians probed the area around the Forest City settlement, burned a few farmhouses, took about sixty horses, and attacked an isolated cabin, killing a man and capturing his wife. When her infant son started to cry, a warrior grabbed the child by the feet, raised him overhead, and smashed the boy's skull against a rock.

Little Crow's group, led by White Spider, was even less successful at Hutchinson. There, too, they found the whites taking refuge behind the sturdy log walls of a hastily built stockade. The town was defended by more than one hundred armed men, including the remnants of Captain Strout's command. Being careful to stay out of rifle range, the Indians managed to loot and burn some houses and steal a few wagons, horses, and oxen.

All the Indians returned to camp near the Upper Agency the next day. Little Crow, with a few of his followers, took a little longer because he chose to go first to his old home at the Lower Agency. On the long return trip, he wondered aloud to Joe Campbell whether he could revive the idea of a negotiated settlement with the soldiers. Now that the Sioux had failed to take Forest City and Hutchinson, the braves might be more receptive to the idea. He resolved to raise the issue again when they reached camp.

To Minnesota's Governor Ramsey, it looked as though his entire state was aflame and under siege from border to border and beyond. Thousands of people had fled their homes from the Iowa boundary to more than a hundred miles north of the Sioux reservation. Reports inundated the governor's office daily of fresh disasters and towns under attack. The Indians appeared to be everywhere—Birch Coulee, Forest City, Hutchinson.

And then Fort Abercrombie was under siege in the far northwest corner of the state, some 165 miles from the Lower Agency. A force of 150 warriors, apparently Wahpetons and Sissetons, had made the assault. The fort held out, but the raids caused hundreds more settlers in Minnesota and the neighboring Dakota Territory to flee. The town of Sioux Falls was abandoned by its residents and burned by the marauding Indians. It was a disaster, and the only armed force Ramsey had to combat it was Sibley's. But Sibley, whose force was concentrated at Fort Ridgely, was reluctant to venture beyond it without additional troops and supplies.

Ramsey appealed to Washington for assistance and to the governors of adjoining states. On September 6, he wrote a long letter to President Lincoln and the heads of the federal departments, requesting three thousand of the best rifles and a large quantity of ammunition. He directed the state adjutant general, Oscar Malmros, to contact Wisconsin's governor with a plea for help.

"The Indian war assumes daily greater proportions," Malmros wrote. "Our people are massacred because we have not a sufficient number of muskets to arm our troops. Can you send us some—say 1000—muskets by express? The emergency is great."

Wisconsin's governor telegraphed the message to Secretary of War Stanton, adding, "I have no arms to send him. What shall I reply?"

Knowing that his letter to the President would take several days to reach Washington, Ramsey also sent a telegram.

> Those Indian outrages continue. I asked Secretary Stanton to authorize the United States Quartermaster to purchase, say, 500 horses. He refuses. The state cannot purchase on as good terms, if at all, as the general government. This is not our war: it is a national war. I hope you will direct the purchase or send us 500 horses, or order the Minnesota companies of horse in Kentucky and Tennessee home. Answer me at once. More than 500 whites have been murdered by the Indians.

Lincoln and Stanton had ignored Ramsey's previous requests for aid, not out of callousness or indifference but because General Lee and his army were threatening the capital. Just the week before, at a place in Virginia called Bull Run, the Union army had been broken and sent scurrying back to the city. At the moment, then, Indian problems in Minnesota seemed insignificant to Washington.

Political pressure was growing, however. Two Minnesota politicians, one in the U.S. House of Representatives and one in the Senate, held important positions on their respective military affairs committees, and they were trying to force Lincoln and Stanton to act. Several representatives from the Dakota Territory also exerted their influence, including a cousin of Mrs. Lincoln's. That pressure, combined with the realization by September 6 that the Sioux uprising was apparently more serious than he had supposed, led Lincoln to conclude that he had to do something to help the people of Minnesota.

He could not spare troops from the Union army, however, nor could he send rifles and ammunition. Yet Lincoln at least needed to give the appearance of helping, to show that he understood the problem. If he could not provide men and supplies, he could send a leader, someone to unify and direct military operations against the Indians. The presence of a high-ranking military man would indicate that the President placed a high priority on countering the Indian raids.

Lincoln happened to have on his hands a major general without a job, who had been removed from his command a few days following his rout at Bull Run. Maj. Gen. John Pope would do nicely. The assignment would take him away from Washington and keep him from commanding any more regular Union forces. He would be placed in charge of the newly created, impressively titled Department of the Northwest, to include the states of Minnesota, Wisconsin, and Iowa, and the territories of Nebraska and Dakota. The headquarters for this largely paper command would be in St. Paul. Let Governor Ramsey bother Pope with his continual pleading rather than Lincoln and Stanton in Washington.

On Lincoln's instructions, Secretary of War Stanton drafted the order to General Pope that same day, September 6, and couched it in terms that he hoped would soothe Pope's vanity and boost his morale. After informing him of the appointment, Stanton wrote the following.

> The Indian hostilities that have recently broken forth and are now prevailing in that department require the attention of some military officer of high rank, in whose ability and vigor the government has confidence, and you have therefore been selected for this important command. . . . You will employ whatever force may be necessary to suppress the hostilities, making your requisitions upon the proper departments for whatever may be needed for that purpose. . . .
>
> In conclusion, I will add that you cannot too highly estimate the importance of the duty now entrusted to you, and you have been assigned to it because of the high confidence of the government that you have the personal and military qualities to meet the emergency.

General Pope did not appreciate being shunted off to the

wilderness, away from the main battle arena, and he was not taken in by the flowery but empty phrases. Soldiers go where they are ordered, however, and they work like hell to show they are good enough to be returned to the kind of command for which Pope had so recently demonstrated he was unfit. He left Washington as soon as he could, arriving in St. Paul on September 17, prepared to make quick work of this little tin-pot Indian war.

In the meantime, Governor Ramsey turned his pen to the future of Minnesota's Indians, loosing a frenzy of invective designed to inflame further an already angry populace.

> The Sioux Indians of Minnesota must be exterminated or driven forever beyond the borders of the state. The public safety imperatively requires it. Justice calls for it. . . . The blood of the murdered cries to heaven for vengeance on those assassins of women and children. . . . Amenable to no laws, bound by no moral or social restraints, they have already destroyed . . . every pledge on which it was possible to found a hope of ultimate reconciliation. They must be regarded and treated as outlaws.

It was not the time to speak of treaties and councils and smoking the pipe together. It was a time for revenge, for ridding Minnesota of the Indian menace. Newspapers throughout the state and beyond its bloody borders reiterated Ramsey's call. Retribution was to be exacted not only from the Sioux but from every Indian of every tribe that trod Minnesota's soil. All would have to pay, the guilty and innocent among the Sioux, and the Winnebagos and the other peaceful bands that were not allied with the uprising. It was not the time for talk, only for more killing.

Many of the newspapers that were calling down the scourge of the Almighty on every Indian within a thousand miles were also calling down the wrath of the governor on Henry Sibley for continuing to sit out the war at Fort Ridgely. They asked whether he ever intended to march into Indian country and put the rascals down, once and for all. One paper called him the "state undertaker, with his company of grave diggers," a clear reference to Birch Coulee. The only time Sibley had sent troops against the Indians, they had gone not to fight, not to seek out Indians and destroy them, but to dig graves.

There were other charges against Sibley, as well—rumors that he was seeking to make a treaty with Little Crow. People had seen the note he had left at Birch Coulee, and they were saying that he wanted a peaceful settlement so that his trader friends could resume their lucrative business of cheating the Indians. Others said that he was trying to make a treaty to save his mixed-blood relatives.

Thus Ramsey was coming under increasing pressure to fire Sibley. What may have made him resist was a long letter from Sibley's military chaplain, the Reverend Stephen Riggs. On September 11, Riggs wrote to defend Sibley's cautious approach to the war. At first, Riggs had agreed with the popular criticism that Sibley was acting too slowly, and he had urged the colonel to send out troops to try to liberate the white captives. What changed his mind, Riggs said, and now led him to counsel restraint, was the disaster at Birch Coulee. More than the individual depredations on the isolated settlements and the attacks on Fort Ridgely and New Ulm, the Indians' boldness in assaulting a force of more than 150 soldiers and then attacking—or so it was told—the 240-man relief party gave them an aura of invincibility in the eyes of many at the fort.

What the Sioux had accomplished at Birch Coulee went far beyond the killing of some two dozen soldiers, Riggs explained to Governor Ramsey.

> It satisfied us all that the greatest caution and prudence are demanded in conducting this campaign. At present the Indians have all the advantage in this war. Their passing with certainty from place to place on horseback, their mode of shooting and fleeing, their perfect knowledge of the country, its ravines and hiding places, their bushwacking and ambushing, all give them a de-

cided advantage in fighting with our troops. The
lesson we have learned at Birch Coulee will not,
I trust, soon be forgotten. Wisdom should be justified of her children. In looking at the past and
the present, I am satisfied that Colonel Sibley
has acted wisely in not advancing until he is well
prepared for offense and defense. The safety of
his command requires it.

The lesson of Birch Coulee—to Riggs and Sibley and others—was that the Sioux were more than mortal men. They
were regarded as unbeatable by any but an immensely superior
force. Sibley was correct to wait for additional troops and ammunition, Riggs concluded. These cautious men overlooked
the lesson that should have been learned from Birch Coulee,
however. When Sibley came forward with one thousand men,
which was less than his full command, the Indians retreated
without firing a shot. Had he pursued them, he might have
ended the war decisively, but he did not, and he would not for
another two weeks.

Little Crow received Sibley's message on September 7 after he
returned to Yellow Medicine from the fruitless attacks on Forest City and Hutchinson. He asked Joe Campbell to translate
it for him, then he took it to several other mixed-bloods to
read and interpret. One was Tom Robertson, son of the school
superintendent on the reservation. Robertson and his mother,
sister, and two brothers, had been captured by Little Crow's
band, but they were being treated well. Little Crow brought
Robertson Sibley's note.

"I have had this letter read and interpreted by several,"
Little Crow said, "but I want to be sure what is in the letter,
so I sent for you. Now read it and tell me what it says."

Robertson read the letter and explained it to the chief.

"Now I know," Little Crow told him, "because I know I
can depend on you to tell the truth."

Little Crow was pleased to learn that Sibley was also
thinking of a peaceful settlement as a way out of the war, and
he was certain that this time the warriors would not jeer. This

time, the idea for a council had come from the whites. Composing a reply, however, was not a responsibility Little Crow could assume himself. The other chiefs would have to be consulted. A council would be called, and both sides—the hostiles and the friendlies, the Lower Sioux and the Upper Sioux— would have their say.

The council was summoned immediately, and it quickly became a noisy, turbulent, even hostile confrontation centering on the issue of exchanging the prisoners for a negotiated peace. Shakopee and Red Middle Voice, the most vociferous of the hostiles, and the ones who bore the greatest responsibility for starting the war, did not attend the meeting, but they sent warriors to speak for them. One of these was Mazzawamnuna.

"You men who are in favor of leaving us and delivering up the captives talk like children," he said. "You believe, if you do so, [that] the whites will think you have acted as their friends and will spare your lives. They will not, and you ought to know it. You say that the whites are too strong for us, and that we will all have to perish. By sticking together and fighting the whites, we will live, at all events, for a few days, when, by the course you propose, we would die at once. Let us keep the prisoners with us and let them share our fate. That is all the advice I have to give."

Rdainyanka, whose father-in-law was the peace chief Wabasha, spoke passionately in favor of continuing the fight and keeping the prisoners. He reminded the council of how the whites had always treated the Dakotas.

> Ever since we [made treaties] with them their agents and traders have robbed and cheated us. Some of our people have been shot, some [hanged], others placed upon floating ice and drowned, and many have been starved in their prisons. It was not the intention of the [Sioux] nation to kill any of the whites until after the four men returned from Acton and told what they had done. When they did this, all the young men became excited and commenced the massacre. The older ones would have prevented it if they could,

but since the treaties, they had lost all their influence. We may regret what has happened, but the
matter has gone too far to be remedied. We have
got to die. Let us, then, kill as many of the whites
as possible, and let the prisoners die with us.

Paul Mazakutemani came next, the only representative of
the friendlies to speak that day. To make sure everyone heard
him, he stood atop a barrel and shouted his words. He began
by accusing the Lower Sioux of initiating the war without con-
sulting the Wahpetons and the Sissetons of the Upper Sioux.
If they had counseled with their brothers first, Mazakutemani
said, they would have advised the Lower Sioux, and their own
young braves, not to fight with the whites.

By your involving our young men without con-
sulting us, you have done us a great injustice. I
am now going to tell you something you don't
like. You have gotten our people into this difficulty through your incitements, and I shall use
all the means I can to get them out of it without
reference to you. I am opposed to their continuing this war, or of committing further outrages,
and I warn them not to do it. I have heard a great
many of you say that you were brave men and
could whip the whites. This is a lie. Persons who
will cut women's and children's throats are
squaws and cowards. You say the whites are not
brave. You will see. They will not, it is true, kill
women and children, as you have done, but they
will fight you who have arms in your hands. I am
ashamed of the way you have acted toward the
captives. Fight the whites if you desire to, but
do it like brave men.

The last speaker was from an Upper Sioux tribe that had
been involved in the killings around Lake Shetek.
"I am an Upper Indian," he said, "but I am opposed to

what Paul advises. I hope our people will not agree with him. We must all die in battle or perish with hunger, and let the captives suffer what we suffer."

Little Crow did not speak. It was his duty to reflect the consensus of the council, and it was being made clear to him that the Lower Sioux would not turn their captives over to the Upper Sioux to be returned. The prisoners could not be used to bargain with for settlement terms. Sibley had asked Little Crow whether he had any proposals to make. Without the prisoners, Little Crow did not, but he had to send some reply in the hope that it might lead to a meeting to discuss peace. The answer decided on by the council was a mixture of explanations, excuses, and threats. The friendlies and the hostiles quarreled over the wording and frequently amended it. Joe Campbell attempted to render it into English.

Dear Sir,
    For what reason we have commenced this war, I will tell you. It is on account of Major Galbraith. We made a treaty with the government, and beg for what we do get and then can't get it till our children are dying with hunger. It is the traders who commenced it. Mr. A. J. Myrick told the Indians they would eat grass or dirt. Then Mr. Forbes told the Lower Sioux that they were not men. Then Roberts was working with his friends to defraud us out of our moneys. If the young braves have pushed the white man, I have done this myself. So I want you to let Governor Ramsey know this. I have a great many prisoners, women and children. It ain't all our fault. The Winnebagoes were in the engagement, and two of them was killed. I want you to give me an answer by the bearer all at present.

Yours truly,
Friend Little Crow

Two mixed-bloods, Tom Robertson and Tom Robinson, agreed to carry the note to Fort Ridgely. Little Crow gave them a mule-drawn buggy, and they started in midafternoon.

Both men were worried that they would be shot as soon as they
came within sight of the fort, because they had nothing white
to wave, not even a handkerchief. Along the way, they found
a fragment of a white sheet tied to a pole over an Indian grave.
They took it with them, even though it had a large blue circle
painted in the center. When they stopped near an abandoned
farmhouse to give the mule a rest, they found a keg of soap
powder inside. They took it down to the river and spent a half
hour washing out the blue dye. Now they had a white flag.

As they neared the fort, Colonel McPhail and a squad of
soldiers rode out to meet them. They escorted the two couriers
to the post, gave them something to eat, and questioned them
about conditions in the Indian camp. The men were interro-
gated separately, and Robertson was able to pass on a verbal
message from the peace chiefs, namely that there was dissension within the Indian nation and that there was a large faction,
the friendlies, who wanted to release the white captives.

Robertson was taken to Colonel Sibley to relay that message directly. He also told Sibley that a large party of braves
was just as determined to keep the prisoners, kill them if necessary, and carry on the war. "They assure me," Sibley wrote
in his diary, "that the Indians are determined to give us battle,
at or near the Yellow Medicine, and are sanguine of success. I
do sincerely hope they will not change their program."

The news of division within the Indian camp was welcome
to the soldiers. Because of it, Sibley felt free to take a hard
line with Little Crow. He wrote a brief reply—no niceties, no
courtesies—just a statement of blame and a demand as to what
would be necessary to get peace talks under way.

Little Crow:
    You have murdered many of our people without any
sufficient cause. Return me the prisoners, under a flag of
truce, and I will talk to you like a man. I have sent your
message to Governor Ramsey.

                                        H. H. Sibley
                                        Colonel Commanding
                                        Military Expedition

The two couriers departed Fort Ridgely early the next morning to return to Little Crow's camp. They found the Indians packing to leave. Two miles away, the friendlies were also preparing to go. Both groups thought it would be wise to put some distance between themselves and Sibley's army, and they had decided to make a new camp near Lac qui Parle, at the mouth of the Chippewa River, twelve miles upriver from Yellow Medicine.

Sarah Wakefield and her two children were part of the five-mile-long wagon train of Indians and their white captives. "The sun is very powerful on these prairies," she recalled, "and the dust was stifling, and the perspiration and dust did not add to my looks. I would hear the Indians say, 'White woman got a dirty face,' but had no idea how I look until I went to the river—my looking glass—to arrange my dress. The last few miles we traveled that day, I experienced more pain than I ever did in my life before. I might have been tracked by the blood that ran from my feet and legs, cut by the tall, dry grass."

Late in the afternoon, the column reached the Sisseton village of Red Iron near the junction of the Chippewa and Minnesota rivers. Red Iron himself and 150 of his warriors lined up across the path to confront Little Crow's party. They fired their guns in the air as a warning. Red Iron told Little Crow that he and his people could not go beyond the village, for that would leave the Sissetons to bear the brunt of Sibley's wrath when the soldiers came looking for Little Crow.

A few of Little Crow's men took offense and shots were fired on both sides, but no one was hit. A council was summoned for all the chiefs. Red Iron and his leaders did most of the talking.

"You commenced the outbreak," Red Iron told Little Crow's group, "and must do the fighting in your country. . . . I cannot bear the thought of everything of mine being destroyed, therefore I shall stay here where I belong until General Sibley comes here, and I will shake hands with him, and then he may do what he pleases with me."

Waanatan echoed these thoughts and added, "I live by the

white man and the buffalo. These people who have done this act have destroyed everything I have—the treaties with the whites and everything else—and for that reason I shall óbject to their going across my land."

Little Crow agreed not to cross Red Iron's land, and the resistance he encountered from Red Iron's people further depressed his spirits. He retained so little power and influence. All seemed to be draining away like the rain falling on the parched earth. He watched helplessly as many of the Mdewakantons, his own people, led by Wabasha, Wacouta, and Taopee, moved over to where the Sissetons and Wahpetons had erected their tents. Everyone knew about the two couriers who had taken Little Crow's letter to Fort Ridgely. The word was that Sibley had promised to spare those Indians who had not joined the uprising or harmed any whites.

Over the next few days, Little Crow spent a great deal of time talking with Susan Brown, the wife of former Indian agent Joe Brown, who was being held captive with several of her children. Her seventeen-year-old son, Samuel, remembered how unhappy Little Crow seemed.

"Little Crow is losing his hold upon the young men and this fact worries him greatly, and the old warrior is getting heartily discouraged. He told Mother today that he intended to spend the coming winter in the Green Lake region of the Big Woods and kill as many whites as he could, but if he should get killed himself it would be all right. He did not want to be caught and hanged."

Little Crow had not abandoned all hope, however. There was still his old friend Henry Sibley. Although Sibley's message had not been encouraging—indeed, its tone had been insulting—Little Crow felt that he should try once more to arrange a peaceful settlement. This time, he would emphasize the friendly relations they had once known, in the hope of rekindling them. First, however, he would remind Sibley of the large number of captives he held. On September 12, he wrote the following, signing himself "Your truly friend."

> We have in Mdewakanton band one hundred fifty-five prisoners. . . . They are at Lake qui Parle

now. The words that I sent to the governor I
want to hear from him also, and I want to know
from you as a friend what way that I can make
peace for my people. In regard to prisoners they
fare with our children or ourself just as well as
us.

Little Crow gave the note to the couriers Tom Robertson
and Tom Robinson and told them to leave for Fort Ridgely at
dawn. That night, Good Thunder visited Robertson and told
him that some of the friendlies wanted him to take a note to
Sibley on their behalf. Robertson agreed, and he wrote down
what the chief dictated by the light of a candle while they huddled under a blanket so that no one would see them. Robertson
thought that some of the hostile Indians suspected him of making secret deals with the whites on behalf of the friendlies. If
they knew about the letter Good Thunder was asking him to
write, they would surely kill him.

You know that Little Crow has been opposed to
me in everything that our people have had to do
with the whites. He has been opposed to everything in the form of civilization and Christianity.
I have always been in favor of, and of late years
have done everything of the kind that has been
offered to us by the Government and other good
white people. He has now got himself into trouble that we know he can never get himself out
of, and he is trying to involve those [of us] in the
murder of the poor whites that have been settled
in the border; but I have been kept back with
threats that I should be killed if I did anything
to help the whites. But if you will now appoint
some place for me to meet you, myself and the
few friends that I have will get all the prisoners
that we can, and with our families go to whatever
place you will appoint for us to meet. . . . Return
the messenger as quick as possible. We have not
much time to spare.

The letter was signed by chiefs Wabasha and Taopee.

"Little Crow evidently begins to quake," wrote Henry Sibley in his diary after receiving the two messages from the Indian camp. "I expect to reach him and fight him within a week." He was pleased to hear from the peace chiefs, for it confirmed what the couriers had told him on their last visit about the disagreement within the Sioux nation. Still, as Sibley told Oscar Malmros, the adjutant general, the whole thing might be a trick, a bit of treachery under cover of a flag of truce. He intended to remain wary and vigilant.

Sibley decided that there was no need to give further encouragement to Little Crow, or even to try to deal with him any longer. If the news of the dissension was not a ruse, then the Indians were hopelessly divided. All Sibley had to do was be patient, and the friendly Indians would solve the problem of the prisoners themselves. He had been right not to move too quickly against them. Had he marched against the Indians earlier, before this friction developed, then his attack would probably have united all the Indian bands and sealed the fate of the captives. Sibley was well pleased with this conclusion.

He sent replies to both notes, a perfunctory one to Little Crow and a conciliatory one to Wabasha and Taopee. The success of his mission clearly lay with the latter.

"I have received your letter today," Sibley wrote to Little Crow. "You have not done as I wished in giving up the prisoners taken by your people. It would be better for you to do so. I told you I sent your former letter to Governor Ramsey, but I have not yet had time to receive a reply. You have allowed your young men to commit some murders since you wrote your first letter. This is not the way to make peace."

To the friendlies, he wrote that he had come with a large force of soldiers to punish those Indians who murdered white settlers. He did not intend to punish innocent Indians.

"If you and others who have not been concerned in the murders and expeditions will gather yourselves, with all the prisoners, on the prairie in full sight of my troops, and when the white flag is displayed by you, a white flag will be hoisted in my camp, and then you can come forward and place yourselves under my protection."

He informed Wabasha and Taopee that his troops would be ready to march in three days. Under no circumstances should the friendly Indians try to approach them except in daylight with a flag of truce. As an inducement to the friendlies, and a warning to the hostiles, Sibley added:

"I shall be glad to receive all true friends of the whites with as many prisoners as they can bring, and I am powerful enough to crush all who attempt to oppose my march, and to punish those who have washed their hands in innocent blood.

"I sign myself the friend of all who were friends of your great American father."

13

I AM ASHAMED TO CALL MYSELF A DAKOTA

"At last we left!" Joe Coursolle wrote. It was September 19, and Sibley's army, now 1,619 strong, marched out of Fort Ridgely that afternoon. "Our company was in the lead and the column stretched back through the woods farther than I could see. I was glad we had the cannons with us. The big guns scared the daylights out of the Sioux."

Sibley was feeling less desperate about his supplies. The week before, he had received fifty thousand cartridges, and a few days after that, additional rations and clothing arrived. He also took command of a regiment of experienced combat troops, 270 infantrymen of the Third Minnesota who had been in the fighting in Tennessee. They were well trained, thoroughly drilled soldiers, and their presence increased the confidence and morale of Sibley and his other units.

The colonel did not stop complaining about insufficient provisions, however. "I have been sadly crippled for want of ammunition and rations, as well as proper clothing for the men," he wrote to Judge Flandrau a few days after the ammunition and supplies had arrived. "I have no mounted force except about 25 men, and they are far from efficient." To his new commander, General Pope, headquartered in St. Paul, Sibley grumbled that he hadn't enough bread, bullets, blankets, clothing, mules, oats, hay, pork, or horses. Unless he received more provisions soon, he warned, he might have to fall back.

"If I had 400 or 500 good mounted men I would feel more certainty in bringing this campaign to a speedy and successful issue. If the Indians decide to fight us—as I hope they will—we shall have a bloody and desperate battle, for it is a life-and-death struggle with them; but I have little doubt that we can whip them, although my troops are entirely undisciplined."

General Pope learned as soon as he arrived in St. Paul that he did not have enough troops to fight even this little tin-pot war. According to his adjutant, he reacted like a "bear with a sore head." Pope appeared to be "ambitiously crazy," the adjutant observed, and imagined himself to be the "most talented general in the world and the one most wronged."

Determined to succeed in this Minnesota backwater, to prove himself fit for a more prestigious assignment, Pope realized that he would need a larger army, one more appropriate for a two-star general. He wrote to Sibley that he was prepared to bring to the state all the troops necessary to end the war. And he fired off messages to his superiors in Washington, emphasizing the strategic importance of his new command. Sibley was delighted; Washington was not pleased.

Pope described to General Halleck at the War Department a widespread Indian uprising all along the frontier that threatened to depopulate the entire region. "Time is everything here, and I must take unusual means to hasten matters." He immediately ordered the purchase of 2,500 horses. He requested that the governor of Wisconsin detach three or four regiments originally intended for the Union army, and asked him, as well as the governor of Iowa, not to send any more troops to fight the Confederates without notifying him first. He believed he needed those soldiers to fight the Indians instead.

Halleck, however, curtly informed Pope that he did not believe Pope required so many troops to bring a relatively small band of Indians under control. He also denied Pope's requisitions for supplies and ammunition, saying that they were beyond "all our expectations, and involve an immense expenditure of money. . . . The organization of a large force for an Indian campaign is not approved by the War Department, because it is not deemed necessary."

Pope was furious. How was he supposed to win a war without adequate supplies and with untrained militia units? He fired off a telegram to Halleck, accusing him of misunderstanding the seriousness of the uprising.

> You have no idea of the wide, universal, and uncontrollable panic everywhere in this country. Over 500 people have been murdered in Minnesota alone and 300 women and children [are] now in captivity. The most-horrible massacres have been committed; children nailed alive to trees and houses, women violated and then disemboweled—everything that horrible ingenuity could devise. It will require a large force and much time to prevent everybody leaving the country, such is the condition of things.
>
> I am acting as vigorously as I can, but without means. There is positively nothing here. It has been assumed that of course there would be no trouble, and everything has been taken away. There is not a wagon, mule, or horse belonging to the United States in this department.

Despite Pope's impassioned pleas, Halleck and Stanton could spare no troops. Pope would have to improvise, to do this job himself, if he ever hoped to join the real war again. Reluctantly, he accepted the fact that his future depended on a man he had never met, a trader and politician with no military experience, a man people in St. Paul described as being slower than molasses. Pope was determined to fire Sibley up or put someone else in charge. "I cannot urge upon you too strongly," he wrote to Henry Sibley, "the necessity of marching as rapidly as possible upon the Sioux." Two days later, the colonel departed Fort Ridgely.

*   *   *

"We moved like snails," Joe Coursolle recalled. "I could have crawled on my stomach and made faster time. Again we cursed Sibley. He was so slow! Every day we started the march in the middle of the [morning], halted for a noon meal, camped at four o'clock, dug rifle pits, and built barricades. Why waste such precious time? We would never catch the Indians dawdling like this."

Little Crow's scouts reported daily on the progress of the four-mile-long column. The white captives heard the talk and wondered why their rescuers were taking so long. The Sioux taunted the whites about the soldiers' lack of speed. One told Sarah Wakefield that the whites must not care much for their women and children; if they did, they would surely travel faster. The distance from Fort Ridgely to Yellow Medicine, twelve miles from the Indians' new camp, was only forty miles. A horse-drawn wagon could make it in a day; it would take Sibley four.

The first day, the soldiers covered only two miles because they left late and had to stop to build a boat so they could cross to the south side of the river. When the advance party reached the other side, they saw a man, half-starved and unkempt, who stumbled toward them, muttering in German. He mistook the soldiers for Indians, pulled out a knife, and started to hack at his own throat, trying, in his fear, to kill himself. The blade was too dull to draw blood, and the soldiers disarmed the crazed man and sent him back to the fort.

Sibley made camp not far from the abandoned Lower Agency, and some of his men took advantage of the chance to explore the houses that had belonged to the farmer Indians. They returned laden with buffalo robes and trinkets. They also found the body of Philander Prescott, the interpreter who had been slain early in the uprising. He was given a proper burial.

The next morning, as the column passed Prescott's grave, Sibley found a message from the Sioux. Little sticks had been placed upright in the fresh dirt—738 of them—each one representing a brave who was waiting for the soldiers. Several times throughout the day, the troops spotted clusters of Indians on horseback. They kept their distance, observing the army's movements. Each time the soldiers topped one of the many rolling hills that contoured the prairie, they saw the Indians watch them for a while and gallop away.

Sibley found another message, a note attached to a wooden fence near the Redwood River. The letter, left by Little Crow's scouts, urged the soldiers to press on. The Dakotas were waiting for them at Yellow Medicine. And as the column approached the bridges spanning the creeks and rivers, they often saw smoke rising from them. The Indians had set them afire, although they did not succeed in destroying them.

After the army made camp that evening, three of the men set out to explore the valley. They were John Other Day, who was the expedition's scout, a cousin of Andrew Myrick's, and a third man whose name is not known. The valley seemed forbidding, dense with tall grass, overgrown cornfields, and the occasional isolated cabin. The men rode through the fields, stopping at a house about two miles from the camp. They tied their horses to a plum tree and sat down on the ground to sample the fruit.

John Other Day's horse sported a distinctive gaudy red headdress, and it was instantly recognized by two Indians lying concealed in the high grass. It was a perfect spot for an ambush. One raised his rifle and took aim at Myrick. His companion stopped him. He knew that John Other Day was fearless and would kill them both. As much as the Sioux hated John Other Day, they also feared him. He had killed several braves in quarrels in his younger days, and although he had become a Christian and a farmer, he went about armed and remained hot-tempered and dangerous.

After gorging on the plums, John Other Day walked up to the house and went inside, leaving his horse by the tree. Myrick and the other man followed him, leading their horses up to the door. The men had seen moccasin tracks nearby, and fresh plum pits on the ground, evidence that Indians had been there no more than an hour before.

Myrick entered the cabin; the third man waited outside. The place had been ransacked, but they found a trunk belonging to Philander Prescott. Its contents were strewn about the room. They rummaged through the attic and went into the cellar. Myrick thought it a foolish thing to do, but he was not about to have his bravery questioned by a mixed-blood, so he followed John Other Day downstairs. While they lingered in the cellar, the two Indians outside made off with John Other Day's horse.

When John Other Day got back to camp, he took a lot of kidding about the mishap. Sibley, in particular, took great delight in laughing at him, saying that the Sioux were too sharp for him. At first, Sibley refused to issue John Other Day another horse, teasing that if he could not keep one, then why should he be trusted with another? John Other Day became angry, and he vowed that when they did battle with the Sioux, he would capture two horses to make up for the one he had lost.

On the following day's march, the soldiers came across the decomposed body of George Gleason. Two large stones were embedded in the skull. They buried him and moved on. The evening of September 22 found them bivouacked at Wood Lake—the Sioux called it Lone Tree Lake—two miles from the Yellow Medicine River. Sibley arranged his camp in three lines, loosely forming a triangle. The Sixth Minnesota was arrayed to the left of the lakefront, the Third on the crest of the south slope of a ravine, and the Seventh behind the ravine. Sibley's scouts had told him that they had seen no traces of Indians near Wood Lake, so he saw no need to take extra precautions to guard the encampment. Pickets were ordered out for the night, but they were stationed quite close to the perimeter. Sibley felt there was nothing to fear. He did not expect to meet the Sioux for another day or two, at least.

Little Crow knew exactly where Sibley's army was, as well as every detail of the encampment, and he was determined to wipe out the invaders. He summoned his warriors, announcing that every brave fit to fight should prepare for battle to slaughter the white soldiers. Honors and gifts were promised to any man who captured the American flag or brought back the scalp of Sibley or the traders Forbes, Roberts, and Myrick. All ablebodied men were pressured to join the attack. Little Crow tried, though without success, to persuade the Sissetons and

Wahpetons to unite with him, but the antagonism between the hostiles and the friendlies had grown intractable because of several incidents over the past few days.

Ugly and potentially explosive confrontations had occurred. Little Crow's braves had knocked over tepees in the friendly camp, and more than once both sides faced each other over gun barrels. So far, shouts and gestures had been traded, but not bullets. Several times, the friendlies vowed to die like men in battle, fighting the hostiles rather than submitting to them. If pushed hard enough, they were indeed ready for such a fight, even though they were outnumbered five to one. The friendlies eventually withdrew to establish a separate camp west of the Chippewa River, but they remained within sight of the main village and they managed to conduct a few more white captives to the safety of their lodges.

Some of the friendlies suggested taking the whites to Fort Ridgely, but Paul Mazakutemani argued against it, saying that they should wait until they could free all of the captives. If only a few were released, he said, the lives of those still in the hands of the hostiles would be in greater danger. Rumors ran through both camps more than once that Little Crow was urging his braves to kill all the captives.

Fear gripped the prisoners each time they heard the rumors. And now they had a new worry. Suppose Little Crow won the battle against Sibley's troops? What would happen to them then? If the warriors returned victorious, drunk with success—and alcohol—they might well run amok, killing the whites, their protectors, and the rest of the friendly Sioux.

Sarah Wakefield had been told by Chaska that he had to ride with Little Crow to fight Sibley. If he refused, he would be shot. He urged her to remain in the lodge with his mother and not to try to slip away to the friendlies' camp while the warriors were away.

"You stay where you are," he said. "Don't go up to the friendly camp. Don't you talk to any half-breed or white women. If you do, you will be killed."

After Chaska left, his cousin explained to Sarah the reason for the warning. Little Crow, he said, planned to attack the friendlies' camp when he returned. Everyone there would be killed.

Little Crow and his chiefs planned their attack carefully. Even Shakopee, who had avoided most of the previous councils, participated, and he and Little Crow both recommended that the Indians attack the soldiers that night while most of the camp was asleep. They believed that a massed charge from all sides, with much shouting and shooting, would leave many whites dead in their beds and send the rest fleeing in panic over the prairie.

Other chiefs spoke against the plan, including several who did not want Little Crow to win and who wanted to make peace with the whites at once. Their most persuasive argument was put forth by Solomon Two Stars, who said that a night attack was "so cowardly as to be unworthy of a Dakota brave and of the great chief who proposed it." Attacking in daylight, he added, was more manly and courageous, and showed greater proof of bravery, than sneaking up on an enemy under cover of darkness.

He proposed a new plan, which Little Crow and the others immediately accepted. "I have been told," Solomon Two Stars said, "that over here in the west [the Indians] would lie in ambush for the troops, and when they came up to them the Indians would rush in, cutting the command in two, and then would kill them all. I think that would be a better plan for you."

An ambush it would be, and Little Crow knew the ideal spot for it. When the army broke camp in the morning and continued on toward the Indian village, the soldiers would have to take the road that ran along the Yellow Medicine River. About a mile beyond the lake, it wound between a heavily wooded ravine and a long, low hill. Little Crow proposed to place warriors at both sites, where the prairie grass provided good cover. That way, he could attack the head, tail, and flanks of the column all at once.

Little Crow's scouts had observed that Sibley did not send patrols ahead of his main force to reconnoiter the terrain, nor did he position outriders. The horsemen were clustered at the head of the long column rather than being deployed as a roving screening force, as was usual for the cavalry. There was no chance, then, that Sibley would discover the Indians before they opened fire. Little Crow had drawn up a good plan.

The Indians rode out of camp that night full of confidence. "We will have plenty of pork and hardtack tonight," one wrote. They brought along wagons to haul back their loot. There would be blankets and rifles and enough ammunition to fight the whites for another year. When they reached the ambush site, they moved stealthily among the trees, settling down in the undergrowth to wait for morning.

Little Crow walked up to the top of a bluff overlooking the neat rows of tents that marked Sibley's camp. He stood there for a long time, watching and listening to the soldiers laughing and singing. In a few hours, the fate of the Sioux nation, and of Little Crow as one of its leaders, would be decided for all time. If they won, if they sent Sibley's troops back to Fort Ridgely in tatters, it would be months, perhaps years, before the army would dare return to the Dakota Territory. If they won and returned to their village in triumph, those Indians who had deserted him and joined the friendlies would return, and the power of the friendlies would wither like a tree whose roots have been severed. There would be no more talk of freeing the captives. They would remain under Little Crow's control.

And if the Indians won, the whites would be willing to make a peaceful settlement with Little Crow. They had no more armies to spare for Minnesota, nor the temerity to risk another massacre, and certainly not the courage to maintain a prolonged war in which their women and children would remain prisoners indefinitely.

If they won, the Dakotas would live again as their fathers had lived, as they were meant to live. The braves were in place. The trap was ready. All was in the hands of the gods. On the prairie below Little Crow, the soldiers were laughing and singing.

The men of Company G of the Third Minnesota were dissatisfied with the rations Sibley provided, and they decided that they could do better on their own. They had learned a thing or two about scrounging when they were down in Tennessee with the Union army. Some of the soldiers had heard that there

were several Indian farms about five miles away, where the
fields were bursting with potatoes, melons, and sweet corn.
The men of Company G thought it would be a good idea to
stock up, and so at seven o'clock in the morning, before Sibley's army was ready to break camp, they took four wagons and
headed off in the direction of the Upper Agency, hoping to
find the farms.

"They came on over the prairie," Big Eagle recalled,
"right where part of our line was. Some of the wagons were
not in the road, and if they had kept straight on would have
driven right over our men as they lay in the grass. At last they
came so close that our men had to rise up and fire. This
brought on the fight, of course, but not according to the way
we had planned it. Little Crow saw it and felt very badly."

One soldier was shot in the leg—he later died from the
wound—and the others jumped down from their wagons to return the fire. Upon seeing how many Indians there were, the
troops of Company G raced back to camp on foot. The Third
Minnesota's new commander, Maj. Abraham Welch, saw his
men under fire about a half mile from the camp, and without
waiting for orders from Sibley, he formed his regiment and
charged. Welch's 270 men, aligned by companies in prescribed
military formation, pushed the Sioux back several hundred
yards in a fierce firefight.

"The savages formed a semicircle in our front," Sgt. Ezra
Champlin wrote, "and to right and left, moving about with
great activity, howling like demons, firing and retreating. Their
quick movements seemed to multiply their number." The
troops were in danger of being cut off and surrounded a mile
from the camp. Sibley, alerted to the threat, sent an officer
forward to tell Major Welch to fall back.

"Get back to camp the best way you can," the officer
shouted, but Welch was not about to retire when he was convinced that he was winning. Sibley, however, failed to support
him. Instead of sending additional units up to assist the Third
Minnesota, he dispatched a second order to Welch to fall back.
In the confusion, the wrong bugle call was sounded, and the
withdrawal threatened to become a rout. The well-trained men
of the Third quickly regained control and set up a strong defensive position on the perimeter of the camp.

Welch took a hit in the leg, and Sergeant Champlin and another man had to help him walk. Three soldiers ran past them, heading back to camp. Welch was irate.

"Go back and fight, you white-livered cowards," he shouted. "Go back and fight or I'll shoot you." The would-be deserters decided they had a better chance with the Indians than with Welch, and they stopped and returned to the front. Sergeant Champlin assisted the major to a safe spot behind some wagons, but Welch became indignant. He pointed to the top of a hill and said he wanted to be taken there so he could watch the battle.

Sibley saw a group of Indians emerge from a ravine on his right, and he ordered Lt. Col. William Marshall of the Seventh Minnesota forward with his five companies and one of the Sixth's. Capt. Mark Hendrix accompanied them, bringing his six-pound howitzer to spew canister shot at the Indians. In short order, the braves fled, and the howitzer fire was directed into the ravine, where another Indian party was waiting to attack. They waited no longer but fled as fast as they could run.

To the left of Marshall's force, Sibley sent two companies of the Sixth under Maj. Robert McLaren to break up another Sioux advance. In less than two hours, marked mostly by desultory fire from both sides under cover, the Indians left the field. The battle of Wood Lake was over, and with it all hope of victory for the Dakotas of Minnesota. It had been a decisive win for the army, due in no small measure to the fact that a few soldiers had accidentally discovered the Indians. As a result, no more than 300 of the 740 warriors came within firing distance of the battleground.

Sibley lost seven killed and thirty-four wounded, and the Indians lost Mankato, one of their most able chiefs, who was cut down by the howitzer. The Sioux also had fifteen other men killed and about fifty wounded. John Other Day killed two Indians himself, to redeem his pledge to obtain two horses in return for the one stolen from him.

The bodies of the dead Indians were scalped by the soldiers, an act that infuriated Sibley. "The bodies of the dead," he wrote in his general orders of the day, "even of a savage enemy, shall not be subjected to indignities by civilized and Christian men."

One Indian, discovered alive but badly wounded on the battlefield, was treated with some compassion. He had sustained a gunshot through the lungs and there was little chance that he would survive. Two soldiers brought him to a tent and gave him water. They spread a coat over him to keep him warm and reported that they saw a look of gratitude in his eyes before he died.

A group of Wahpetons, who had joined Little Crow for the fight at Wood Lake, sent a note to Sibley under a flag of truce. They said that they wanted peace with the whites and asked for permission to retrieve their dead and wounded. Sibley hastily wrote a reply.

> When you bring up the prisoners and deliver them to me under the flag of truce I will be ready to talk peace. The bodies of the Indians that have been killed will be buried like white people, and the wounded will be attended to as our own; but none will be given until the prisoners are brought in. I will wait here a reasonable time for the delivery of the prisoners, if you send me word [that] they will be given up.

With the Indians beaten and retreating from Wood Lake, with at least some of them asking for peace, and with the white captives fewer than a dozen miles away, Sibley decided not to break camp but to wait for an answer from the Indians. Apparently, he gave no thought to pursuing his demoralized enemy, taking advantage of the confusion of their retreat, and rescuing the prisoners himself.

Instead, he wrote to Governor Ramsey that he might have to retreat himself if he did not receive more supplies. "I am very much in want of bread rations, 6-pounder ammunition, and shells for the howitzer, and unless soon supplied I shall be compelled to fall back, which, under present circumstances, would be a calamity, as it would afford time for the escape of the Indians with their captives."

If only he had had five hundred cavalry, he added, he could have brought the present campaign to a successful close.

*   *   *

Little Crow rode slowly back to his village in the company of Wabasha, an old friend but one who had spoken out against the war in the council at Little Crow's house six weeks earlier. They talked about the future of the Dakotas, about what they would do now that their uprising had been crushed. Little Crow announced that he would leave the village at dawn, taking along whoever wished to go with him. Wabasha did not try to change his mind. He knew it would be pointless. He felt that Little Crow was right to leave, to be far away when the soldiers came to their camp.

Wabasha said that he would stay, but he asked Little Crow to release the whites still held by the Mdewakantons. He hoped that if Sibley found the prisoners alive, under the protection of the friendlies, he might allow the Indians to resume their lives on the reservation instead of banishing them to the distant territories. Little Crow did not commit himself either way, but when they reached the camp, he found that the decision about the prisoners was no longer entirely in his hands.

The friendlies now held most of the whites and had brought them into their own village of about one hundred lodges. They had fortified the camp with holes, trenches, and earthen breastworks to defend themselves from Little Crow's warriors. The friendlies were determined to fight the hostiles if necessary in order to save the lives of the captives.

When Little Crow's braves saw what had happened in their absence, they urged the chief to attack the friendlies at once and retrieve the prisoners. At first, Little Crow agreed, but then he changed his mind, recognizing that many of the captives would likely be killed or wounded in such a battle, which would make things worse for those Indians who chose to stay behind and wait for the soldiers. Also, many of the Indians in the friendly camp were Little Crow's relatives, and he had no wish to harm them, especially since war with the friendlies would not change his own fate or that of the men who decided to go with him.

Heartbroken and despondent, Little Crow instructed his wives to prepare for a long journey. While they were packing their belongings, he summoned a few friends to bid them fare-

well. Joe Campbell came to Little Crow's tepee with great re-
luctance. He feared the chief's wrath because he had been
cooperating secretly with the friendlies, but he went to see Little Crow anyway, believing it was his duty to honor the chief's
summons.

To Campbell's relief, Little Crow greeted him warmly and
asked whether there was anything he could do for Campbell
before he left in the morning. Campbell said that he would
like to see Little Crow stay and surrender to Sibley. It would
be better for his people, Campbell said. Little Crow laughed.

"The long merchant Sibley would like to put the rope
around my neck," Little Crow said, "but he won't get the
chance."

"I don't think they will hang anybody," Campbell said.
"They never did before."

"No, Cousin," Little Crow said, "anything else but to
give myself up to hang by the neck like a woman. If they
would shoot me like a man I would, but otherwise they will
never get my live body."

Campbell asked Little Crow whether he would release the
rest of the prisoners.

"Yes, you shall have them," Little Crow said.

He ordered his warriors to send the rest of the white captives over to the friendlies' camp. It was a measure of how little
authority Little Crow retained that some braves protested, and
a few refused to obey, keeping their captives for several
months more. However, most of the Indians released their prisoners—about forty-six in number—after Little Crow pleaded
with them to do so.

"Let them alone," he told his men. "Too many women
and children have been killed already. If you had killed only
men, we could make peace now."

In the morning, Little Crow and the other chiefs who had
decided to leave were packed and ready. More than one hundred warriors chose to accompany him, and even more followed
Shakopee, one of the war chiefs who had fomented the uprising. Red Middle Voice, who had also urged war, was leaving,
too, along with Hapa and the four Rice Creek Indians who had
murdered the settlers at Acton because of a taunt about stealing
some eggs.

Little Crow gathered his men around him. There was one more speech he wanted to make. It was about their defeat the day before at Wood Lake.

"I am ashamed to call myself a Dakota," Little Crow told them. "Seven hundred of our best warriors were whipped yesterday by the whites. Now we had better all run away and scatter out over the plains like buffalo and wolves. To be sure, the whites had wagon guns and better arms than we, and there were many more of them. But that is no reason why we should not have whipped them, for we are brave Dakotas and whites are cowardly women. I cannot account for the disgraceful defeat. It must be the work of traitors in our midst."

He led his band north, across the Minnesota River, and climbed out of the valley that had been the Dakotas' home for many years. When he reached the bluff on the far side, he reined in his horse and looked back over the lush terrain.

"We shall never go back there," he said.

Shortly after Little Crow and the others left, Wabasha sent Joe Campbell to Wood Lake to tell Colonel Sibley that the captives were in the hands of the friendly Indians, and that those braves who had made war on the whites were gone. Campbell informed Sibley that the road to the Indian village was safe, and that the prisoners were awaiting his arrival.

Sibley did not immediately act on this information. He waited three more days before going to reclaim the captives, three days to make a journey that could easily have been managed in an afternoon. He did, however, send a message to Wabasha and the other friendly chiefs.

> My friends. I call you so because I have reason to believe that you have had nothing to do with the cruel murders and massacres that have been committed upon the poor white people who had placed confidence in the friendship of the Sioux Indians. I repeat what I have already stated to you, that I have not come to make war upon those who are innocent but upon the guilty. I have waited here one day, and intended to wait still another day, to hear from the friendly half-

breeds and Indians, because I feared that if I advanced my troops before you could make your arrangements, the war party would murder the prisoners.

Now that I learn from Joseph Campbell that most of the captives are in safety in your camp, I shall move tomorrow, so that you may expect to see me very soon. Have a white flag displayed so that my men may not fire upon you.

Shortly after Campbell took Sibley's letter to the Indians, word spread among the captives that rescue was at hand. Assuming that deliverance was only a matter of hours away, the Indians supplied the prisoners with clothing looted from the white settlements, believing that the soldiers would be angry if they saw their women and children dressed as Indians.

Sarah Wakefield had one of her own dresses returned to her. Chaska, and others who had cared for her, asked her to write a letter attesting to her good treatment and to their efforts to protect her and her children from the hostile Indians. She said goodbye to Chaska and his mother, with whom she had lived for six weeks, then took her children to the center of the Indian encampment, where the captives were congregating around a large American flag. Chaska's mother cried when they left.

"You are going back," she told Sarah, "[to] where you will have good warm houses and plenty to eat, and we will starve on the plains this winter. Oh, that 'bad man,' who has caused us so much trouble." She was referring to Little Crow.

Sarah Wakefield and the others waited with mounting anxiety. Suppose Little Crow and his band returned before the soldiers arrived? As night passed and another day dawned without any sign of Sibley, their worry seemed all the more real. The Indians, too, were fearful. Chaska came to tell Sarah that it would be safer for him to go away because Sibley might be planning to kill all the Indians. Sarah reminded him that Sibley had promised to shake hands with the friendlies and not punish them. She was sure he would keep his word. She pleaded with Chaska to stay and he finally, reluctantly, agreed. He expressed his misgivings, however. "If I am killed," he told her, "I will blame you for it."

The Indians and their captives waited all that day and another night for Sibley, and the next day and night, as well. During the second night, an Indian scout who had been tracking Sibley's column reported back to say that he could not understand why the soldiers had covered only eight miles that day. The scout also said that Sibley had made camp after spending hours digging entrenchments, despite Wabasha's message that the road was safe. The tension in the friendlies' camp was almost unbearable, for Indians and whites alike. Didn't Sibley realize that Little Crow could come back and slaughter them all while the soldiers were wasting time digging entrenchments?

At noon on the following day, Sibley's army approached the Indian village. The troops marched triumphantly to a point five hundred yards from the perimeter and set up their camp, which they dubbed "Camp Release," with the howitzers trained on the largest cluster of Sioux lodges. When the troops were first sighted by the captives, the joy was unrestrained. Some of the prisoners cried, some became hysterical, others fell to their knees to pray. A few fainted.

Sam Brown, the seventeen-year-old son of the former Indian agent Joe Brown, described the scene. "No grander sight ever met the eyes of anybody than when the troops marched up with bayonets glistening in the bright noonday sun and colors flying, drums beating, and fifes playing. I shall never forget it while I live. We could hardly realize that our deliverance had come."

The Indians, driven by their fear and an eagerness to please, jumped about and shouted as though the soldiers' arrival meant salvation for them, and each man made sure to carry some bit of white cloth as a flag of truce, or a badge of surrender.

"White rags were fastened to the tips of tepee poles," Brown recalled, "to wagon wheels, cart wheels, to sticks and poles stuck in the ground, and every conceivable object, and in some grotesque manner and ludicrous way.

"One Indian who was boiling over with loyalty and love

for the white man threw a white blanket on his black horse and tied a bit of white cloth to its tail, and then that no possible doubt might be raised in his case, he wrapped the American flag around his body and mounted the horse and sat upon him in full view of the troops as they passed by, looking more like a circus clown than a friendly Indian."

At precisely two o'clock that afternoon, having prolonged the captives' ordeal for another two hours, Col. Henry Sibley marched to the Indian camp, attended by his staff, senior officers, and two companies of infantry. He moved smartly to the center of the circle formed by the lodges and called the Indian leaders to assemble. When they had gathered around him, he spoke to them about what he called "the late proceedings." He repeated what he had told Joe Campbell, that all Indians guilty of crimes against whites would be punished. He demanded that the prisoners be turned over to him instantly.

The chiefs agreed, but first they had their own speeches to make. Such was the way with councils. One by one, they condemned the Indians who had made war on the settlements and assured Sibley that they had not committed any crimes themselves. They would not dare shake his hand, they told him, if their own were stained with blood. And solemnly each chief came forward to shake hands with Sibley and his officers. Paul Mazakutemani, the spokesman for the friendlies, took Sibley's hand and said:

"I have grown up like a child of yours. With what is yours, you have caused me to grow; and now I take your hand as a child takes the hand of his father. My hand is not bad. With a clean hand I take your hand. I know whence this blessing cometh. I have regarded all white people as my friends, and from this I understand this blessing has come. This is a good work we do today, whereof I am glad. Yes, before the great God, I am glad."

At last, the speeches came to an end and it was time for the prisoners to be formally set free. They numbered 269 in all, 162 mixed-bloods and 107 whites. They walked and ran and stumbled, laughed, cried, and shouted as they made their way from the Indian camp to the soldiers'.

"The woe written in the faces of the half-starved and

nearly naked women and children would have melted the hardest heart," wrote one officer. "Some seemed stolid," Sibley recorded, "as if their minds had been strained to madness and reaction had brought vacant gloom, indifference, and despair. They gazed with a sad stare. Others acted differently. The great body of the poor creatures rushed wildly to the spot where I was standing with my brave officers, pressing as close to us as possible, grasping our hands and clinging to our limbs, as if fearful that the Red Devils might yet reclaim their victims."

For a few of the whites and the Indians, there were heartfelt and tearful farewells. Snana felt as though she was losing yet another child when she said goodbye to young Mary Schwandt. "When I turned this dear child over to the soldiers my heart ached again," she said, "but afterward I knew that I had done something which was right."

Chaska's mother tore her shawl in two and gave half to Sarah Wakefield. The two women clung to each other, crying, until Chaska came to escort her to Sibley. Sarah saw that Chaska was trembling with fear.

"You are a good woman," he told her. "You must talk to your white people, or they will kill me. You know I am a good man and did not shoot Mr. Gleason, and I saved your life. If I had been a bad man I would have gone with those bad chiefs."

Sarah assured him that he need not worry. No one was going to harm him. And true to her word, Sarah told Sibley how Chaska had helped and protected her and her children, and how more than once he had saved their lives. Sibley and his officers shook hands with Chaska and praised him for his actions. Sarah noticed that he seemed greatly relieved.

Joe Coursolle raced through the Indian village shouting the names of his daughters. Suddenly, the little girls stood before him, skinny, dirty, and dressed in rags.

"The Indians didn't hurt us," the older one said, "but we didn't have good things to eat like Mama makes. Sometimes we got awful cold. We slept on the ground. We didn't even have a blanket. And, oh, we were so lonesome. We wanted to see you and Mama and Cistina Joe and Duta."

Joe held them both in his arms and walked them back to Camp Release. He told them that their baby brother, Cistina Joe, had gone to a happy place, along with their dog. He did not tell them that he had killed Duta with his own hands to prevent him from barking and revealing his hiding place to the Indians. Maybe when they were older, he could tell them.

The soldiers greeted the captives with tenderness and concern, showering them with clothing and blankets. They prepared tents for their use, and they gave the children candy and sang to them around camp fires. They tried to ease the pain they saw in their eyes, but for some, nothing could be done to make a victim—or a family—whole again.

Nancy Faribault and her husband had sat down to a meal when a three-year-old girl, the daughter of friends, walked into their tent. She joined them at the table.

"This is not like the dinner Mama made the day Papa was killed," the child told them. "The Indians killed my papa on his very birthday. We were going to have a good dinner. Mama made a cake and everything nice, and Papa came home with a load of hay, and the Indians shot him. But my papa isn't dead for sure. He is in heaven with God. You know, Mrs. Faribault, God is everywhere."

They could not eat another bite.

14

VENGEANCE IS MINE

It was time for retribution, and the cry for it—the demand for it—came with "a wail and a howl," according to the Reverend Stephen Riggs. It came in letters to Sibley, in official orders and reports, in newspaper editorials, and in remarks from the soldiers at Camp Release. "They must be exterminated," a newspaper editor wrote, "and now is a good time to commence doing it." Another writer claimed that the "government [should] treat them for all time to come as outlaws, who have forfeited all right to property and life."

Two days after the release of the white captives, General Pope wrote to Sibley that the atrocious behavior of the Sioux called for "punishment beyond human power to inflict. There will be no peace in this region by virtue of treaties and Indian faith. It is my purpose utterly to exterminate the Sioux if I have the power to do so. . . . Destroy everything belonging to them and force them out to the plains, unless, as I suggest, you can capture them. They are to be treated as maniacs or wild beasts."

The Dakotas learned of this call for revenge as soon as the soldiers did. The day after her release, Sarah Wakefield walked from Camp Release to the Indian camp to get some of her belongings, and there she found Chaska, as anxious as before the surrender. He told her that the whites were rounding up the warriors, and he was certain he would be killed. Sarah, too, sensed the changed attitude toward the Indians, and this time she urged Chaska to flee.

"No," Chaska told her. "I am not a coward. I am not afraid to die. All I care about is my poor old mother. She will be left alone." He said he was sorry that Sarah had persuaded him to stay yesterday, when he might have gotten away safely. His mother was very angry with her. Sarah was chagrined.

That night, in the company of Sibley's officers and several former captives, she overheard Captain Grant say that the soldiers had taken seven "black devil Indians" into custody and would hang them the next day. She asked whether one of them was Chaska.

"Yes," Grant said, "and he will swing with the rest."

"Captain Grant," Sarah said, in the hearing of everyone in the tent, "if you hang that man, I will shoot you."

Everyone fell silent and stared at her as though she was insane. The stories about Sarah Wakefield were already spreading throughout Camp Release. Oh yes, she's the one who became a squaw, the one who's always defending the Indians. Sarah realized that her threat to Captain Grant was a mistake—it would not help Chaska—and she tried to make light of it.

"But," she said, "you must first teach me to shoot, for I am afraid of guns, unloaded even."

No Indians were hanged the next day, but a process was set in motion that would result in hangings in the future. Sibley established a five-man military commission to try those men accused of committing outrages against the settlers, and to execute those found guilty. It was necessary, he wrote to Pope, to make an example of the Indians who had perpetrated crimes against the whites. By then, Sibley's men had arrested sixteen braves from the friendly camp, Chaska among them. Sibley knew that many of the guilty had already fled, however. If he was going to hang them, he would have to catch them first.

Most of the Indians who had committed the murders and atrocities during the uprising had, indeed, gotten away, some heading north with Little Crow and still on the move. Others had not gone so far but had merely crossed the river where they could keep in touch with the situation and return to the Indian camp if all seemed well. Others set up their tepees out on the prairie and waited.

Gradually, during the first week after the soldiers arrived, up to eight hundred Sioux men, women, and children surrendered to them under flags of truce. Sibley sent groups of mixed-bloods into the countryside to tell the holdouts that anyone who surrendered would be treated as a prisoner of war. That was not the most desirable fate, but the alternative, with winter approaching, was starvation. The number of Indians crowding into the friendlies' village soon grew so large that a separate camp was established nearby.

A week later, General Sibley (recommended for the promotion by President Lincoln, although the U.S. Senate would take a while to confirm it) sent two detachments of troops upriver to bring in by force all the Indians they could find. No mercy would be shown unless they surrendered immediately. Messengers distributed Sibley's warning, along with the promise that innocent braves would not be harmed if they gave themselves up.

"Unless these people arrive very soon," Sibley added, "I will go in search of them with my troops and treat them as enemies; and if any more murders and depredations are committed upon the white settlers, I will destroy every camp . . . I can find, without mercy."

By October 11, Sibley decided that his efforts had netted all the Indians he was going to get. He had avoided making mass arrests because he knew that word would spread and prevent other Indians from surrendering. Now it was time to get tough. He sent additional troops to reinforce the guard at the second Indian camp and purged it of eighty-one men, who were chained in pairs at the ankles and led away.

Two days later, he mounted a larger operation. A contingent of 1,250 Indians had been sent, under guard, to Yellow Medicine to dig potatoes and gather corn for the soldiers, and to help feed all the Indians now in captivity. Of this group, 269 warriors had been earmarked for arrest. Agent Tom Galbraith was in charge. Acting under Sibley's orders, he told young Sam Brown to inform the Indians that a roll call would be taken in the morning and that every man would have to be counted in order to receive his annuity. This was standard procedure. The Sioux were glad to learn that they would receive the annuity payments after all that had occurred. It was a ruse, however, and, Brown said, "it worked like a charm."

At eight o'clock the next morning, the Indians lined up outside the ruins of the agency's large stone warehouse building. Only the outer walls remained intact. Galbraith, the officer commanding the guard detachment, and several clerks were seated at a table, with pens, paper, and bottles of ink before them, the familiar scene for an annuity distribution. As each family stepped up to the table, the name was recorded on a list, and a soldier escorted them to the far end of the warehouse, where Sam Brown was waiting.

Brown motioned the women and children to move on, but he told each man to go through a doorway. As heads of families, he explained, they had to be counted separately because the government planned to pay a bonus. No one suspected a trick, not even when Brown asked them to leave their weapons—their rifles, tomahawks, and knives—in a barrel by the door. The weapons would be returned shortly, he said. It all went off without a hitch. As soon as the Indians passed through the door, they were stopped, shackled, and led away.

As far as Sibley was concerned, the guilty had now been arrested. The trials could begin.

"This power of life and death is an awful thing to exercise," Sibley wrote to his wife, "and when I think [that] more than three hundred human beings are subject to that power, lodged in my hands, it makes me shudder. . . . I shall do full justice, but no more. I do not propose to murder any man, even a savage, who is shown to be innocent."

Sibley himself did not sit on the court, but he appointed five of his officers to do so. No one served as counsel for the defense. The five members of the military commission were the sole judges—decisions of life and death were theirs to make, not Sibley's. He chose Isaac Heard, a lawyer who had fought at Wood Lake, to be court recorder, and the Reverend Stephen Riggs to be what Heard called the "grand jury." It was Riggs who would decide, based on his interrogation of the captives, which Indians would be brought to trial. At least that was Sibley's intention. However, in the face of mounting public pressure for vengeance, for retribution, the plan had to be abandoned.

As Riggs explained it, "instead of taking individuals for trial, against whom some specific charge could be brought, the plan was adopted to subject all the grown men, with a few exceptions, to an investigation of the commission, trusting that the innocent could make their innocence appear." Thus, all Indians were considered guilty by the military commission until proven innocent, and that proof had to be presented by the accused.

Riggs shared the widely held belief that most, if not all, of the Indians in Sibley's hands were guilty of harming white settlers during the uprising. He wrote to President Lincoln that the majority of the Indians charged should be executed to meet the "demands of public justice," although Riggs did express concern about the manner in which the trials were being conducted. His doubts about the fairness of the proceedings increased daily, and he later concluded that most of the Indians were "condemned on general principles, without any specific charges proved." Nevertheless, Riggs played out his role as grand jury, and almost all of the charges brought against the defendants were based on his recommendations.

The first man to be tried was a twenty-seven-year-old mulatto named Joseph Godfrey, of French Canadian and black parentage, who had married a Sioux woman and lived with the Indians for about five years. He was charged with two counts of murder, one specific and the other general, the latter the result of being with other Indians when killings occurred. The complaints against Godfrey were based on testimony from Mary Schwandt, Mattie Williams, David Faribault, and Mary Woodbury. Although none of the witnesses could swear that they saw Godfrey kill anyone, they all recalled seeing him in war paint and clothing as a member of several war parties. They also heard him brag about killing at least seven whites, and he appeared to support the murder of whites as eagerly as the Indians did.

Godfrey, in his defense, argued that he was compelled to accompany the war parties because he had been threatened with death. He had boasted about killing settlers only to retain the goodwill of the Indians. He admitted to fighting on the side of the Indians at Fort Ridgely, New Ulm, Birch Coulee, and Wood Lake, and he participated in several raids on settlements. He denied killing anyone, but he did admit to striking a white man with the dull edge of a hatchet to satisfy the demands of the warriors who were with him.

Although neither guilt nor innocence was clearly established, Godfrey was sentenced to death. However, he made a favorable impression on the judges and the court recorder. "He had such an honest look and spoke with such a truthful tone," Heard recalled. And because Godfrey agreed to testify against the Indians, his sentence was commuted to ten years in prison.

Godfrey became "the means of bringing to justice a large number of savages," Heard said. "His observation and memory were remarkable. Not the least thing had escaped his eye or ear. Such an Indian had a double-barreled gun, another a single-barreled, another a long one, another a short one, another a lance, and another one nothing at all. One denied he was at the fort. Godfrey saw him there preparing his sons for battle, and recollected that he painted the face of one red, and drew a streak of green over his eyes."

An avenging angel, Godfrey's eyes were all-seeing, his finger pointing, his soft gentle voice condemning. The whites had no more effective witness than Godfrey. The Indians came to call him Otakle—He Who Kills Many.

Chaska was put on trial for being present when George Gleason was killed. Despite Sarah Wakefield's testimony on his behalf—she said clearly that it was Hapa who killed Gleason, and she reminded the court that Chaska had protected her during the six weeks in captivity—the commission found him guilty of murder and sentenced him to death. The judges considered it strange that a former captive would offer testimony favorable to an Indian.

Sarah was incensed, and she protested to the judges, continuing to proclaim Chaska's innocence. "Many things I need not have said . . . but everyone ought to know that my mind was in a dreadful state." The more she spoke—the more enraged and bitter she sounded about Chaska's fate—the less credence others placed on her words. They suspected that she had personal reasons for her pleas. "They soon at camp began to say that I was in love [with Chaska]," she wrote later, "that I was his wife; that I preferred living with him to my husband, and all such horrid, abominable reports."

Whites and Indians alike shunned her. Chaska's mother burst into tears at the sight of her and reproached her for not saving her son's life. "He saved your life many times," the old woman reminded her. "You have forgotten the Indians now [that] your white friends have come."

Before Sarah Wakefield left Camp Release, she visited Chaska in his tent. He was chained up with twenty other Indians, and it pained her to see him in such conditions. He refused to shake her hand, and he accused her of lying about him to the soldiers. Sarah broke down in tears, a fact noted with disapproval by the camp guards, when Chaska began to recount all that he had done for her and her children. She told him that she had sacrificed all her friends in her efforts to save him, and she was finally able to persuade him that she was not responsible for his being brought to trial.

"I said I would like to shake hands and bid him goodbye in friendship. He shook hands with me, and that is all that passed between us. I never saw him again."

Not all of the men who were tried and convicted were innocent; some had committed heinous crimes. However, most of those guilty of murder, rape, and other atrocities had escaped the trials simply by leaving before Sibley had arrived at the Indian camp. Many of those judged guilty were convicted on the basis of flimsy or questionable evidence, and most of those sentenced to death were condemned for merely being present at the battles of Fort Ridgely, New Ulm, Birch Coulee, or Wood Lake. As soon as a defendant admitted to being at one of those places and shooting at the whites, he was sentenced to hang. Before long, the five members of the military commission became so familiar with the details of those battles that they found it possible to dispose of a case in less than five minutes. Up to forty men were tried in a single day.

The Indians did not understand the proceedings and had no one to act on their behalf, or even to explain to them what was going on. Most of them, when questioned, readily admitted to participating in the fighting. They were, after all, warriors, doing battle with an enemy who had cheated and starved them and taken their land. When they realized that admitting to this meant they would hang, many of the men concocted stories to try to show that they had not killed anyone.

About two-thirds of the Indians said they had fired their weapons, but they also claimed that they had shot no more than two or three times and never hit anything because they were such poor marksmen. One man said that he could not possibly have harmed anyone because his gun was too short. Others testified that they had not fired a gun at all, that they were too young, their hearts too weak, they were too old and feeble. Some said they had slept through the battles or spent their time roasting corn, hiding behind rocks, or being sick.

Those Indians accused of stealing also invented explanations. One man justified his theft of a horse by saying that it was only a small horse and did not really count. Another admitted to taking a pair of oxen but said he had to because his wife needed them.

After days of listening to such testimony, the judges became inured to all protestations of innocence. If an Indian had been at New Ulm or Fort Ridgely, Birch Coulee or Wood Lake, he was guilty as sin and deserved to die.

By the third week of October, more than one hundred Indians had been sentenced to death, but there were still more than three hundred waiting in chains for their turn to appear before the military commission. Sibley had not carried out any of the executions because he was unsure of his authority to do so. He wrote to General Pope, and Pope, in turn, kicked the problem upstairs by writing to the War Department. Until an answer was received from Washington, the condemned men would remain alive.

Sibley had another problem. He was running low on food for his men and for the Indians, as well as on forage for the animals, and winter was fast approaching. If he stayed too long at Camp Release and snow made the roads impassable, they could all be stranded and starve. He decided that it was time to move everyone back to the Lower Agency. On October 23, the tents were struck, the Indian prisoners loaded in wagons, and Camp Release was abandoned to winter.

Throughout the month, Sibley had sent out patrols to hunt for food, bury bodies, and search for survivors. There were plenty of bodies, often lying in clusters of a dozen or more. In one house, soldiers found a human skull and a dead hog, which had apparently been feasting on the body. The troops encountered many wild and starving dogs as well as dead and dying oxen, cattle, and buffalo, frothing at the mouth and writhing in agony from hydrophobia. A spate of prairie fires had erased all traces of many victims; they were never found or counted.

On one patrol, two soldiers approached a cabin not far from the Upper Agency. They pushed open the door and found on the floor an emaciated woman and her three-year-old daughter. The woman, nearly blind, assumed that the visitors were Indians, and she begged them not to kill her. She had been hiding for more than two months, since the day the uprising began. Her husband and relatives had all been killed. She was identified as twenty-eight-year-old Justina Boelter, who had fled her home with two children, ages three and five. In five weeks, they had found in the fields only a few cucumbers and potatoes to eat. The older girl died of starvation, but Justina was too weak to bury the body or even to leave her daughter's side.

"The body now became offensive," she wrote later, "and I crawled off some ten feet from the place where the dead child lay." Justina stayed in that spot for five days, unable to move, subsisting on the leaves of a grapevine. "The flies had now become so troublesome near the dead child that I was unable to remain longer by it. The strength I had gained from the grape leaves enabled me to remove some fifty yards away." She and the three-year-old spent another two weeks outdoors, until frost killed the leaves.

With great effort, Justina dragged herself a quarter of a

mile to a farm, where she unearthed a small cucumber and a few potatoes, and took the food back to her young daughter. Snakes found their hiding place, and the weather became so cold that she realized they would freeze to death if they did not get indoors. She decided to strike out for home—she had never been more than a mile or two away. If she was to die, let it be there.

The house had been ransacked, but three young turnips had sprouted from seeds the Indians accidentally scattered on the ground when they carried off their plunder back in August. Justina and the child settled in, and there they stayed until the soldiers came upon them. They were the last victims of the great Sioux uprising ever to be found alive.

The trials resumed at the Lower Agency in a log house that had survived the assault at the beginning of the war, although its owner had not. Many white settlers thought it fitting that the trials conclude at the site of the Indians' first attack. The remaining cases—272 prisoners—were disposed of within ten days. When the commission completed its work on November 5, it had tried a total of 392 Indians and sentenced 16 to jail terms and 307 to death. Sibley approved all the sentences except one. He reduced the sentence of John Other Day's brother from death to imprisonment, in part because the evidence seemed less than conclusive but also because John Other Day, who had saved the lives of many whites, made an impassioned appeal.

Sibley wanted to carry out the executions as soon as possible, and so did Pope, but both remained uncertain about their authority to do so. No answer had been received from the War Department to Pope's query on the matter, and neither man was willing to proceed without authorization. Pope, increasingly impatient and irritated by the delay, took the extraordinary step on November 7 of telegraphing to President Lincoln the entire list of names of the condemned Indians, which by then had been cut to 303. The cost was a staggering four hundred dollars. The expenditure was seen as so excessive that *The New York Times* suggested in an editorial that the amount be deducted from Pope's salary.

The President replied three days later, asking for the complete trial records for each man, and suggesting pointedly that they be sent by mail. Lincoln wanted to determine in each case who was guilty of murder or rape, and who had been convicted solely because he had participated in a battle. Pope was incensed by Lincoln's meddling, by the refusal to countenance hanging them all, and he fired off an angry reply—by mail. "The only distinction between the culprits is as to which of them murdered most people or violated most young girls. All of them are guilty of these things in more or less degree." Nevertheless, Pope eventually complied with Lincoln's request.

While waiting for the President's decision, Sibley decided to move the rest of the Sioux to Fort Snelling, where it would be easier to feed them. There were 1,658 Indians—men, women, and children—and they were bundled into wagons that formed a train four miles long. With an escort commanded by Lt. Col. William Marshall, the column left the Lower Agency on November 7 and reached the town of Henderson four days later. The citizens were waiting for them.

Sam Brown recalled that the streets were "crowded with an angry and excited populace, cursing, shouting, and crying. Men, women, and children armed with guns, knives, clubs, and stones rushed upon the Indians as the train was passing by, and before the soldiers could interfere and stop them, succeeded in pulling many of the old men and women and even children from the wagons by the hair of the head and beating them. . . . I saw an enraged white woman rush up to one of the wagons and snatch a nursing babe from its mother's breast and dash it violently upon the ground."

The soldiers dragged the white woman away and handed the battered infant back to its mother; it died within a few hours. A drunken white man approached a wagon and aimed his pistol at Sam Brown's uncle, one of the friendly Indians who had helped to save the white captives. Colonel Marshall rode up, saber drawn, and knocked the man's gun out of his hand. The soldiers drove the crowds back and hurried the wagon train through town as fast as they could.

They reached Fort Snelling on November 13. The Indians were confined in a fenced camp of tepees on the north side of the river. It was a gloomy, inhospitable site, on bottomland that turned to mud and offered no protection from the icy winter winds. Settlers ran off the Indians' few horses and oxen and taunted them until eventually they grew bored. The army allotted the Indians only meager rations, typically bread for the adults and crackers for the children.

An epidemic of measles broke out among the young. The Indians, who had never known the disease, blamed it on the crackers. The death rate was high, but the Sioux could do nothing but wait for the Great Father to decide their future. Those who had not been charged with a crime, those who had risked their own lives to save the whites, and even those who had argued against the outrages of the uprising were all being punished. In the winter of 1862, being an Indian was crime enough.

Two days after the wagon train of Indians left the Lower Agency for Fort Snelling, Sibley marched the rest of his troops and the Indian prisoners to Camp Lincoln, a stockade erected near the town of South Bend. The prisoners were crowded into small carts that held four apiece. "We were bound securely," one man recalled, "and on our journey resembled a load of animals on their way to market." Their route took them through New Ulm, whose citizens were busy recovering the bodies of those who had been killed in the two Indian attacks, preparing them for a proper burial.

When the townspeople of New Ulm spotted the caravan approaching, they went berserk. Frenzied white men and women attacked the Indian prisoners with pitchforks, hoes, clubs, and rocks. One woman beat a warrior with her fists, breaking his jaw and toppling him from the wagon. Sibley did not dare order his troops to fire on the crowd, fearing that they would turn on his men, but he was able to drive the whites back with a bayonet charge. One soldier and fifteen Indians sustained serious injuries before the wagon train could pass out of sight.

There was more trouble at Camp Lincoln. On December 4, word spread that settlers from the town of Mankato planned to storm the stockade and they were urging every able-bodied man in the area to join them. About 150 men gathered that night at the Mankato House Hotel to bolster their courage with whiskey provided by a generous citizen. Camp Lincoln's commanding officer, Col. Stephen Miller, heard about the mob and ordered a company of cavalry to meet it on the road.

The men left the hotel and headed for the stockade, stopping before they reached it to allow the stragglers in the rear time to catch up. While they waited, perhaps sobered a bit by the cold night air, the men conferred about just what it was they were going to do when they got to the camp. No one seemed to be sure; much of their passion had been spent. Most of them were unarmed, and without a leader to rally them, they milled around shouting and cursing the Indians. They were still arguing when the cavalry arrived.

Capt. Horace Austin ordered his troopers to encircle the crowd and place the men under arrest. He announced that he would escort them to Camp Lincoln, where Colonel Miller wanted to have a talk with them. The men of Mankato did not think much of the idea and refused to go, until Austin ordered his men to draw sabers.

Subdued, the men walked on, prodded by the cavalry, until they reached Miller's headquarters. The colonel asked what they were doing out on the road at midnight. Some said they were on their way to visit friends across the river. Others admitted that they were going to the stockade, but only out of curiosity. They just wanted to see the savages, not harm them. Miller said that he would let them go if they would promise to do their visiting and gawking at a more reasonable hour. They agreed, feeling more than a little sheepish.

The trouble had passed, but Sibley was worried that it would happen again. A larger and more determined lynch mob might succeed. A lot of people were madder than hell that President Lincoln was taking so long to approve the death sentences, and the longer he took, the angrier the people became. On December 6, Sibley expressed his opinion about the danger in a letter to department headquarters in St. Paul.

"Colonel Miller informs me that large numbers of citizens are assembling, and he fears a serious collision. I have authorized him to declare martial law, if necessary, and call to his assistance all the troops within his reach. He thinks it will require 1000 true men to protect the prisoners against all organized popular outbreaks." In closing, Sibley revealed what may have been his real motive: to force the President to speed up his decision and proceed with the executions. "Please telegraph the facts to the president, and ask instructions. Any hour may witness a sad conflict, if it has not already occurred."

Two days later, in another report, Sibley escalated the danger he perceived from angry civilians, especially if Lincoln saw fit to pardon the Indians.

> Dispatches and private letters just received indicate a fearful collision between the United States forces and the citizens. Combinations, embracing thousands of men in all parts of the state, are said to be forming, and in a few days our troops, with the Indian prisoners, will be literally besieged. I shall concentrate all the men I can at Mankato. But should the president pardon the Indians, there will be a determined effort to get them in possession, which will be resented, and may cost the lives of thousands of our citizens. Ask the president to keep secret his decision, whatever it may be, until I have prepared myself as best I can. God knows how much the excitement is increasing and extending.

Sibley was seeing lynch mobs where none existed, charging that more lives might be lost to aroused citizens than had been taken in the Indian uprising. It might take, he predicted, almost as many troops to defend the Indians now as it had taken to subdue them. His fears were shared by Governor Ramsey, who issued a proclamation calling on the people of Minnesota to desist from disorderly demonstrations. The public must not take the law into its own hands. Justice will be done eventually, Ramsey explained, although he agreed that it was certainly taking a long time.

"Our people, indeed, have had just reason to complain of the tardiness of executive action in the premises, but they ought to find some reason for forbearance in the absorbing cases which weigh upon the president."

The people must be patient, Ramsey said, but he also noted that if the President decided not to execute the Indians, then perhaps the state would settle the issue on its own.

In Washington, President Lincoln was inundated with telegrams, letters, resolutions, and visitors, all hoping to influence his decision about the convicted Sioux Indians. The pressure was intense on both sides of the issue—from those urging leniency, mercy, and compassion, and those calling for the immediate execution of all 303 of the condemned. It was, in part, a conflict between East and West, between those living in such cities as Philadelphia and Boston, far from the threat of Indian depredations, and those in the plains, forests, and valleys of Minnesota, burying their dead, tending their wounded, and grieving for their losses.

Governor Ramsey wrote to Lincoln to urge the speedy execution of the Indians. He predicted that if they were pardoned, "private revenge would on all this border take the place of official judgment." That theme, that the people would exact retribution if the President did not, rang clearly through most of the communications Lincoln received from the frontier.

General Pope wrote that unless the guilty were hanged, there would be an "indiscriminate massacre" of all the Indians, including innocent women, children, and old men. "The troops are entirely new and raw," Pope said, "and are in full sympathy with the people on this subject. I will do the best I can, but fear a terrible result." General Sibley agreed that a general massacre of the Indians was inevitable if the executions were not carried out soon.

A U.S. senator and two congressmen from Minnesota informed Lincoln that if he failed to order the executions, "the outraged people of Minnesota will dispose of the wretches without law. These two people[s] cannot live together. We do not wish to see mob law inaugurated in Minnesota, as it certainly will be, if you force the people to do it. We tremble at the approach of such a condition of things in our state."

The citizens of St. Paul sent a resolution to the President demanding not only the execution of the convicted Indians but also the banishment of every Sioux from the state. "The blood of hundreds of our murdered fellow citizens cries from the ground for vengeance. 'Vengeance is mine, I will repay, saith the Lord,' and the authorities of the United States are, we believe, the chosen instrument to execute that vengeance. . . . The Indian's nature can no more be trusted than the wolf's. Tame him, cultivate him, strive to Christianize him, as you will, and the sight of blood will in an instant call out the savage, wolfish, devilish instincts of the race."

Equally fervent appeals for mercy reached Lincoln from friends of the Indians, from those who opposed the death penalty, and from persons who considered the Indians to be legitimate prisoners of war. William Dole, the Commissioner of Indian Affairs, protested that it was unfair to punish men who had laid down their arms and surrendered. Quakers and clergymen appealed for mercy, pointing to the terrible image of 303 human beings dangling from a gallows in this supposedly civilized nation. Such a picture, they warned, would haunt the United States for generations to come and make Americans look like barbarians in the eyes of the world.

Some argued the diplomatic benefits of pardoning the Indians, an action that could help Washington in the war against the Confederates. The Southern cause was receiving sympathetic hearings in England and France, while the Union was trying to dissuade those governments from officially recognizing the Confederate States. A mass killing of more than three hundred Indians by the federal government would present a stark contrast to the courtly, noble, and gracious South.

The most intense personal pressure brought to bear on Lincoln came from a relative of General Halleck's, the articulate, well-born, highly educated forty-year-old bishop of Minnesota's Protestant Episcopal Church, Henry Benjamin Whipple. Whipple journeyed to Washington to give the President an eloquent account of the reasons for the Indian uprising—the broken treaties, the routine cheating by the traders, the near-starvation conditions, and the missed annuity payment. He reminded Lincoln that the Sioux had long suffered in silence.

Whipple was a forceful and energetic speaker who brooked no interruption, not even from the President of the United States. Lincoln was impressed, at least with the man's spirit.

"He came here the other day," Lincoln told a visitor, "and talked with me about the rascality of this Indian business, until I felt it down to my boots."

In the end, adherence to the law influenced Lincoln's decision more than passion and eloquence, bigotry and threats of retaliation. He had given the trial records to two young attorneys, George Whiting and Francis Ruggles, and asked them to prepare an abstract of their findings. Based on his reading of their analysis, Lincoln concluded that only thirty-nine Indians were "guilty of individual murders and atrocious abuse of their female captives."

On December 6, he wrote, in his own hand, the order to Sibley to execute those thirty-nine prisoners found guilty of murder and rape; he appended the names in a long list. The others who had been convicted—those judged guilty solely of participating in battles—were to be held "subject to further orders, taking care that they neither escape nor are subjected to any unlawful violence."

Lincoln need not have been concerned about unlawful violence. Although many citizens of Minnesota were disappointed by his decision, and quite a few were angry, they did not rise up and seek vengeance on their own. Sibley, and Governor Ramsey, had underestimated them.

On Monday, December 22, 1862, the thirty-nine condemned men were separated from the others and taken to a room in a stone building next to the log jail. There they were chained to the floor. Identifying the Indians scheduled to be executed had proved difficult; there were often several with the same or similar names—four Chaskays, for example, and three Washechoons. During the trials, each warrior had been assigned a number, and Lincoln's list and execution orders had been drawn up in accordance with those numbers. Unfortunately, no one connected with the military commission remembered which number belonged to which Indian.

To keep from hanging the wrong men, Joe Brown was called on to examine the Indians and select the ones on the President's list. Brown was the logical choice for the task—no one knew the Indians as well as he did—but he admitted that he did not recognize them all. He was, he said, pretty sure he had chosen the correct ones.

At 2:30 P.M., Colonel Miller and the Reverend Riggs entered the prisoners' room. Miller had come to tell them that they were soon to die. Riggs acted as translator.

"The commanding officer at this place has called to speak to you upon a very serious subject this afternoon. Your Great Father in Washington, after carefully reading what the witnesses have testified in your several trials, has come to the conclusion that you have each been guilty of wantonly and wickedly murdering his white children; and for this reason, he has directed that you each be hanged by the neck until you are dead, on next Friday, and that order will be carried into effect at ten o'clock in the forenoon."

The Indians took the news impassively, as though they had been expecting it. They grunted in acknowledgment and puffed calmly on their pipes. One knocked the ashes from his pipe onto the floor when the date and time of the execution were announced. Another rubbed some kinnikinnick in his hand, preparing to stuff it into his pipe's bowl.

Riggs continued to translate Colonel Miller's words, telling the prisoners that they could select a spiritual adviser—Catholic or Protestant—to visit them over the next few days. The President's letter was read, first in English and then in Dakota. Miller concluded with an appeal for them to turn to religion—the white man's religion—for solace.

"Say to them now," he directed Riggs, "that they have so sinned against their fellow men that there is no hope for clemency except in the mercy of God, through the merits of the blessed Redeemer; and that I earnestly exhort them to apply to that, as their only remaining source of comfort and consolation."

After Colonel Miller left, Riggs spent several hours talking with the prisoners and writing down their remarks. Most protested their innocence but said that they recognized that because so many whites had been killed by the Sioux, it was necessary to kill some Indians in return. Most remained composed when they spoke to Riggs, and when a few became excitable, the others quieted them and told them to tell the truth. Riggs wrote letters for them to their friends and relatives, tell-

ing them that the men expected to go to live with the Great
Spirit after death, so there was no reason for sadness.

Rdainyanka wrote bitterly to his father-in-law, the peace
chief Wabasha, who had urged him to surrender to the whites.

> You have deceived me. You told me that if we
> followed the advice of General Sibley, and gave
> ourselves up to the whites, all would be well; no
> innocent man would be injured. I have not
> killed, wounded, or injured a white man, or any
> white persons. I have not participated in the
> plunder of their property; and yet today I am set
> apart for execution, and must die in a few days,
> while men who are guilty will remain in prison.
>
> My wife is your daughter, my children are
> your grandchildren. I leave them all in your care
> and under your protection. Do not let them suf
> fer; and when my children are grown up, let
> them know that their father died because he fol-
> lowed the advice of his chief, and without having
> the blood of a white man to answer for to the
> Great Spirit.
>
> My wife and children are dear to me. Let
> them not grieve for me. Let them remember that
> the brave should be prepared to meet death; and
> I will do as becomes a Dakota.

The list of those to be executed was published in newspapers across the state. In the town of Red Wing on the border
with Wisconsin, eighty miles northeast of Mankato, Sarah
Wakefield read the list while she was visiting with friends. She
was relieved that Chaska's name was not on it. "I noticed the
name of Chaskadon, but knew it was not Chaska's number,
and that he was not guilty of the crime that Chaskadon was
being punished for." She did not plan to attend the hangings.

On Wednesday, Christmas Eve, each condemned man was allowed to send for any relatives and friends from the stockade
near Mankato, to say farewell. Joe Brown was present and was

much moved by the sadness of the occasion. The braves passed on messages to be conveyed to loved ones still held at Fort Snelling. Many left word for their children, exhorting them to adopt Christianity and to remain friendly with the whites.

Some were too overcome with emotion to talk, but others joked and chatted as though they were sitting around a camp fire. One old warrior asked a friend to tell his family not to mourn. He was old and would not have lived much longer, anyway. His death, he said, should be seen as nothing more than moving to a better world. "I have every hope of going direct to the abode of the Great Spirit, where I shall always be happy."

His remark was overheard, and another Indian prisoner commented on it.

> Yes, tell our friends that we are being removed from this world over the same path they must shortly travel. We go first, but many of our friends may follow us in a very short time. I expect to go direct to the abode of the Great Spirit, and to be happy when I get there; but we are told that the road is long and the distance great. Therefore, as I am slow in all my movements, it will probably take me a long time to reach the end of the journey, and I should not be surprised if some of the young, active men we will leave behind us will pass me on the road before I reach the place of my destination.

On Thursday, the Dakota women who had been put to work as cooks for the prisoners were allowed to visit. The men gave them gifts to pass on to their families—locks of hair, blankets, clothing, and their other few possessions. They would have no further use for them. No sadness or solemnity was expressed, no wailing or tears. No Sioux warrior would show weakness in front of women.

The clergymen also called on them that day—Father Ravoux, the Reverend Riggs, and the Reverend Williamson. They talked to the men about the salvation of their souls. About thirty asked Father Ravoux to baptize them in the Catholic faith, to the disappointment of the Protestant ministers, who had worked for many years trying to convert the Indians. There was, however, a nondenominational reason for the Indians' choice. One of the condemned men was a mixed-blood who had become a Catholic, and the others were simply following his example.

Isaac Heard, the military court recorder, and Col. William Marshall visited the Indians, out of curiosity more than anything else. Heard wrote:

> They were all fastened to the floor by chains, two by two. Some were sitting up, smoking and conversing, while others were reclining, covered with blankets and apparently asleep. . . . The majority of them were young men, though several were quite old and gray-headed, ranging perhaps toward seventy. One was quite a youth, not over sixteen. They all appeared cheerful and contented, and scarcely to reflect on the certain doom which awaited them. [They] looked as innocent as children. They smiled at your entrance, and held out their hands to be shaken, which yet appeared to be gory with the blood of babes. Oh treachery, thy name is Dakota.

Later that same day, the brave called Round Wind received a reprieve from President Lincoln. He had been convicted on the testimony of two German boys who said they saw him kill their mother. The ministers Williamson and Riggs had appealed to Lincoln, arguing that Round Wind had been on the opposite side of the river at least ten miles from where the woman had been killed. Round Wind was escorted back to the log jail, and thirty-eight men were left to die.

Friday morning, December 26: The time had come. The three clergymen visited the prisoners again, and Father Ravoux urged them to be strong, to show no signs of fear. As he spoke, one of the older men, Tazoo, began to chant the mournful Dakota death wail. The others picked it up and soon the rhythmic chanting filled the room with wild, unearthly sound. It stopped as suddenly as it had begun. The Indians puffed on their pipes, sitting calmly, until someone started the chant again.

The Reverend Williamson spoke to them, and his remarks were followed by another chorus of death wails. "The last was thrilling beyond expression," wrote a reporter. "The trembling voices, the forms shaking with passionate emotion, the half-uttered words through set teeth, all made up a scene which no one who saw [it] can ever forget.

"The influence of the wild music of their death song upon them was almost magical. Their whole manner changed after they had closed their singing, and an air of cheerful unconcern marked all of them. It seemed as if, during their passionate wailing, they had passed in spirit through the valley of the shadow of death, and already had their eyes fixed on the pleasant hunting grounds beyond."

The Indians laughed and bade one another cheerful farewells and wishes for pleasant journeys to the spirit land. They shook hands with the whites and pointed their fingers skyward. "Me going up," one said. When the soldiers came for them, they shook hands with them, too, and when they were led outside, they rushed toward the gallows, gladdened to be going to the abode of the Great Spirit, where they would be free again.

Two days later, Sarah Wakefield read a newspaper account of the execution and was horrified to find her name and that of Chaska in the article. He had been hanged by mistake, in place of Chaskadon, who had killed a pregnant woman and cut the fetus out of her body.

"Mrs. Wakefield, Dear Madam," the Reverend Riggs wrote to her two months later. "In regard to the mistake by which Chaska was hanged instead of another, I doubt whether I can satisfactorily explain it. We all felt a solemn responsibility and a fear that some mistake should occur. . . . When the name Chaska was called in the prison on that fatal morning, your protector answered to it and walked out. I do not think anyone was to blame. We all regretted the mistake very much."

15

THE HILLS WERE SOON COVERED WITH GRAVES

Little Crow was a wanted man with a price on his head. "I have ordered $500 reward for him dead or alive," Pope wrote to General Halleck on October 7, "so as to make him an outlaw among the Indians. Nearly the whole of his band have deserted him and are coming in begging for mercy."

With fewer than three hundred of his people, Little Crow headed northwest and deeper into winter with each passing mile. The prairie grass turned brown and the trees were already bare of leaves. The sky became leaden and the breeze that blew in the Indians' faces was a harbinger of the icy winds that would soon sweep down from Canada. There would be no forage for the ponies and no fields to strip of corn and cucumbers. The days ahead looked as bleak as the skies.

Yet Little Crow held out hope for the future. Indeed, he had grand plans. He wanted to forge a mighty alliance of the Sioux tribes of the western plains—the Yanktons, Yanktonais, and Tetons—and to obtain guns and ammunition from the British in Canada. He envisioned a massive, well-provisioned army marching from the west across Minnesota to chase the whites out of his homeland forever.

By the end of the month, he had camped with a band of Sissetons, led by Standing Buffalo, some twenty miles north of Big Stone Lake, about eighty-five miles from the Upper Agency. Little Crow appealed to Standing Buffalo for help in continuing the war against the whites. Some of Standing Buffalo's warriors had been involved in the second attack on Fort Ridgely, although the chief had not been in favor of it. He feared retaliation from the army and was, therefore, not receptive to Little Crow's plea for aid.

While Standing Buffalo and his leaders discussed the matter in councils, a Sioux scout—a farmer Indian now employed by the military—arrived with a message from General Sibley, asking Standing Buffalo to refuse all assistance to Little Crow. Sibley further requested that the Sissetons surrender.

Little Crow addressed the council, using Sibley's note to promote his own position. Sibley's army, Little Crow told them, would soon reach the Sisseton camp and would kill Standing Buffalo and all the Sioux they found there, no matter which tribe they belonged to or whether they favored war or peace. Some of the Sissetons became so concerned by Little Crow's picture of disaster that they fled the village without waiting for the council's decision.

When Standing Buffalo and his leaders finally reached a conclusion, he summoned Little Crow. "You have already made much trouble for my people," Standing Buffalo said. "Go to Canada or where you please, but go away from me and off the lands of my people."

Little Crow moved on, leading his warriors far northwest again, onto the barren plains of the Dakota Territory. They camped for a week near Devil's Lake, more than 200 miles from Standing Buffalo's village, then veered southwest, traveling another 160 miles to join a tribe of Yanktons along the Missouri River. The Yanktons were no more interested in following Little Crow to war than Standing Buffalo had been, but they did allow him to stay and share their food. He visited other nearby Yankton villages, urging the warriors to ally themselves with his band, but he met with no success. At one encampment, he pleaded with the people repeatedly, for almost a month, until they broke camp and left in anger. He had suggested that they attack a trading post at Fort Pierre. Not only did they refuse, but they sent some of their men to guard the post in case Little Crow attacked it on his own!

Rebuffed again, he gathered his band and journeyed north for four days, up the Missouri River, trying to enlist support from the Mandan, Ree, and Gros Ventre tribes. Although the Sioux had warred with those nations in the past, Little Crow now approached them as a friend.

A group of Little Crow's braves approached one village, signaling that theirs was a peacemaking mission and indicating clearly that they were not a war party. They whooped, yelled, danced, and fired their guns in the air, making as much noise and commotion as they could, and displaying a peace pipe at the same time. These actions were traditionally accepted as showing a desire among the tribes to hold a council, to put past grievances and disputes behind them, at least for the moment. However, the Mandans, Rees, and Gros Ventres were unreceptive and unfavorably disposed toward the Sioux. Some warriors opened fire as soon as the Sioux came within range. Others slipped behind Little Crow's party, and almost succeeded in cutting off their retreat. Taken by surprise and vastly outnumbered, the Sioux turned and fled, leaving eight braves behind, all dead. Obviously, Little Crow would find no help there. Only one option was left to him: He would have to go north to Canada.

Some of Little Crow's Mdewakantons and a number of Standing Buffalo's Sissetons had already crossed the border into Canada. In late December, that party arrived at Fort Garry, sixty miles north of the border, now the site of Winnipeg. The Indians hoped to exploit what they considered to be a long-standing relationship with the British, dating from the War of 1812, when they had given the British considerable assistance. Little Crow's grandfather had been a prominent Sioux leader in that conflict. The Sioux believed that the British were, therefore, beholden to them forever, a view not shared by the British in 1862.

The British did not offer the Sioux delegation an effusive

welcome. They told the Indians that it would be better for everyone if they did not come to Canada. They were concerned that if the Sioux migrated north in large numbers, they would take over British territory, straining the area's food supply, almost all of which had to be shipped from the East. The Indians might also provoke a war with the local Cree and Chippewa tribes, which were old enemies of the Sioux. Or, if the Sioux were able to persuade these former enemies to unite with them, they might all decide to turn on the whites. For several reasons, then, the presence of the Sioux could mean only trouble for the British, and although they did not try to force them to leave, they offered no assistance beyond a little food, and they made no promises for the future.

Small bands of Mdewakantons and Sissetons continued to filter across the border into Canada and set up camps. They carried little sustenance with them, but they did bring many of the goods they had stolen from the white settlements. The local traders eagerly swapped food for this merchandise, dangerously depleting the only food stocks available to the white population. No wagon trains were expected from the East with additional provisions until late spring or early summer.

Little Crow, still smarting from his failure to unite the tribes but heartened by the reports he was receiving from Canada, decided to go himself in late April of 1863. Fewer than one hundred people remained with him. They stopped first at the border town of St. Joseph, where he sought advice from Father Alexis André, a Catholic priest. Little Crow told the priest that he planned to ask the British for a parcel of land on which he and his people could start a new life. To demonstrate his loyalty, he had advised his men to wear the British medals and decorations that had been awarded to their grandfathers in the War of 1812, and he raised a large British flag over his camp. He told Father André of all the help the Mdewakantons had once given the British and of the promise made at that time to aid the Indians should they ever need it. Now was the time to call on that promise.

He sent two messengers to Fort Garry with instructions to call on the governor of the Hudson's Bay Company, Alexander

Dallas, and to tell him of the strong friendship the Sioux felt toward the people of Canada. Without waiting for them to return, Little Crow led his party toward Pembina, a few miles south of the border, the next stop on the road to the fort. He reached it on May 24 and tried to parley with the local Indians. Most of the chiefs refused to meet him, and others openly expressed their hatred. One chief who did receive him draped himself in an American flag, leaving no doubt about his allegiance.

Little Crow pushed on and arrived in grand style at Fort Garry on May 27. He and his followers formed a colorful parade as they made their way down the main street on horseback and in wagons. Men and women had decked themselves out in the finery taken from the whites—broadcloth coats and trousers, leather leggings, silk dresses, dainty parasols. According to his biographer, Little Crow "upstaged the women, appearing in a black coat with velvet collar, a breech cloth of broadcloth, and deerskin leggings. He wore one fine shawl around his neck and another around his waist as a sash. As a sidearm, he carried a seven-shooter, a showy but delicate weapon."

He met with Alexander Dallas to say that he offered peace and friendship to the Canadian people but war "to the knife" against the United States. It was for that war, he told Dallas, that he needed help. The Indians were fighting "with a rope around their necks," and Little Crow hoped he could count on the British to supply them with weapons and ammunition to continue their fight. When the British had needed assistance in 1812, Little Crow reminded him, the Indians had come to their side without question or hesitation.

Despite his spectacular appearance, Little Crow did not make a good impression. Some of those present said that he behaved in an insolent and arrogant manner. He was described as abrupt, demanding, and curt. Dallas refused his request for guns and ammunition, whereupon Little Crow retorted that he did not need them, anyway; the Sioux had more than enough to kill all the Americans. He threatened to use St. Joseph as a base of operations for conducting raids into Minnesota, but he stopped just short of daring Dallas to stop him. As the three days of talks wore on, however, Little Crow became more conciliatory, and he asked Dallas to intercede with Sibley to stop the war and free the Sioux who were being held as prisoners in Minnesota.

Little Crow knew about the mass hangings at Mankato and the miserable conditions under which the rest of the Sioux were living. He expressed concern about their welfare and their future, and he prodded Dallas to write to Sibley to try to secure their release. Remind Sibley, he urged, that Little Crow had turned over the white captives at Camp Release. Now it was Sibley's time to reciprocate.

Dallas finally agreed to write to Sibley, although nothing ever came of it, but that was the only request he granted. He remained adamant on the matter of weapons. He gave the Indians some food and a few presents as a perfunctory gesture of friendship and was relieved when Little Crow announced that the talks were over and he was leaving. Dallas did not hesitate to suggest that it would be best if Little Crow did not return to Canada.

When the Sioux party reached St. Joseph on their way south, scouts informed them of major troop movements in the Dakota Territory. General Pope had formed two armies, one of 3,300 infantry under Sibley, who, of course, had asked for more troops, and another of 4,000 cavalry under Gen. Alfred Sully. Both armies moved out in mid-June, Sibley from Minnesota heading west and Sully from the lower border of the Dakota Territory heading north. The plan was to form a pincer movement, joining forces not far from Devil's Lake, to trap the Sioux who were still roaming the Dakota Territory. Pope was looking for some eight hundred Indians from the Lower Agency and up to four thousand from the Upper Agency, plus unknown thousands of Yanktons and Yanktonais. Forewarned of every movement of the American armies, many of the Indians crossed into Canada. Red Middle Voice, who, with Shakopee, bore primary responsibility for fomenting the August uprising, met his death as he fled north, killed by a roving band of Chippewas.

Pope's military expedition was not a success. The jaws of the pincers never closed. The soldiers drove the Sioux farther from Minnesota, but only for a time. As soon as the troops withdrew, the Indians returned to their camps in the Dakota Territory, within striking distance of the Minnesota reservation. There were a few battles, and men on both sides died, more Indians than soldiers. Several Indian villages were burned and about a hundred people taken captive—women, children, and some braves. In general, however, the operation—expensive, cumbersome, and slow—failed to live up to Sibley's and Sully's expectations, and it shattered Pope's dream of a victory that would restore him to a prominent command. Many felt that the seven thousand troops could have been put to better use against the Confederates.

However disappointing the campaign was to the army, its effect on Little Crow was devastating. Although he never came within sight of those long blue-coated columns, the threat of the advancing armies itself was sufficient to scatter his remaining band. Most of the warriors left him, saying that they would rather give themselves up to Sibley than be caught with Little Crow in a trap. The Sissetons and Wahpetons were also angry with him. It was bad enough that they had lost their annuity payment because of Little Crow. Now the army was chasing them farther from their home. They might never be able to return.

Sibley won his war against Little Crow not on the battlefield but by attrition, leaving him with only a handful of supporters, few supplies, and no hope for reclaiming his territory. The chief was finally forced to recognize that he would never forge an alliance of the Indian nations and return to the land of his fathers at the head of an avenging army. Of the hundreds, the thousands, of Sioux he had once led, who had come to him for guidance and counsel, only seventeen remained— sixteen men and one woman, including his sixteen-year-old son and a son-in-law. They would follow him wherever he chose to go, they pledged, and Little Crow did not hesitate. He knew where he would lead them—back to Minnesota, back to the Big Woods that covered much of the eastern portion of the state, the place where he had spent his childhood. Little Crow was going home.

He was going home to die. "When we were coming

back," his son, Wowinape, recalled, "he said he could not fight the white men, but would go below and steal horses from them, and give them to his children, so that they could be comfortable, and then he would go away off. Father also told me he was getting old, and wanted me to go with him to carry his [medicine] bundles."

Men who carried medicine bundles were, in Sioux lore, assured long life and happiness. It was expected that Sioux warriors facing death would pass them on to their next of kin. When a chief handed down the bundles, it symbolized the passing of leadership from one generation to the next.

Little Crow's small party traveled from Devil's Lake in the Dakota Territory to the vicinity of Hutchinson, north of Yellow Medicine, a distance of about 350 miles. They arrived in late June, and a few braves immediately split off to pursue their attacks on the white settlers. One group came across Amos Dustin, riding in his ox cart with his mother, his wife, and their three children. They were found a week later, but only Mrs. Dustin and two children were alive, and she died a few days later from arrow wounds. In another incident, a white man traveling alone was murdered. The brave responsible brought Little Crow the man's gray coat, and the chief wore it frequently in the days ahead.

Two days later, a quarrel erupted among the Indians. Several of the men, and the woman, decided to return to Canada; the rest of the party went south. Little Crow did not accompany either group. He wanted to stay where he was, in the Big Woods, with his son, the only companion left to him. They camped about six miles north of the town, near Scattered Lake. It was a good place, and a good time. Already the berries were ripening on the vines.

In the late afternoon hours of July 3, Little Crow and Wowinape were picking raspberries in a small clearing in the woods. Not far away, Nathan Lamson and his son, Chauncey, were out hunting. When they spotted the two Indians through the trees, they dropped to the ground and inched toward a poplar tree with a flurry of vines around its base. It was as close as they dared get. Nathan Lamson steadied his rifle against the trunk, took aim at the older of the two Indians, and fired. Little Crow yelled, threw back his hands, and fell to the ground.

"He was hit the first time in the side," his son said, "just above the hip. His gun and mine were lying on the ground. He took up my gun and fired it first, and then fired his own. He was shot the second time when he was firing his own gun. The ball struck the stock of his gun, and then hit him in the side, near the shoulders. That was the shot that killed him. He told me that he was killed, and asked me for water, which I gave him. He died immediately after."

Little Crow had shot the elder Lamson in the left shoulder blade, causing only a flesh wound. Lamson crawled away from the tree to reload his rifle when Little Crow and Chauncey fired at the same time. Chauncey's bullet was the one that proved fatal for Little Crow. The boy ran off, making no effort to determine his father's condition. The elder Lamson, thinking that more Indians might be around, hid in the bushes and waited, his rifle and revolver at the ready. After the sun set, he took off his white shirt so that he would not be spotted in the darkness, then he slipped away, reaching his home at about two o'clock in the morning.

Wowinape wrapped his father's body in a blanket, put new moccasins on his feet to help on the journey to the abode of the Great Spirit, and left him on the ground in the Big Woods. There was nothing more he could do for Little Crow.

Twenty-six days later, Wowinape was captured by Sibley's troops near Devil's Lake. He was tried by a military commission and sentenced to death but was released from prison in 1866. He converted to Christianity and founded the first YMCA for the Sioux. In 1864, Nathan Lamson was awarded five hundred dollars by the Minnesota legislature for killing Little Crow.

On the morning of July 4, a cavalry detachment sent out from Hutchinson found Little Crow's body, scalped it, and brought it into town, where it became a major attraction that Independence Day of 1863. The corpse was dumped in the middle of the main street. Boys stuffed firecrackers in the ears and nose and set them off. By evening, however, people had lost interest, and the body was tossed in an offal pit on the outskirts of town.

Sometime later, a cavalry officer retrieved it and cut off the head with his saber. The town's doctor, John Benjamin, placed the head in a kettle of lime to preserve it. The scalp lock and two forearm bones, showing deformities from earlier gunshot wounds, were put on display at the State Historical Society in St. Paul. In 1896, the skull was added to the exhibit.

Henry Sibley was outraged and disgusted by this treatment of the chief's remains. He wrote that it was "not to the credit of Christian civilization or the culture of the superior races. . . . All that is redeeming in humanity protests against the acquisition; a spectacle which can only feed the temper of a barbarous mind, and excite the moral disgust of every man, unblunted by a spirit of revenge."

In 1971, more than one hundred years later, Little Crow was reunited with his people. The remains were buried in a family plot in South Dakota, with Little Crow's grandson, Wowinape's son, in attendance.

There were many other Indians to be dealt with, and the net of retribution was cast far and wide. Two of the most wanted chiefs—Shakopee, who had pressured Little Crow to go to war, and Medicine Bottle, who had fought at Fort Ridgely—were traced to Canada. At Pembina, near the border, Maj. Edwin Hatch, in command of a battalion, took it upon himself, without orders, to attempt to kidnap the Sioux chiefs and bring them back to Minnesota to stand trial.

On Christmas Day, 1863, Hatch sent one of his lieutenants to Fort Garry, across the border, to offer a reward of hundreds of dollars for the delivery of Shakopee and Medicine Bottle to the Americans. Two civilians, John McKenzie and Onisime Giguere, agreed to undertake the commission. They went to the Sioux camp, some twenty-five miles away, and told the chiefs that the British intended to stop issuing them rations. They offered to escort the chiefs to Fort Garry to talk to the provincial governor himself and plead their case. The chiefs agreed.

Along the way, they stopped at McKenzie's house for refreshment. The Indians were plied with whiskey and wine, generously laced with laudanum—a tincture of opium popularly used as a sedative. It took a full day of drinking for the mixture to have the desired effect, but once Shakopee fell unconscious, a handkerchief soaked in chloroform was held over his nose to make sure that he did not awaken too soon. Medicine Bottle proved tougher, and it required several men to subdue him. The chiefs were strapped to dogsleds and transported to Major Hatch, waiting with his troops on the U.S. side of the border. McKenzie and Giguere had to wait more than three years for their payment; in 1867, the Minnesota legislature finally appropriated the sum of one thousand dollars for their services.

Because of a shortage of officers at Fort Snelling to serve on a military commission, it was almost a year before Shakopee and Medicine Bottle were brought to trial. Witnesses called by the prosecution provided only hearsay evidence, and most of them could not offer even that. The Sioux chiefs had no witnesses to summon on their behalf, nor did they cross-examine those called by the government. They denied killing whites during the uprising, and they voiced their objections to being kidnapped from a foreign country where the United States had no jurisdiction. Shakopee and Medicine Bottle were sentenced to death by hanging.

General Sibley issued a statement in support of the verdict. He wrote that it was well known that the two chiefs had committed or at least instigated the atrocities of the uprising in 1862, and that the testimony of the government witnesses provided overwhelming proof of their guilt. As to the charge that they had been kidnapped, that was nonsense! British subjects handed them over to American authorities because they were anxious to get rid of them. No American civilians or soldiers, he declared, had been involved in any attempt to seize or abduct the Indians. (It is possible that Sibley did not know the truth of Major Hatch's involvement.) Finally, Sibley argued that if the government failed to hang the Indians, it would have a bad effect. Once again, an example must be made.

On August 29, 1865, President Andrew Johnson confirmed the death sentences. When told the news, Shakopee said, "I am no squaw. I can die whenever the white man wishes." Medicine Bottle agreed.

Father Ravoux was with the two men at their death, as he

had been with the thirty-eight Sioux hanged at Mankato nearly three years earlier. On the day before the execution, the *St. Paul Pioneer* printed an editorial, noting that no "serious injustice will be done by the execution tomorrow, but it would have been more creditable if some tangible evidence of their guilt had been obtained. . . . no white man, tried before a jury of his peers, would be executed upon the testimony thus produced. The general supposition that they are guilty, is very likely correct, but their execution will, nevertheless, establish the precedent of hanging without proving. . . . About the only admirable element in the whole course of the cases was the serene and dignified behavior of the chiefs in their last hour."

An apocryphal tale is told of their last moments. It was said that when Shakopee and Medicine Bottle mounted the steps to the gallows, a steam locomotive—one of the first to cross the state—hooted its mournful whistle in the distance. Shakopee gestured toward the train. "As the white man comes in," he said, "the Indian goes out."

And what of the more than sixteen hundred Indian men, women, and children penned up in the stockade at Fort Snelling after the mass hangings in December of 1862? None of them had been convicted of any crime, or had even been brought to trial. Many were from the friendlies' camp, the Indians who had protected the white captives before Sibley arrived with his troops. Some were mixed-bloods who had been prisoners themselves. With their homes and farms destroyed in the uprising, they had no place to go, and they willingly entered the stockade in order to have food and shelter for themselves and their children. The conditions were appalling; measles and other diseases were widespread.

"Amid all this sickness and these great tribulations," wrote Gabriel Renville, "it seemed doubtful at night whether a person would be alive in the morning. We had no land, no homes, no means of support, and the outlook was most dreary and discouraging. How can we get lands and have homes again, were the questions which troubled many thinking minds, and were hard questions to answer."

Rumors fed their fears. The Indians heard about the thirty-eight hangings at Mankato and believed them to be only the first installment of wholesale executions. Some people said that all the men and boys were to be killed. The rest would become slaves, transported to the South, where they would die of fevers. Others would be sent to a barren island far away and left to fend for themselves. The guards at the stockade could tell the Indians nothing of their fate; they knew no more than the Sioux. In truth, no one in authority had yet decided what to do with them.

With little to occupy their minds but fear, and with only the missionaries to show them any kindness, it was perhaps not surprising that a great religious fervor swept the Indian camp. Their own gods had failed them, their conjurers and medicine men had been unable to prevent disaster, and they turned to the white man's God for salvation, for relief, for answers.

The Reverend Samuel Hinman, whose church Little Crow had attended, preached to the Sioux at Fort Snelling, along with John Poage Williamson, a missionary who lived at the Upper Agency. Both men spoke Dakota and could offer the Indians comfort in their own language. They held prayer meetings, first only for those who had been baptized, but soon their tent was crowded with Indians wanting to learn more about the whites' all-powerful God.

When winter came in its full fury, the services were moved indoors to a dark attic room above the warehouse. Often up to five hundred Indians sat cross-legged on the floor. "In that low garret," the Reverend Stephen Riggs wrote on a visit to the camp, "when hundreds were crouched down among the rafters, only the glistening eyes of some of them visible in the dark, we remember how the silence was sometimes such that the fall of a pin might be heard."

Hundreds clamored to be baptized, and out in front of the warehouse, Williamson made a huge bonfire of the charms and medicine bundles the Indians surrendered to him when they rejected their own religion for his. In twenty-five years of proselytizing, the missionaries had never known such success. In a quarter of a century, they had converted no more than sixty Sioux. Now they brought that many and more to their God in a single afternoon.

If the white man's God was omnipotent, so, too, must be his words, and the garret became a school as well as a church. Men, women, and children were taught to read and write English, moving their fingers slowly along the lines of the Bible and school primers, painstakingly printing the alphabet on slates and scraps of paper. They studied and prayed industriously, believing that their lives depended on mastering the white man's ways.

The missionaries became targets of bigotry and hatred for their work among the Indians. Hinman was assaulted by a gang of white men who forced their way into the stockade and beat him unconscious. Riggs, Williamson, and Bishop Whipple were subjected to verbal abuse and threats. After Whipple visited the Indian encampment to conduct a confirmation service, he was blasted in newspapers across the state.

AWFUL SACRILEGE, a headline roared. "Holiest rites of the Church given to red-handed murderers." "God was mocked," another newspaper wrote, "and his religion burlesqued by the solemn farce of administering the sacred ordinances of baptism and confirmation to a horde of the treacherous fiends at Fort Snelling."

At a prison in Mankato, the more than three hundred Indians whose death sentences had been commuted, plus those who had been given prison terms, also experienced a mass religious conversion. Dr. Thomas Williamson from the Upper Agency, the father of the missionary who was saving souls at Fort Snelling, preached every Sunday. During the week, Robert Hopkins, a Christian mixed-blood, held three daily prayer sessions. The guards were permitted to remove the chains from the Indians so they could participate in these services, and they prayed and sang for hours at a time. They studied the English language, as though by learning to read and write, they could absorb the white man's power.

Williamson and Gideon Pond, a Presbyterian minister, baptized 274 of the prisoners. Pond recalled that some of the Indians told him that "their whole lives had been wicked, that they have adhered to the superstitions of their ancestors until they have reduced themselves to their present state of wretchedness and ruin. They declare that they had left it all, and will leave all forever; that they do and will embrace the religion of Jesus Christ, and adhere to it as long as they live. . . . They say that before they came to this state of mind, this determination, their hearts failed them with fear, but now they have much mental ease and comfort." The Indians would soon need all the mental comfort they could muster.

The majority of the white population of Minnesota was demanding that every Indian, whether guilty or innocent, be banished from the state. Governor Ramsey himself had expressed that sentiment in September 1862, before the uprising had ended. The Sioux, he wrote, must either be exterminated or driven forever beyond the state's borders. They must be dealt with harshly—everyone agreed with that—and there was no dearth of ideas about how this should be accomplished.

One proposal was to ship the Sioux, Chippewas, and Winnebagos—a total of 47,000 Indians—to an island in Lake Superior, to manage on their own. "Let not the work of the Lord be done negligently," one proponent of this idea urged. Another suggestion was to send the convicted men to the Dry Tortugas, a desolate island group off the Florida Keys. General Pope said that the Indians should be treated the same way the state governments treated lunatics—feed and clothe them cheaply, out of their annuities, deprive them of weapons and whiskey, and confine them somewhere far away. Sibley wanted to transport the Indians to a reservation near Devil's Lake in the Dakota Territory, station a cordon of troops around them, and reduce them to a state of servitude.

Perhaps the most vindictive was the Indian agent Tom Galbraith. "They must be whipped [and] coerced into obedience," he wrote. "After this is accomplished, few will be left to put on a reservation; many will be killed; more must perish from famine and exposure, the more desperate will flee and seek refuge on the plains or in the mountains. . . . A very small reservation should suffice for them."

On February 16, 1863, less than two months after the hangings at Mankato, the U.S. Congress passed a bill abrogating and annulling all past treaties with the Sioux and appropriating the annuity money to use as a fund to reimburse white victims of the uprising. Additional punitive legislation followed, and by March 3, the fate of all Indians in Minnesota had been decided. The Winnebagos, few of whom had participated in the war, would be banished along with the Sioux. Their land, and that of the Sioux—a million choice acres of rich farmland—would be made available for public sale. The Indians would be relocated to a site not yet designated, but one certain to be well beyond the borders of Minnesota.

Those Indians convicted of crimes against whites were to be housed in military barracks at Camp McClellan, near Davenport, Iowa, 250 miles south. They were taken from Mankato on the morning of April 22, aboard the steamboat *Favorite*. The men were chained together and guarded by four companies of infantry, to protect them from angry mobs.

The townspeople crowded the dock to watch the boat leave, but they made no protests. "All believe [the Indians] richly deserve hanging," a writer for the *Mankato Weekly Record* observed, but since the President had not seen fit to do that, "the next best thing was to take them away." Another newspaper, commenting sarcastically on the Indians' shipboard prayer meeting, wrote that it would be a fine thing if the boat's boiler exploded.

At Camp McClellan, the men were confined in four flimsy barracks buildings, with inadequate clothing and only enough fuel to heat the place for half a day at a time. Many of the Indians developed tuberculosis, and the death rate soared; 120 men died in three years of captivity. During the summer, their lot improved when they were allowed to work on farms and sell homemade trinkets to the settlers. They were permitted to leave the camp without guards, and none of them tried to escape. Many asked to join the army, but the Secretary of War turned down their requests.

Dr. Williamson remained with the Indians at Camp McClellan for two years, continuing to teach religion and English. Some of the money the Indians earned from selling their handicrafts was used to purchase books. Williamson divided the men into groups, according to their native villages, and held regular classes, plus morning and evening sessions for singing and prayers.

The following year, at his urging, forty men were officially pardoned. Two years later, the remainder of the Sioux received pardons and were allowed to rejoin their families. It is ironic that these prisoners, who had been convicted of crimes against the white settlers, lived better than the larger group of friendly Sioux confined at Fort Snelling, and better than the Winnebagos who were guilty of nothing more than being Indians. All of them paid a terrible price.

At Fort Snelling, thirteen hundred Sioux were still captive by the spring; three hundred had died over the winter. As the grass grew green, the Indians remained uncertain about their fate. No one told them of the government's plan until May 4, when 771 of them, mostly women and children, were jammed aboard a small river steamer, the *Davenport*. They were being taken by a circuitous route to a reservation in the Dakota Territory. Transporting them by train and wagon would have been faster and more direct, but Sibley insisted on a boat, arguing that it would be cheaper and would keep the Indians safe from attacks by angry whites. Also, it would make it more difficult for any of the Indians to escape.

When the steamer docked at St. Paul, an outraged crowd lobbed stones at the Indians, injuring several of the women. The forty-man army escort fixed bayonets and prepared to charge the crowd, but the assault quickly stopped. Four days later, the *Davenport* reached St. Louis, after a journey of 450 miles down the Mississippi. The Indians were transferred to the *Florence*, which departed on May 9 for the 350-mile voyage up the Missouri River to St. Joseph.

A second shipment of Sioux left Fort Snelling on May 5. The 547 Indians were accompanied by the missionary John Poage Williamson. "The last [Indian] was counted on at dusk," he recalled, "after which, an escort of soldiers being brought aboard, we shoved off. . . . We are, however, hardly under way when from all the different parts of the boat where they are collected, we hear hymns of praise ascending to Jehovah—not loud, but soft and sweet, like the murmur of many waters. Then one of them leads in prayer, after which another hymn is sung; and so they continue till all are composed; and drawing their blankets over them, each falls asleep."

They traveled as far as Hannibal, Missouri, where they were loaded into freight cars, sixty persons to a car, for a two-day trip across the state to St. Joseph, arriving on May 11. The men were herded into tents to await the arrival of the *Florence*, with its cargo of women and children.

The ship, already overloaded, arrived several days later, and the second group of Indians was shoved aboard. The resulting overcrowding was made more unbearable by the searing heat. Williamson protested to the captain and to the officer in charge of the guard detail, but there was nothing to be done. "When 1300 Indians were crowded like slaves on the boiler and hurricane decks of a single boat," wrote Williamson, "and fed on musty hardtack and briny pork, which had not had half a chance to cook, diseases were bred which made fearful havoc."

The Indians reached their new home on June 1, after a difficult and dispiriting journey of nearly a month. The real horror awaited at the end of the *Florence*'s gangplank, however. They had been brought to a place still spoken of with great emotion. The Santee Sioux had come to Crow Creek.

"It is a horrible region," wrote Isaac Heard, "filled with petrified remains of the huge lizards and creeping things of the first days of time. The soil is miserable; rain rarely ever visits it. The game is scarce, and the alkaline waters of the streams and springs are almost certain death."

An Indian historian described Crow Creek as a place of "drought-stricken desolation, a land with no lakes, almost no timber." And the Commissioner of Indian Affairs called it "one wilderness of dry prairie for hundreds of miles around."

Nothing grew there. Nothing could grow there. It was a barren stretch of emptiness for as far as the eye could see—and beyond. There was not a house within fifty miles, no game, no berries, no edible roots. Weakened and diseased from their terrible journey, the Sioux began to die within days of their arrival, three or four every day. In a few weeks, 150 were dead, and by the end of the summer, the number had climbed to 300. "For a time," Williamson said, "a tepee where no one was sick could scarcely be found, and it was a rare day when there was no funeral. So the hills were soon covered with graves."

Clark Thompson, the Indian agent who had chosen the site, set about surveying and building, to establish at least the appearance of a functioning government reservation for the thirteen hundred Sioux, and the two thousand Winnebagos who arrived later in June. Temporary structures were erected to house the agency's white personnel, and a stockade four hundred feet square was put up to protect them from any marauding Indians. A road to the river was laid out and a sawmill constructed so that timber could be cut for additional buildings. A parcel of land was plowed and seeded, but nothing took hold in the inhospitable soil.

Food was the major concern. There never seemed to be enough left for the Indians. During the first summer, they were given only small quantities of flour and pork, and by the fall, even that ration was reduced. A wagon train reached Crow Creek on December 2, but the only sustenance provided for the Indians was more flour and pork, of a type that had been condemned as unfit for the soldiers. It was considered good enough for the Indians, however.

The cattle that had hauled the wagons were a source of beef, but they had traveled more than three hundred miles with nothing to eat but the dry prairie grass. They were fed no more until they were slaughtered a month later. Their meat, such as it was, was stored outdoors in the snow. When some of it was offered to the Sioux the following June, it was black.

Thompson decided that the rations would feed more people if they were pooled. He ordered that a vat be built out of green cottonwood boards to serve as a communal cooking pot. A visiting army surgeon, Dr. Samuel Haynes, left with vivid memories of what he saw thrown into that vat.

> Beef, beef heads, entrails of beeves, some beans, flour, and pork. I think there were put into the vat two barrels of flour each time, which was not oftener than once in twenty-four hours. This mass was then cooked by the steam from the boiler passing through the pipe into the vat. When that was done, all the Indians were ordered to come with their pails and get it. . . . It

was about the consistency of very thin gruel. The
Indians would pour off the thinner portion and
eat that which settled at the bottom. . . . I
passed there frequently when it was cooking, and
was often there when it was being issued, and it
had a very offensive odor; it had the odor of the
contents of the entrails of the beeves.

This unpalatable soup was issued every other day—to the
Sioux one day and the Winnebagos the next. On the days they
received the soup, they were given no additional food. Many
Indians refused to eat the slop, and it made many others ill,
but there was nothing else. Some banded together and left the
reservation from time to time, to roam the countryside in a
desperate search for something to eat. The lucky ones came
across abandoned army camps where they were able to tear into
nuggets of horse dung to retrieve half-digested corn kernels
and strip rotting flesh from dead horses and mules.

A young Teton Sioux warrior visited his brothers at Crow
Creek during that awful winter. He came from far away to the
west, from the great northern plains where his people still
roamed free, living the way their fathers had lived, where the
white man had not yet come with wagons and trinkets and
whiskey and treaties and soldiers. He was appalled by the pitiful condition of the Santee Sioux, and he listened in silence to
their stories of how the coming of the white man had changed
their lives forever, how the whites had brought sorrow and misery and death. He gazed sadly and with mounting anger at the
remnants of a once proud and noble people.

He resolved that his own Sioux people would be strong
when the white men came to take their buffalo and their land,
as surely they would one day. They would fight as no Indians
had fought before to avoid the fate of the Sioux from Minnesota.

The warrior's name was Tatanka Yotanka. The whites
would come to know him as Sitting Bull.

CHAPTER NOTES

CHAPTER 1: EVERYTHING WENT OFF QUIETLY

"Jesus Christ" chant, West, p. 290. "Their bodies swayed to and fro," Bryant, p. 477. Sibley telegram to Lincoln, Minnesota Board of Commissioners, p. 292.

CHAPTER 2: LET THEM EAT GRASS

"The paymaster did not come," Big Eagle, in Anderson and Woolworth, p. 27. "My Great Father," Standing Buffalo, in Anderson and Woolworth, p. 293. Galbraith described as "supremely confident," Meyer, pp. 109–110. Minnesota as "an Indian paradise," Flandrau (1900), pp. 38–39. "After we have fought for you," Meyer, p. 30. "At some of the villages," Meyer, p. 68. "It was a grand affair," Faribault, pp. 445–446. "When we were at Washington," Meyer, p. 81. "There is one thing more," Anderson, p. 66. Taliaferro–Little Crow conversation, Taliaferro, pp. 253–254. "My boys are soldiers,"

Oehler, p. 26. Galbraith–Little Crow meeting, Folwell, vol. 2, pp. 232–233; Anderson, p. 127. "Let them eat grass," Russo, p. 101. "All is quiet," Bryant, p. 88.

CHAPTER 3: HE IS NOT A COWARD

Story of the four braves from Rice Creek, Folwell, vol. 2, p. 416. "Let us go down and see Little Crow," Oehler, p. 30. Description of Little Crow, Anderson, pp. 4, 39; Oehler, p. 17. Meeting of Little Crow and other chiefs, Oehler, pp. 31–34; Eastman, pp. 66–67; Little Crow, in Anderson and Woolworth, pp. 40–42.

CHAPTER 4: THE INDIANS ARE RAISING HELL

"During the whole of the night," Coursolle, in Anderson and Woolworth, pp. 57–58. "I will kill the dog," Heard, p. 62. "Myrick is eating grass," Big Eagle, in Anderson and Woolworth, p. 56. "I am an old man," Prescott, p. 254. "He was usually very polite," Heard, p. 66. "I was forced to do the cruelest task," Coursolle, in Anderson and Woolworth, p. 59. "This is my friend and comrade," McConkey, p. 59. Helen Carrothers story, Tarble, pp. 26–30. Jonathan Earle story, Bryant, pp. 280–281. Marsh expedition, Carley (1976), p. 15. Battle report of Sergeant Bishop, Minnesota Board of Commissioners, pp. 168–169. "The guttural speakers," Anderson, p. 138. Sarah Wakefield story, Wakefield, pp. 11–14. "Some of you say you have horses," Heard, p. 75. Messages from Lieutenant Gere, Carley (1976), p. 26.

CHAPTER 5: OH GOD! OH GOD!

Helen Carrothers–Little Crow conversation, Tarble, p. 32. Description of Wabasha, DeCamp, pp. 358–359. "Go into the house," Bryant, p. 289. "This is my squaw," Bryant, p. 290. "One of them laid his hands," Bryant, pp. 339–340. "Are we going to be killed," DeCamp, p. 362. "I told them," DeCamp, p. 363. Sarah Wakefield story, Wakefield, p. 15. "And this Other Day," Bryant, p. 123. Stephen Riggs story, Riggs, pp. 181–186. Justina Krieger story, Bryant, pp. 303–315.

CHAPTER 6: WITH THE UTMOST PROMPTITUDE

"In a state of excitement," Flandrau, in Fridley, Kellett, and Holmquist, p. 34. "All is clatter," Bryant, p. 428. Dispatch from Ramsey to Fort Snelling, Minnesota Board of Commissioners, p. 165. Sibley background and speeches, West, pp. 47, 150–152. "Sad to say," McConkey, p. 81. "To your posts!" Folwell, vol. 2, p. 363. "They made a motley, straggly column," Clapesattle, p. 31. "You ought not to kill," Oehler, p. 59.

CHAPTER 7: THERE WAS DEATH BEHIND

Alomina Hurd story, Bryant, pp. 368–370; Hibschman, p. 13. Charley Hatch story, Hibschman, p. 15. Lavina Eastlick story, Bryant, pp. 347–349. Old Pawn story, Hibschman, pp. 19, 23. Tommy Ireland story, Hibschman, p. 27. Fort Ridgely attack, Lightning Blanket, in Anderson and Woolworth, p. 155; Coursolle, in Anderson and Woolworth, p. 159. "We will fix you," Faribault, p. 138. Letter from Sibley to Ramsey, Minnesota Board of Commissioners, p. 193.

CHAPTER 8: OVER THE EARTH

Lavina Eastlick story, Bryant, pp. 352–353; Hibschman, p. 31. Sarah Wakefield story, Wakefield, pp. 16–21. Jannette DeCamp story, DeCamp, p. 365. Mary Schwandt story, Schwandt, p. 469. Anderson family story, Bryant, p. 400. Ramsey proclamation, Minnesota Board of Commissioners, pp. 193–194. Sibley letters, Minnesota Board of Commissioners, p. 196; Carley (1962), p. 101.

CHAPTER 9: THERE WAS NO TIME FOR MOURNING

Joseph Coursolle story, Coursolle, in Anderson and Woolworth, pp. 159–160. Charles Flandrau story, Flandrau, in Fridley, Kellett, and Holmquist, pp. 38–39. Flandrau message to Sibley, Minnesota Board of Commissioners, p. 198. Flandrau's report of the battle of New Ulm, Minnesota Board of Commissioners, pp. 203–207; Flandrau (1900), p. 154; Flandrau, in Fridley, Kellett, and Holmquist, p. 46.

CHAPTER 10: A HEARTRENDING PROCESSION

Lavina Eastlick story, Bryant, pp. 355–357, 363; Hibschman, p. 33. Justina Krieger story, Bryant, p. 317. Helen Carrothers story, Tarble, pp. 40–41. Sarah Wakefield story, Wakefield, pp. 24–28. Snana story, Snana, in Anderson and Woolworth, p. 143. Mary Schwandt story, Schwandt, pp. 470–471. Flandrau orders, Flandrau, in Fridley, Kellett, and Holmquist, p. 50. Rudolph Leonhart recollections, Leonhart, in Fridley, Kellett, and Holmquist, p. 52. Poison barrel story, Fridley, in Fridley, Kellett, and Holmquist, p. 22. "A more heartrending procession," Flandrau (1900), p. 157. Sibley letter to his wife, Carley (1962), p. 102. Sibley letters to Ramsey, Minnesota Board of Commissioners, pp. 198–200. Criticisms of Sibley, Oehler, p. 140; Folwell, vol. 2, p. 176. "There are horsemen," Bryant, p. 195. Arrival of McPhail's troops, McConkey, p. 93. Arrival of Sibley's force, Folwell, vol. 2, p. 173.

CHAPTER 11: LAY ON YOUR BELLIES AND SHOOT!

Sarah Wakefield story, Wakefield, pp. 32–33. Gabriel Renville story, Gabriel Renville, in Anderson and Woolworth, pp. 186–187. Paul Mazakutemani story, Mazakutemani, in Anderson and Woolworth, pp. 195–197. Victor Renville story, Victor Renville, in Anderson and Woolworth, p. 193. Burial party from Fort Ridgely, Minnesota Board of Commissioners, pp. 219–220. Justina Krieger story, Bryant, pp. 318–319. Report of battle of Birch Coulee, Minnesota Board of Commissioners, pp. 212–223; Coursolle, in Anderson and Woolworth, pp. 162–165; Big Eagle, in Anderson and Woolworth, pp. 150–152; Oehler, p. 181. Sibley report to adjutant general, West, p. 461. "Well, let them come," Carley (1976), p. 59. Grant statement, Minnesota Board of Commissioners, p. 219. "To avoid any pass or defile," West, p. 460. "If Little Crow has any proposition," West, p. 262.

CHAPTER 12: WE MUST ALL DIE IN BATTLE

Wisconsin governor to Stanton; Ramsey to Lincoln; Stanton to Pope; Minnesota Board of Commissioners, p. 225. "The Sioux

Indians of Minnesota," Folwell, vol. 2, p. 255. Riggs letter to Ramsey, Minnesota Board of Commissioners, p. 227. Thomas A. Robertson story, Robertson, in Anderson and Woolworth, p. 178. Council of Upper Sioux and Lower Sioux, Heard, pp. 147–153. "They assure me," West, p. 267. Sibley–Little Crow correspondence, West, pp. 263–267. Sarah Wakefield story, Wakefield, p. 42. Little Crow–Red Iron meeting, Star, in Anderson and Woolworth, p. 204; Anderson, p. 156. Brown story, Samuel J. Brown, p. 174. Wabasha letter, West, p. 264.

CHAPTER 13: I AM ASHAMED TO CALL MYSELF A DAKOTA

Joseph Coursolle story, Coursolle, in Anderson and Woolworth, pp. 239, 241. Sibley to Flandrau, Minnesota Board of Commissioners, p. 231. Sibley–Pope correspondence, Minnesota Board of Commissioners, pp. 234, 237. Pope–Halleck correspondence, Minnesota Board of Commissioners, pp. 232, 238, 239. Sarah Wakefield story, Wakefield, pp. 45–50. Little Crow confrontation with chiefs, Anderson, p. 159; Gabriel Renville, in Anderson and Woolworth, p. 231. "We will have plenty of pork," Faribault, p. 245. "They came on over the prairie," Big Eagle, in Anderson and Woolworth, p. 236. Report of battle of Wood Lake, Minnesota Board of Commissioners, pp. 244–247; Folwell, vol. 2, p. 182. Sibley letter to the Wahpetons, Minnesota Board of Commissioners, p. 249. "I am very much in want of bread rations," West, p. 471. Campbell story, Cecelia Campbell, in Anderson and Woolworth, p. 253; Anderson, p. 161. "I am ashamed to call myself a Dakota," Oehler, p. 197. "We shall never go back there," Anderson, p. 161. Sibley letter to the friendlies, Minnesota Board of Commissioners, pp. 249–250. Brown recollections, Samuel J. Brown, p. 10. Paul Mazakutemani statement, Mazakutemani, in Anderson and Woolworth, p. 256. "The woe written in the faces," Heard, p. 186. "Some seemed stolid," West, p. 275. Snana story, Snana, in Anderson and Woolworth, p. 258. Nancy Faribault story, Faribault, pp. 247–248.

CHAPTER 14: VENGEANCE IS MINE

"A wail and a howl," Meyer, p. 124. Pope letter to Sibley, Minnesota Board of Commissioners, p. 257. Sarah Wakefield story, Wakefield, pp. 53–59. "Unless these people arrive," West, p.

476. Brown story, Samuel J. Brown, pp. 226–227. "This power of life and death," Folwell, vol. 2, p. 204. Stephen Riggs story, Riggs, p. 207; Meyer, p. 127. Godfrey story, Heard, pp. 189, 254, 266. Justina Boelter story, Bryant, pp. 329–330. Lincoln-Pope correspondence, Minnesota Board of Commissioners, pp. 289–290. "We were bound securely," Crooks, in Anderson and Woolworth, p. 261. Sibley letters to department headquarters, West, pp. 285–286. "Our people, indeed," Bryant, p. 469. Ramsey letter to Lincoln, Minnesota Board of Commissioners, p. 289. "The outraged people of Minnesota," Bryant, p. 459. "The blood of hundreds," Ellis, p. 13. "He came here," Folwell, vol. 2, p. 208. Lincoln's decision, West, pp. 287–288. "The commanding officer," Bryant, pp. 471–472. "Say to them now," Heard, p. 275. Rdainyanka's letter, Heard, p. 284. "Yes, tell our friends," Execution, p. 6. "They were all fastened," Heard, pp. 287–288. "This last was thrilling," Bryant, p. 475.

CHAPTER 15: THE HILLS WERE SOON COVERED WITH GRAVES

Pope letter to Halleck, Minnesota Board of Commissioners, p. 266. Little Crow and his followers, Anderson, pp. 168–176. Wowinape recollections, Wowinape, in Anderson and Woolworth, p. 280. "Not to the credit," West, p. 333. "I am no squaw," Folwell, vol. 2, p. 449. "Serious injustice," Folwell, vol. 2, p. 450. "As the white man comes in," Carley (1976), p. 75. Gabriel Renville story, Gabriel Renville, in Anderson and Woolworth, p. 234. "In that low garret," Riggs, p. 219. "Awful sacrilege," Meyer, p. 139. "Their whole lives have been wicked," Riggs, p. 368. "Let not the work of the Lord," Folwell, vol. 2, p. 258. "They must be whipped," Meyer, p. 142. "All believe," Meyer, p. 143. Williamson recollections, Barton, pp. 75–77; Folwell, vol. 2, p. 259. "It is a horrible region," Heard, p. 295. "Drought-stricken desolation," Meyer, p. 146. "Beef, beef heads," Manypenny, pp. 137–138. Sitting Bull story, Dee Brown, p. 65.

BIBLIOGRAPHY

Anderson, Gary Clayton. *Little Crow: Spokesman for the Sioux*. St. Paul: Minnesota Historical Society Press, 1986.

———, and Woolworth, Alan R., eds. *Through Dakota Eyes: Narrative Accounts of the Minnesota Indian War of 1862*. St. Paul: Minnesota Historical Society Press, 1988.

Barton, Winifred W. *John P. Williamson: A Brother to the Sioux*. New York: Fleming H. Revell, 1919.

Big Eagle. Account in Anderson and Woolworth; originally published 1894.

Brown, Dee A. *Bury My Heart at Wounded Knee: An Indian History of the American West*. New York: Holt, Rinehart and Winston, 1970.

Brown, Samuel J. "In Captivity: The Experience, Privations and Dangers of Samuel J. Brown, and Others, While Prisoners

of the Hostile Sioux, During the Massacre and War of 1862."
Mankato, MN: *Daily and Weekly Review*, 1896; in *Garland Library of Narratives of North American Indian Captivities*, vol. 76.
New York: Garland Publishing, 1977.

Bryant, Charles S. *A History of the Great Massacre by the Sioux Indians, in Minnesota, Including the Personal Narratives of Many Who Escaped.* Cincinnati: Rickey & Carroll, 1864.

Buell, Salmon A. "Judge Flandrau in the Defense of New Ulm During the Sioux Outbreak of 1862." *Collections of the Minnesota Historical Society*, vol. 10, 1900.

Campbell, Antoine J. Testimony in Anderson and Woolworth; testimony taken 1901.

Campbell [Stay], Cecelia. Account in Anderson and Woolworth; narrative given 1882.

Carley, Kenneth. "The Sioux Campaign of 1862: Sibley's Letters to His Wife." *Minnesota History* (September 1962): 99–114.

———. *The Sioux Uprising of 1862.* St. Paul: Minnesota Historical Society, 1976.

Clapesattle, Helen. *The Doctors Mayo.* Minneapolis: University of Minnesota Press, 1941.

Coursolle, Joseph. Story in Anderson and Woolworth; story told to son and grandson; grandson provided narrative 1962.

Crooks, George. Account in Anderson and Woolworth; newspaper interview 1909.

Daniels, Asa W. "Reminiscences of Little Crow." *Collections of the Minnesota Historical Society*, vol. 12, 1905.

DeCamp [Sweet], Jannette E. Sykes. "Mrs. J. E. DeCamp Sweet's Narrative of Her Captivity in the Sioux Outbreak of 1862." *Collections of the Minnesota Historical Society*, vol. 6, 1894.

* * *

Eastman, Charles Alexander. *Indian Heroes and Great Chieftains*. Boston: Little, Brown, 1918.

Ellis, Richard N. *General Pope and U.S. Indian Policy*. Albuquerque: University of New Mexico Press, 1970.

"Execution of Thirty-Eight Sioux Indians at Mankato, Minnesota, December 26, 1862." Special edition of the *Mankato Record*, reprinted in the *Mankato Daily Review*, December 26, 1896; in *Garland Library of Narratives of North American Indian Captivities*, vol. 76. New York: Garland Publishing, 1977. Includes general and special orders, the death warrant, the names of the condemned, letters from the condemned, and an account of the execution.

Faribault [McClure-Huggan], Nancy. "The Story of Nancy [Faribault] McClure: Captivity Among the Sioux." *Collections of the Minnesota Historical Society*, vol. 6, 1894.

Flandrau, Charles E. *The History of Minnesota, and Tales of the Frontier*. St. Paul: E. W. Porter, Pioneer Press, 1900.

———. "The Battle of New Ulm and Orders for the Evacuation of New Ulm"; in Fridley, Kellett, and Holmquist.

Folwell, William Watts. *A History of Minnesota*, 4 vols. St. Paul: Minnesota Historical Society, 1924.

Fridley, Russell W. "Charles E. Flandrau, Defender of New Ulm"; in Fridley, Kellett, and Holmquist.

———, Kellett, Leota M., and Holmquist, June D., eds. *Charles E. Flandrau and the Defense of New Ulm*. New Ulm, MN: Brown County Historical Society, 1962.

Gray, John S. "The Santee Sioux and the Settlers at Lake Shetek." *Montana, the Magazine of Western History* (Winter 1975): 42–54.

Heard, Isaac V. D. *History of the Sioux War and Massacres of 1862 and 1863*. New York: Harper & Brothers, 1864; Millwood, NY: Kraus Reprint Co., 1975.

Hibschman, Harry Jacob. "The Shetek Pioneers and the Indians." Privately printed; in *Garland Library of Narratives of North American Indian Captivities*, vol. 104. New York: Garland Publishing, 1976.

Lass, William E. "The Removal from Minnesota of the Sioux and Winnebago Indians." *Minnesota History* (December 1963): 353–364.

Leonhart, Rudolph. "The Exodus from New Ulm"; in Fridley, Kellett, and Holmquist.

Lightning Blanket. Account in Anderson and Woolworth; originally published 1908.

Little Crow. Speech in Anderson and Woolworth; speech delivered 1862.

McConkey, Harriet E. Bishop. *Dakota War Whoop: Indian Massacres and War in Minnesota of 1862–1863*. St. Paul: Clerk's Office of the District Court, 1863; Minneapolis: Ross & Haines, 1970.

Manypenny, George W. *Our Indian Wards*. Cincinnati: Robert Clarke, 1880; New York: Da Capo Press, 1972.

Marshall, S. L. A. *Crimsoned Prairie: The Indian Wars*. New York: Charles Scribner's Sons, 1972.

Mazakutemani, Paul. Statement in Anderson and Woolworth; written in Dakota, translated and published 1880.

Meyer, Roy W. *History of the Santee Sioux: United States Indian Policy on Trial*. Lincoln: University of Nebraska Press, 1980.

Minnesota Board of Commissioners on Publication of History of Minnesota in Civil and Indian Wars. *Minnesota in the Civil*

and Indian Wars, 1861–1865, vol. 2: Official Reports and Correspondence. St. Paul: Pioneer Press, 1893. Contains letters, dis-
patches, executive orders, battle reports, and other materials to
and from Ramsey, Flandrau, Sibley, Galbraith, Pope, Halleck,
Stanton, and others.

Minnesota Historical Society, St. Paul, Division of Library and
Archives, Sioux Uprising Collection (4 boxes). Contains letters,
reminiscences, reports, diaries, and other materials detailing
personal experiences of whites and Indians related to the Sioux
uprising of 1862.

National Archives, Washington, D.C., Record Group 46 (Senate records of Sioux war trials, 1862).

Newcombe, Barbara T. "A Portion of the American People:
The Sioux Sign a Treaty in Washington in 1858." *Minnesota
History* (Fall 1976): 82–96.

Nichols, David A. "The Other Civil War: Lincoln and the Indians." *Minnesota History* (Spring 1974): 2–15.

Oehler, Charles M. *The Great Sioux Uprising.* New York: Oxford
University Press, 1959.

Other Day, John. Interview in Anderson and Woolworth; newspaper interview 1862.

Prescott, Philander. *The Recollections of Philander Prescott: Fron-
tiersman of the Old Northwest, 1819–1862;* ed., Donald Dean Par-
ker. Lincoln: University of Nebraska Press, 1966.

Quinn, George. Account in Anderson and Woolworth; newspaper interview 1898.

Renville, Gabriel. Memoir in Anderson and Woolworth; written in Dakota, translated and published 1905.

Renville, Victor. Account in Anderson and Woolworth; written
1920, published 1923.

Riggs, Stephen R. *Mary and I: Forty Years with the Sioux.* Chicago: W. G. Holmes, 1880; Minneapolis: Ross & Haines, 1969.

Robertson, Thomas A. Reminiscences in Anderson and Woolworth; written 1917, published 1940.

Russo, Priscilla Ann. "The Time to Speak Is Over: The Onset of the Sioux Uprising." *Minnesota History* (Fall 1976): 97–106.

Schutz, Wallace, and Trenerry, Walter. *Abandoned by Lincoln: The Military Biography of General John Pope.* Urbana: University of Illinois Press, 1990.

Schwandt [Schmidt], Mary. "The Story of Mary Schwandt: Her Captivity During the Sioux 'Outbreak'—1862." *Collections of the Minnesota Historical Society*, vol. 6, 1894.

Sibley, Henry Hastings. "Reminiscences, Historical and Personal." *Collections of the Minnesota Historical Society*, vol. 1, 1850.

————. "Sketch of John Other Day." *Collections of the Minnesota Historical Society*, vol. 3, 1870.

———— *Iron Face: The Adventures of Jack Frazer, Frontier Warrior, Scout, and Hunter;* ed., with introduction and notes, Theodore C. Blegen and Sarah A. Davidson. Chicago: Caxton Club, 1950. Written in the 1850s by Sibley and printed serially in a Minnesota newspaper in the 1860s.

Snana. Story in Anderson and Woolworth; originally published 1901.

Solomon Two Stars. Testimony in Anderson and Woolworth; testimony taken 1901.

Standing Buffalo. Letter in Anderson and Woolworth; dictated and transcribed 1864.

Star. Testimony in Anderson and Woolworth; testimony taken 1901.

Taliaferro, Lawrence. "Autobiography of Major Lawrence Taliaferro, Indian Agent at Fort Snelling, 1820–1840." *Collections of the Minnesota Historical Society*, vol. 6, 1894.

Taopee. Statement in Anderson and Woolworth; originally published 1912.

Tarble, Helen M. [Carrothers]. *The Story of My Capture and Escape During the Minnesota Indian Massacre of 1862.* St. Paul: Abbott, 1904; in *Garland Library of Narratives of North American Indian Captivities*, vol. 105. New York: Garland Publishing, 1976.

Terrell, John Upton. *Land Grab: The Truth About "The Winning of the West."* New York: Dial Press, 1972.

———. *Sioux Trail.* New York: McGraw-Hill, 1974.

Trenerry, Walter N. "The Shooting of Little Crow: Heroism or Murder?" *Minnesota History* (September 1962): 150–153.

Wabasha. Statement in Anderson and Woolworth; testimony taken 1868.

Wakefield, Sarah F. *Six Weeks in the Sioux Tepees (Little Crow's Camp): A Narrative of Indian Captivity.* Shakopee, MN: Argus, 1864; in *Garland Library of Narratives of North American Indian Captivities*, vol. 79. New York: Garland Publishing, 1977.

West, Nathaniel. *The Ancestry, Life, and Times of Hon. Henry Hastings Sibley.* St. Paul: Pioneer Press, 1889.

White, Urania S. "Captivity Among the Sioux." *Collections of the Minnesota Historical Society*, vol. 9, 1901; in *Garland Library of Narratives of North American Indian Captivities*, vol. 104. New York: Garland Publishing, 1976.

Williams, J. Fletcher. "Memoir of General Henry Hastings Sibley." *Collections of the Minnesota Historical Society*, vol. 6, 1894.

Wowinape. Statement in Anderson and Woolworth; newspaper interview 1863.

INDEX